The Anxiety Cure

Also by the authors

The Anxiety Cure for Kids: A Guide for Parents

The Anxiety Cure

An Eight-Step Program for Getting Well

Completely Revised and Updated
Second Edition

Robert L. DuPont, M.D.
Elizabeth DuPont Spencer, M.S.W.
Caroline M. DuPont, M.D.

WILEY

John Wiley & Sons, Inc.

Published by John Wiley & Sons, Inc., Hoboken, New Jersey
Published simultaneously in Canada

For general information about our other products and services, please contact our Customer Care Department within the United States at (800) 762-2974, outside the United States at (317) 572-3993 or fax (317) 572-4002.

Wiley also publishes its books in a variety of electronic forms. Some content that appears in print may not be available in electronic books. For more information about Wiley products, visit our web site at www.wiley.com.

Library of Congress Cataloging-in-Publication Data:
DuPont, Robert L., date.
    The anxiety cure : an eight-step program for getting well / Robert L. DuPont, Elizabeth DuPont Spencer, Caroline M. DuPont.—Completely revised and updated 2nd ed.
        p.   cm.
    Includes bibliographical references and index.
    ISBN 0-471-46487-2 (pbk.)
    1. Anxiety—Treatment—Popular works. 2. Anxiety—Popular works. I. Spencer, Elizabeth DuPont, 1966–   II. DuPont, Caroline M., 1968–   III. Title.

RC531.D87 2003
616.85'2230651—dc21
                                                        2003049666

This book is dedicated to our spouses,
Helen, Spence, and Paul.
You are our strongest allies,
our unfailing supporters,
and our best friends.

CONTENTS

PART ONE: Learning about Anxiety

PART TWO: The Anxiety Cure:
Eight Steps to Getting Well

FOREWORD

Welcome to *The Anxiety Cure*, a warm, wise, and thoroughly wonderful book for people with anxiety disorders and for everyone who cares about them. As a clinician, educator, and patient advocate, and having overcome my own debilitating height phobia, I know firsthand the importance of offering those who suffer from an anxiety disorder accurate, up-to-date, and inspirational information. This book clearly accomplishes this while also outlining roles for family members and welcoming them into the healing process, should they care to participate. Friends and family members involved with someone who is actively seeking treatment for an anxiety disorder, as well as one who is reluctant to try to get better, will find help in this book.

This is a book about which I care a great deal. Its warm tone, caring message of hope, and clear path to getting well will bring lifesaving help to individuals and families in all parts of the country. This book will help you make the best use of modern medicines and of the new nonpharmacological treatments for anxiety disorders. Using the eight steps detailed in this book, you will cover all the important paths to finding your road to recovery. Among other things, you will learn ways to cope with anxiety, evaluate your need for medication and therapy, and recruit your own support person to help you on your journey to win your own "anxiety cure."

Let me introduce the team of authors: a father and his two daughters, each a mental health professional specializing in the treatment of anxiety disorders. Bob and Caroline are psychiatrists, and Elizabeth is a clinical social worker. This book is the culmination of a dream of sharing their family story and their new treatment techniques for anxiety. They work together in Rockville, Maryland, as researchers and treatment providers. While not listed as an author, the fourth member of this family team, Bob's wife and Caroline and Elizabeth's mother, Helen, is an important part of this story, too, since she runs the family and also manages their practice.

The authors came to this work through their own family's confrontation with anxiety. Their initial recognition of the problem and their determined efforts to find effective ways to overcome handicapping anxiety are the driving force behind *The Anxiety Cure*. The authors share their own and other anxiety sufferers' hard-won knowledge as they show you both the pains of the anxiety disorders and the joys of release. They make anxiety understandable and ultimately manageable by characterizing panic as a "dragon." They show you how the dragon gets its influence over you so that you can tame it, rather than cowering from its terrifying displays of power.

Bob and I met when we teamed up to create the Phobia Program of Washington in 1978. Over the next five years the Phobia Program grew to have active treatment centers in six East Coast cities, treating in that brief time over ten thousand patients suffering from an anxiety disorder. We also teamed up to found the Phobia Society of America (PSA) in 1980. Bob served as its first president. Later, PSA became the Anxiety Disorders Association of America (ADAA), of which I have served as president for more than a decade.

I first met Caroline and Elizabeth when they were in elementary school, and as a family friend and Bob's professional alter ego, I shared their growing up and their educations. I experienced with them Caroline's early anxiety problems and her eventual mastery of her anxiety. I came to have a special relationship with her as we traveled together speaking about anxiety disorders in children, a serious and largely untreated problem that is still underappreciated by most anxiety experts and by parents, teachers, and pediatricians. Caroline has a fabulous gift not only for telling her story but also for bringing others, including children, to an understanding of the problem of clinically significant anxiety and what to do about it, a skill that she has carried into her professional career. Elizabeth brings with her a practical, optimistic, can-do approach with an incredible amount of empathy for those suffering from anxiety disorders. These are special young women who have great gifts as therapists, teachers, and writers.

As you work toward overcoming your anxiety problem, I hope you will turn to ADAA and to other local and national organizations that are devoted to helping people with anxiety disorders. These organizations, which are listed at the end of this book, can provide you with additional information and resources, as well as helpful networking opportunities.

Get ready for an adventure with these three to guide your travels through this book. It is an unforgettable trip with a priceless reward at the end: freedom from the prison of anxiety.

—JERILYN ROSS, M.A., L.I.C.S.W.

Guide to the Anxiety Cure Program

This book is for you if you are suffering from an anxiety disorder yourself or are concerned about someone else who suffers from one of these common, painful, and sometimes crippling problems. You will read about our family struggle with anxiety, be introduced to the brain biology of anxiety, and learn about choices in medicines and therapy for treating anxiety. Our program builds on two decades of experience helping thousands of clinically anxious people, as well as their friends and families, to live full lives without being limited by anxiety. The Anxiety Cure is an active, high-impact, goal-oriented treatment program to get you on the road to recovery. This is a program that can be tailored to the needs of each anxious person. You can use this book on your own, or in conjunction with individual or group therapy or medication treatment with a doctor.

This book is different from other books about anxiety disorders in two ways. First, it is written by a family whose perspective is that friends and family members are important in stages of the recovery process. Throughout the book we have special sections for friends and family that will help the people who care about you learn how to help you deal with your anxiety. Second, we have encompassed our two professional areas of training in this book, psychiatry and social work. Psychiatry currently views anxiety as a brain disorder and stresses cognitive-behavioral therapy and medicine. Social work sees a person in an environmental context, so the anxious person's family, job, and community involvements are all useful parts of treatment. We work together in our practice, so we know that these two approaches complement each other well. We have brought this teamwork approach to the Anxiety Cure program.

If you have picked up this book because you are experiencing high levels of anxiety and have never before been in treatment, you may find Part One of this book to be too confusing for now. You may find Part Two, Steps 1 through 8, to be the most helpful parts of this book to get you started. Later you can come back to understanding the brain biology of anxiety. Now you will want to begin to get well without delay.

If you are a friend or family member of someone who suffers from anxiety, you will find help geared especially for you. People who care about a person suffering from an anxiety disorder are frequently unsure about what to do to help. They realize that what they do about the anxiety has an impact on the anxious person, but often no solution seems possible. In *The Anxiety Cure* we outline important roles for caring friends and family. You will find references to what friends and family can do throughout this book. We highly recommend that you read Part One, Chapter 1, "The Anxious Brain," to get a clear understanding that the anxiety disorders are real, biologically based illnesses. See especially the Tips for Friends and Family highlighted at the end of each of the eight steps in Part Two, "Eight Steps to Getting Well." In Part Four you will find Chapter 17, "Anxiety and Friends, Family, and Support People," to be especially helpful.

The Quick Alternative

For some people, reading this whole book, much less doing all the exercises we suggest, will be overwhelming. Try our shortcut if you feel you cannot manage the whole program for one reason or another.

Start the shortcut program by reading the table of contents. Mark the chapters of special interest that you want to read as time permits. Be sure to read the following chapters:

Part One
  Chapter 1, The Anxious Brain
  Chapter 2, The Vocabulary of Anxiety
Part Two
  Chapter 6, Use Wizard Wisdom to Tame the Dragon
  Chapter 7, Practice—Put Yourself in Your Discomfort Zone

The two most important lessons to take away from *The Anxiety Cure* are:

1. Change your thoughts about your anxious feelings so that you recognize the physical symptoms of anxiety as merely false alarms of danger that are being sent to your body because your brain's normal fear response is occurring at the wrong times. Remove the fear of these feelings from these triggering feelings and they subside.

2. Change your behavior of avoidance to actively seek practice opportunities to systematically disconnect the association you now have between anxious feelings and avoided situations. Make your feared experiences familiar and the fear goes away.

If you do those two things—change your thoughts and your behaviors—you will begin to get well from your anxiety problems, even if you do none of the other work suggested in this program. Additional information in this book will speed your cure and help you cope with inevitable setbacks you will encounter on your road to recovery. Even small changes in your thoughts and behaviors are the main engine of recovery from anxiety problems. There is no good reason not to do something about your anxiety problem now. You picked up this book because you are suffering. Even if our ideas sound too hard, or like things that you have tried that have not worked before, it is important to try something new to get well. Many paths can lead to a cure. You must start somewhere to find the one that will work for you. Give the short program a try. When you encounter problems, take time to read the rest of the book and do the other suggested exercises. Above all, *get started!*

ACKNOWLEDGMENTS

We would not have been able to write this book without the generous help of our colleagues, friends, and family. First we want to thank our editor at Wiley, Thomas Miller. Without his hard work and vision, this book would not exist. Thank you also to our copy editor for the first edition, Shelly Perron, and for this edition, Miriam Sarzin, and to our production editor for the first edition, Benjamin Hamilton, and for this edition, Hope Breeman, for checking all the details.

Our families have encouraged us to keep writing about the ways that we have found to overcome anxiety in our personal and professional lives. Thank you for your love and support, Helen, Bill, Paul, Spence, Robert, David, and Colleen. Thanks to Janice Carroll for the fierce dragon illustration.

We acknowledge our reliance on the pioneers who created the modern treatments for anxiety disorders. Over the past thirty years we have worked with thousands of professional colleagues, each of whom has contributed to our understanding of these cunning, baffling, and powerful diseases. While we cannot here name all of these experts upon whose strong shoulders we now stand as we look to a future when all who suffer from an anxiety disorder can learn what is wrong with them and what to do about it, we call your attention to seven early leaders who created the modern "phobia clinic," a professional organization dedicated to helping people crippled by anxiety regain control of their lives. Manuel Zane, M.D., and Doreen Powell developed the White Plains Phobia Program while Arthur Hardy, M.D., and Nancy Flaxman built the TERRAP program in California, which later spread thought the nation. Martin Seif, Ph.D., from the Roosevelt Hospital Phobia Program, also had an early and sustained influence on our work. R. Reid Wilson, Ph.D., was another early leader in this rapidly developing field. In the late 1970s, when new hope emerged for the successful treatment of anxiety disorders, everyone in this field gratefully acknowledged their indebtedness to Claire Weekes, D.Sc., the Australian general practitioner who gave so much to therapists and patients alike through her brilliant, unique, and effective books.

These early leaders all focused on what is now called the cognitive-behavioral approach to the treatment of anxiety disorders. In the 1980s a whole new movement was created on the solid foundations laid in the 1960s and 1970s by Donald F. Klein, M.D., the creative psychiatrist who showed the way using medicines to block panic attacks and other anxiety symptoms. He was later joined by James C. Ballenger, M.D., Bruce Lydiard, Ph.D., M.D., Jonathan Davidson, M.D., and what ultimately became an army of physicians who brought new hope to people with anxiety disorders through medical treatments. In the early 1990s the National Institute of Mental Health (NIMH), under the wise leadership of Fredrick K. Goodwin, M.D., began to nationally disseminate new important information about treating anxiety disorders both through the cognitive-behavioral approach and through medication. We gratefully acknowledge our debts to these few named leaders and to countless other professional colleagues who have helped us to learn about anxiety disorders and to find better ways to help cure them.

We, like everyone who is concerned about anxiety disorders, are indebted to Jerilyn Ross. Jerilyn and Robert DuPont cofounded the ADAA. Jerilyn is not only a brilliant therapist but is also the one person in the world who has been most responsible for the dramatic improvement in the lives of anxious people through her two decades of leadership of the ADAA.

Most of all, we want to thank our patients. You are our teachers and our inspiration as we watch with respect the hard work you do every day to live your lives fully, without restrictions from your anxiety. It is a privilege to be your therapists.

A Family of Mental Health Professionals Deals with an Anxiety Problem

We come to the field of anxiety disorders with strong personal feelings about how much pain anxiety causes its sufferers and their families. While we have pursued our professional lives with excitement as we participate in the research and learning that has improved the help that is available, our personal encounter with anxiety is the driving force behind our focus on this field. To understand our motivation, it is important to understand our family's story. We are a father and two daughters. When Elizabeth was about five years old and Caroline about three, they were briefly locked in a closet together during a game of hide-and-seek. Elizabeth showed no ill effects from the experience, but Caroline developed a disabling claustrophobia. Starting in first grade, she was terrified of having the classroom door closed, and of being in an elevator. This was not only profoundly distressing to Caroline, but it was disruptive for the entire family. Travel was difficult, as elevators would be unexpectedly part of our hotel stay or museum trip, and almost any event could end in tears if Caroline had to go to the bathroom in a place where there was a toilet stall without a space under the door. Our family was, in a sense, trapped with Caroline. We did not have any idea of how to help her with this debilitating fear.

We learned how to treat anxiety with exposure and response prevention as part of the contextual therapy pioneered at the White Plains Phobia Society. This learning took place when Caroline was nine. After several long years of watching her torment and having no idea what to do, we had an understanding and a plan of action. Caroline was suffering because she avoided the places she was frightened of. Because of her avoidance, she could not learn that those places weren't really frightening. We had enabled this fear to continue by mistakenly giving her the idea that those places really were scary every time we let her not go into them. We now understood that her fears were understandable and painful but that she could get over them with practice. That meant she needed to spend a lot of time with us riding in elevators.

Although this family encounter with anxiety happened long ago, the impact on all of us has been profound and lasting. We start our book with our own family story, told in turn by each of the three authors. There is no way to explain the story with the emotional depth that it requires without letting each of us describe the feelings that we endured. While most of this book takes a respectful look at the feelings anxiety causes, and explains how the feelings are misplaced, in this section you can see that we do not come to our recommendation from want of understanding how powerful the emotions themselves are for everyone in the family.

Dr. Robert DuPont's Story: Valuable Lessons

The first time I learned about what I now know to be anxiety disorders was when I was about ten. A favorite aunt was afraid of snakes. At the time, I was fascinated by snakes, so this fear of what fascinated me was incomprehensible. Once when my aunt visited, I caught a snake—something I often did for fun. I brought the snake back and, as my aunt was leaning down, I whipped the snake out from behind my back to show her my treasure. She screamed so loudly that she scared me and I dropped it. My aunt ran away horrified. I was shocked and mystified.

Later, my grandfather developed claustrophobia after he had a retinal detachment and lost some of his peripheral vision. He could no longer sit in the backseat of a two-door car, and he often had to drive with the window open when he sat on the passenger side of the front seat.

I noticed even later that my mother was frightened when one of her children got near an edge that she took to be dangerous. She later admitted to a height phobia. She surely never got on a ladder.

When I was a resident in psychiatry at Harvard Medical School in the early 1960s I treated a female graduate student with a fear of bridges. She was admitted to our psychiatric hospital. All my teachers were psychoanalysts, and I was taught that fears were repressed sexual impulses.

I asked this patient about her sexual thoughts about bridges and crossing them. She checked out of the hospital figuring that the doctors there were even crazier than the patients.

When I started my own private practice, a patient who was an elementary school teacher came to see me because of her inability to drive to and from work. I figured her problem was regression and that she was inappropriately dependent on her husband to drive her back and forth to work because her needs as a child had not been met. We talked about these ideas twice a week for three years. She got less dependent and did well in many ways, but she still did not drive.

One day she brought in an article from *Glamour* magazine about a new treatment for a disorder called "agoraphobia." I read the article and set it aside, returning to my previous approach to helping her, which I was sure was just what she needed. She was not satisfied with this approach, and after a few weeks of encouraging me to take the article seriously, she told me she had found the telephone number of the psychiatrist who was quoted in the article as an expert in this new form of treatment. She gave me his name and phone number. It took me a while to overcome my unreasonable confidence in my own unsuccessful approach, but finally I called Manuel Zane, M.D., at the White Plains Phobia Clinic outside New York City. He took my call and patiently explained to me that this new approach involved going with the patient into the situation that produced the phobic fear and helping the patient manage the overwhelming and terrifying feelings that arose in that situation. Never in all of my training as a psychiatrist had I been advised to go anywhere with patients, most surely not to go driving with them.

I discussed this conversation with my patient, who told me the school year was ending and she had relatives in White Plains. She proposed that we both go to the White Plains Phobia Clinic and see what they had to offer us. After I talked with her husband about this idea and with Dr. Zane, with whom I had developed a relationship by phone, they booked a flight to New York. My patient stayed with her family while I took a hotel room near the hospital. I practically moved in with Dr. Zane and his wife as I worked with him and the wonderful program he founded. I learned about Claire Weekes, M.D., the Australian general practitioner who had written about phobias and anxiety.

In learning about anxiety and its treatment, I felt like a blind person who discovered sight as an adult. My new colleagues and the programs they had founded were my teachers and my role models.

My agoraphobic patient stayed in New York for the summer of 1977 while I returned home. Dr. Zane began to refer patients to me, since he had no one else to send patients to in the Washington metropolitan area for this new way to treat agoraphobia and other anxiety disorders. I felt inadequate to the task as I tried to interest some of the largest clinics and hospitals in the Washington, D.C., area in this new form of treatment. To my surprise, no one was interested. They had not been to the White Plains Phobia Clinic, and they had no idea how inadequate current treatment was and how much better it could be. When I tried to explain it to them, they acted as if I had fallen under the spell of a cult. In desperation I started to put together groups of phobic people much like the groups that Dr. Zane and Dr. Hardy, a psychiatrist from Menlo Park, California, were running. Since Dr. Zane ran groups at his home, I did the same at my home.

Then a young woman named Jerilyn Ross called, saying she had been a high school teacher in New York. Her friends at the Roosevelt Hospital Phobia Clinic told her that I was starting a similar program in Washington, where she had decided to move. She had worked hard to overcome her own phobia and understood the new techniques, based on her work dealing with her own anxiety disorder. She also proved to be the most gifted anxiety disorders therapist with whom I ever worked.

This group of pioneers was a team. I had never had so much fun as a doctor. My family's home in suburban Maryland was bursting at the seams with phobia groups night and day, six days a week. Our neighbors never complained as the patients' cars filled the streets, but normal life at home became so difficult that in 1979 my wife, Helen, helped me to find an office in Bethesda, Maryland. We moved the Phobia Program of Washington out of our basement.

Later Jerilyn and I traveled to the annual White Plains Phobia Program meeting. I proposed that we create an organization to advocate for the needs of patients and therapists as well as to educate them and the public about the new forms of treatment for anxiety disorders. Manuel Zane, M.D., Arthur Hardy, M.D., Martin Seif, Ph.D., Doreen Powell, and Nancy Flaxman, along with Jerilyn Ross and me, founded the Phobia Society of America (PSA). I was the organization's president. We focused on the word *phobia* rather than on the word *anxiety*, since we were providing treatment that helped people overcome their fears of particular activities, such as the agoraphobic's fear of driving, which had gotten me into this new world in the first place. Later the group extended to an interest in using medications to help anxious people. A wider group of leaders was recruited, including the academic leaders, most of whom were committed to using medications to help anxious patients. Reflecting this new, broader focus, the organization was renamed the Anxiety Disorders Association of America (ADAA), and Jerilyn took over as president.

Over the years I have lost track of the patient with whom I traveled to White Plains in 1977. But that trip changed my life at least as much as it changed hers. After a decade of immersion in the problems of addiction to alcohol and other drugs, I began a new life in the world of anxiety disorders.

In 1983 I met Dr. Claire Weekes at a meeting of the Phobia Society of America. I spent most of two days with her. At one point when I was talking alone to Dr. Weekes, I asked her if she'd ever had a panic disorder. She said, "Yes, I have had what you call panic attacks. In fact, I still have them. Sometimes they wake me at night." I told her I was sorry to hear that. She looked at me with shock: "Save your sympathy for someone else. I don't need it or want it. What you call a panic attack is merely a few normal chemicals that are temporarily out of place in my brain. It is of no significance whatsoever to me!"

I was amazed by that response. This remarkable eighty-year-old pioneer was showing me the ultimate in the cognitive restructuring of panic attacks. Dr. Weekes, using the techniques she teaches others through her inspired books, had taken the menacing meaning entirely away from the panic attack. She gave those attacks no power whatsoever, simply letting them pass and getting on with her life. Few sufferers from terribly painful panic attacks ever reach the heights of cognitive restructuring reached by Dr. Weekes, but her message was clear, and it was accessible to all people who would make the effort to learn it: *the bonus people receive for recovering control of their lives from an anxiety disorder is that the techniques learned to overcome panic disorder have a broad application in all of life's other difficult problems.*

These professional developments, however, do not explain my deep and personal interest in this field from the start. Why was I so fascinated by the patient's driving phobia, and why was I so excited by the new treatment I discovered in White Plains? To understand that you have to know that my two daughters, my coauthors on this book, were stuck in a closet for about fifteen minutes when they were small. While Elizabeth showed no ill effects from the experience, Caroline developed a claustrophobia over the following few years. When she started school at age six, she had a terrible time with separation. She would cry and cling when her mother or I took her to school. Helen handled the problem by firmly telling Caroline that everyone in the family had a job and that her job was to go to school. Helen explained that she would be back to pick up Caroline at the end of the school day and that in the meantime her teacher would take good care of her. Then Helen turned Caroline over to her teacher and walked out, despite Caroline's sad tears of entreaty to stay with her.

My approach was different. I sat down and talked with Caroline about her fears. But as we talked, it became clear that Caroline had no idea what she was afraid of and that the longer we talked, the more scared she became.

Once in school, Caroline had another anxiety problem. She was terrified of having a door closed, such as the door to her classroom or the door to a toilet stall. In preschool, her teachers accepted this and left the classroom door ajar, which felt safe to Caroline. At this time, I was not involved in the treatment of anxiety disorders, so I did not label her problem clearly as a psychiatric disorder. What I did see was Caroline's claustrophobia in elevators. When it came time to get into an elevator, she cried and pleaded with us to take the stairs instead, no matter how high we had to go in the building. I tried demanding that she go in the elevator, and she sometimes would, but her distress was so real and so obviously severe that it was a terrible experience for both of us.

When Caroline was nine, I went to White Plains to learn a new way to understand anxiety and its treatment. I had a new way to think about Caroline's problem with elevators and closed doors and a new way to help her: I told Caroline that her fears were understandable and painful but that she could get over them with practice, just as she was then practicing her strokes as a member of the neighborhood swim team. That meant she and I needed to spend time together riding in elevators and closing doors in a gradual way while she was in full control of the exposure.

In the spring of 1978, when Caroline was ten, she proudly announced at my birthday party that she had a special gift for me: she would go with me to a tall building and take the elevator alone to the top and back down again while I waited for her on the ground floor. I could not wait but went that day to the tallest building I could find (which in Washington was about ten stories), and I stood outside that elevator as Caroline pushed the "up" button with a big smile on her face. She had to wait a while to get in an empty elevator, since going on an elevator alone was harder for her than going with other people. Finally a door opened, and there was an empty elevator. Caroline got on, waved good-bye, and disappeared behind the closing doors. It was a long time as I watched the indicator over the elevator record her progress to the top and then back down. At long last the door opened, and my proud and happy ten-year-old daughter leapt into my arms. That was the best birthday present I ever received.

Over the next few years, as I treated more than seven thousand clinically anxious people, many of our family conversations dealt with anxiety in its many disguises. As a family we often went to the local county fair in August. In 1979 I noticed something new: I had a smoldering nameless terror when we got on the Ferris wheel and it stopped at the top of its cycle with our little carriage seemingly swinging wildly in the wind as I looked out over the fair below. I told my daughters that I seemed to have developed a height phobia late in my life or, if I had had it before, I had not noticed it. Starting that year and extending to the present, the girls took turns helping me with my phobia practice as they took me up on the Ferris wheel over and over. I still have twinges when I do it, but I never fail to get on that Ferris wheel each year.

Facing your fears, with the help of those who love you, has become a family coping strategy that goes far beyond just dealing with anxiety. Rather than hide our fears or weaknesses, we have found that talking about them and, even more important, practicing them, is a source of both pride and pleasure for us all. We have learned to turn our problems in life into opportunities and our setbacks into springboards. We learned this valuable lesson from our exposures to Caroline's anxiety. For that gift we are all grateful.

As great a gift as that lesson has been, however, it was not the most recent gift from that dragon. Not only did anxiety give my career a new life and direction, but now, with the writing of this book, I have fulfilled my dream of working with my now-grown daughters on a project we all care about with deep passion. This book, and the loving work we are putting into it together, is another gift from the anxiety that for so many years terrorized our family.

Caroline's Story: Anxiety Is My Companion

Anxiety is my companion. In some ways, I might even say it is my friend. It was not always that way. In fact, for many years we were mortal enemies set on destroying each other. I don't remember when my relationship with anxiety began, but the family story is that when I was about three, I was locked in a dark closet with my older sister, Elizabeth, while playing hide-and-seek. We were not locked in for long, and my sister suffered no ill effects. However, in me it apparently was the trigger for the development of claustrophobia, which is an overwhelming fear of being trapped in a closed space.

By the time I started first grade, I was terrified of being in a room with the door closed. My teacher was a wonderful woman with traditional ways. She believed that the classroom door should be closed when class was in session; she would not change her ways for me, a phobic child. I was terrified. It was the terror that comes from a life-threatening situation, not from a closed classroom door.

One morning my teacher outlined The Plan. Those two words—The Plan—will always be capitalized in my mind. In her no-nonsense way, she explained that the day in her classroom was always the same. She would close the door at the beginning of each class day and open it at the end. I never had to worry that she would close it one day and not open it again. This directly addressed my fears and gave me a way to reassure myself when anxiety hit. From then on, I could cope better with school, and I made it through first grade with few difficulties. The words *The Plan* became a mantra in our home. "Caroline, today this is The Plan," my mother would say as she outlined my activities for the day. The Plan was comforting and reassuring. As long as I understood The Plan, I could cope. The Plan allowed me to know ahead of time what was going to happen on a given day and took away the constant anticipatory anxiety that I would unexpectedly be forced into a fearful situation.

Identifying the problem was only the beginning of my long road to peace and acceptance. For six long years I suffered. My friends and family suffered along with me.

Although I was a happy and outgoing child with family and friends, I was shy at school. I had low self-esteem. I could not spend the night at my best friend's house because she might sleep with her door closed. I could not go places without my mother because I might be trapped by my fear. I was not trapped physically, but I was unable to go where my friends went, so I was trapped by my own fear and I was left behind. I also worried about my family. Every time we were separated, I would think about all of the horrible things that might happen to them. My fears were hard on my family, and I often felt ashamed of the scenes that I caused and the things we all had to miss because of my anxiety and avoidance.

Any closed-in space was a problem for me, but elevators were the worst. I felt that elevators were almost evil. The doors would stay open too long or close too quickly. The elevator would make strange sounds, or the elevator would be stopped too long before the doors slowly opened. In my imagination, any deviation from the expected was the sign that this elevator on *this* ride was going to malfunction.

How could I explain that the fear really did not go beyond the terrible feeling of being trapped? I really did not worry about anything beyond that. Nothing, in my mind, could be worse than that. How could I explain that I never felt trapped in a car when the door was closed? It took longer to get out of a car than to get out of an elevator on the next floor. One scared me, the other never did. I learned that panic is not rational. That just makes it more disturbing and far harder to explain to yourself or to anyone else.

Systematic Desensitization

At about the age of ten, the disparity between my usual happy, outgoing self and the shy, frightened inner self became more obvious to me and to my family. But what could we do? Over the years, my father had become involved in treating several patients with phobias. He learned of a new technique called systematic desensitization. In this process, the phobic person is gradually exposed to the fearful activity until the fear and the activity are no longer matched together. For me, the process involved gradually working up the courage to ride on an elevator alone.

Dad and I started the process of systematic desensitization by sitting at home and talking about elevators. For people who do not have anxiety, it can be difficult to understand that simply talking about the anxious situation can cause terrible feelings of panic. After I became comfortable discussing elevators, we moved up to driving to a building that had an elevator in it and sitting in the parking lot. We sat in the car and talked about the elevator and my fears. During these early stages we also researched the history of elevators and learned how they worked. Eventually, we started going into the building and watching the elevators, then getting in but not letting the door close, then going one floor and walking back down in a stairwell. The big hurdle, which seemed impossible until the very end, was riding in the elevator without my father. Together we came to talk of my fears as a dragon that descended on me. My phobic dragon used fear to cage me. I learned that I had to face and to accept that dragon to regain control of my life.

There was a fairly long gap between the time I was able to ride in an elevator with my father or another trusted adult and the time that I rode in one alone. My hesitation to try this last hurdle must have frustrated and disappointed my father. Finally, I made my decision and did it.

So I rode the elevator by myself and was cured forever, right? Wrong. But the tables had turned on that dragon. I had found the key to conquer my fears. It was many years before I rode in elevators without a second thought, but I never avoided an elevator again. I entered high school with confidence. I began to realize that the lessons I learned were useful and valuable to other people. I began working with my father and his colleague Jerilyn Ross to help other children with anxiety. I spoke on several television programs about my phobia and how I had overcome my fear. The confidence I gained more than made up for the confidence I had lost in the early years.

The lesson I learned not only cured my claustrophobia, it also taught me about life. Many problems in life appear terrifying and unmanageable, but they can be solved by following the same principles that got me on that elevator. Identify the problem, break it down into little steps, take one step at a time, be proud of your successes (even little ones), keep your eye on the goal, and keep moving toward that goal.

Some people ask me if I am still afraid of elevators. I can say with all honesty I am not. The moment I knew that for sure came when I was a resident in psychiatry at Johns Hopkins Hospital. I had been riding elevators without thinking about it for years, but nothing had ever tested my fear of really being trapped. One night I was the doctor on call for the entire psychiatric hospital. *On call* means that besides my normal daily responsibilities, it was my turn to stay the night and take care of any psychiatric patients who required admission or had other problems during the night. I stepped onto the elevator at about 4 A.M. to go down to the emergency room to treat a new patient. I was very tired, and it was clear that I would get no sleep that night. The doors closed, and the elevator began to move. Then it stopped. At first I was calm and pushed the "door open" button. Then I pushed other buttons. Absolutely nothing happened. I began to get scared, my heart pounded, and I felt dizzy. I was trapped! Then it dawned on me: if I was trapped, I could not see the patient in the ER. It was comforting to think that there were other doctors to care for him, so it was not necessary for me to reach the ER right away.

If I was trapped in the elevator at 4 A.M., then nobody would blame me if I lay down on the floor of the elevator and slept a little! Just then, the elevator began to move again, and soon I was busily working in the ER. The significance of finally being trapped in an elevator—my very worst childhood fear—did not strike me until several nights later. I was again stepping onto that same elevator in the middle of the night, and as the doors slid shut, I thought, Oh, I hope the elevator gets stuck for a little while. I would love a rest! When I realized what I had wished for, I laughed out loud.

The Goal of the Anxiety Cure

Live a full, normal life without restrictions because of anxiety disorders.

The realistic goal of treatment is not the elimination of the painful, anxious thoughts and feelings. Getting well from an anxiety disorder means letting go of the wish not to have the uncomfortable feelings of panic and anxiety. Getting well means accepting that the symptoms can come back at any time.

When I started this chapter, I said that "anxiety *is* my companion," not that it *was* my companion. I have learned that anxiety can take many forms and that it can go away completely and then return in another form. But I am not discouraged. Sure, I wish at times that I was not hardwired as an anxious person, but anxiety, though sometimes seriously unpleasant, is not a major factor in my life. Anxiety does not control or limit me. I have used the same skills that I learned in order to conquer my claustrophobia to keep anxiety as only a minor player in my life. I have had people ask how I managed to accomplish some difficult task such as speaking in front of a large group. "You did not look nervous at all!" Nervous? Sure I was nervous, but it's been a long time since being nervous has stopped me from doing what I want to do. I have had a lot of experience living my life while I feel nervous, even very nervous, which now gives me a lot of confidence that I can do whatever I want to do, with or without anxiety.

Elizabeth's Story: A Sister

My story will be a familiar one for friends and family members of sufferers from anxiety disorders. As Caroline's older sister, I was not her parent and not her support person, and yet I spent many years with Caroline as she struggled with her anxiety.

I felt helpless as I watched her suffer. Caroline's childhood fears were terrifying and unsettling for her and for me. I remember the time we were trapped in a closet while playing hide-and-seek as small children.

Although I was five years old, I was not frightened by the experience. Sure, it was dark, and the dust on the closet floor made me sneeze, but I knew that an adult would be along soon to find out where we were. I called out for help. I put my arm around her and felt her shiver with fear in the dark. Could such a short experience explain the terror that she thereafter experienced? It seemed to be the only way to understand why in future years she was so frightened of closed spaces.

I learned to be protective of Caroline, since it was so easy to avoid the things she feared and the consequences were so terrible for her if she had to face her fears. She was eight and I was ten and the dragon of anxiety had convinced both of us to give in to its demands. We would meet at recess in elementary school so I could hold open the door to the bathroom for her. I knew if I didn't do that, she would wait all day to use the bathroom until she got home. On the other side of protectiveness, however, was resentment. I never got to the best swings first on the playground because I had to wait behind with my younger sister. I resented the intrusion of her anxiety into my life. Since I did not know then that it was an illness, I simply saw the problem as Caroline limiting my life.

Caroline's anxiety also limited my life because she was afraid not only for herself but also for the rest of her family, fearing something terrible would happen to the people she loved. This meant that none of us could ride an elevator or walk up the stairs without holding the door open without risking her screams of fear. Sometimes I felt the urge to do something she did not want me to do just to hear her scream. More often I stumbled unaware into a fear-generating situation, like the time I came out of a bathroom in a fast-food restaurant to find her in tears outside the door, certain that I had been locked inside and would never be seen again.

When Dad learned about treating phobias and anxiety and began to help Caroline with her fears, our family life changed dramatically. Suddenly there was a way other than avoidance to help Caroline deal with her fears. We had a language to communicate how scared she was, with the ability to rank the intensity of her fear from 0 to 10. With consistent practice, the fears shrank amazingly quickly. It was a miracle. After all those years of having to submit as a family to the dragon's self-centered will, life was again unmarred by avoidance and tantrums.

It seemed that once Caroline had the tools to deal with anxiety, her fears fell like a row of dominos. Suddenly she could close doors to bathrooms at school, at first with me standing just outside and then on her own.

Having considered myself immune to anxiety problems, I was surprised one day when I stood in front of an elevator and felt my heart hammer and my mouth go dry with fear. I was a student at Columbia University in New York, and I lived on the eighth floor of a freshman dormitory. This occurred several weeks into the fall semester, and I had ridden that elevator daily during that time. Yet suddenly I could not get onto the elevator. My experience made clear to me that anxiety is truly a family disorder.

I got over my brief fear by realizing that I had set myself up for having an anxiety problem. The first weeks of college are tremendously stressful. Additionally, I had been staying up later than I was used to and, consequently, drinking more coffee during the day to stay awake. By that time, after my years of learning about anxiety, I knew to cut back on the coffee, get more sleep, and use relaxation techniques to calm myself prior to attempting to ride the elevator again. I rode the elevator alone the next morning—a quiet time, and after having had a good night's sleep. I had only mild anxiety and have continued riding elevators since. Even now I have some anxiety every time I step into an elevator. I look on the anxiety as a reminder that I need to keep up my own work or risk being entangled with the dragon once again.

People with a family history of anxiety disorders are genetically vulnerable to having anxiety problems. Not everyone is going to have the same degree of difficulty, but I know that I am definitely at risk. I use my knowledge of anxiety treatment to reduce the risk that anxiety will become a problem in my life, and I generally avoid medications and caffeine that might cause me to have a panic attack. When I have a tooth filled, for example, I request novocaine formulated without epinephrine, since I have found that regular novocaine causes me to have unpleasant physical symptoms of anxiety.

Now I have two sons. Will they have anxiety problems? Probably not, but the risk is in our family. I do not wish such a painful problem on my sons, but if either (or both) should develop an anxiety problem, I am ready to help them not only overcome it but also to learn from it as others in my family have—including me.

PART ONE

Learning about Anxiety

CHAPTER 1

The Anxious Brain

Scientists all over the world are now studying the anxious brain. Since the first edition of this book was published in 1998, understanding of the biology of anxiety has changed so profoundly that this chapter has been completely rewritten. It is no accident that so much creative energy, and so much money, is now being spent on the anxiety problem. As recently as the 1980s, the anxiety disorders were thought to be both uncommon and virtually untreatable. Anxiety disorders were considered by most mental health practitioners and researchers to be trivial compared to the "major" mental disorders—the psychotic disorders such as schizophrenia and major depression. People suffering from anxiety were called, disparagingly, "the worried well."

Attitudes within the mental health field toward clinically significant anxiety have changed completely for two reasons. First, modern epidemiological studies of mental disorders, using more scientific diagnostic categories, have shown that the anxiety disorders are the most widespread or prevalent of all of the mental disorders, exceeding even major depression and all of the other affective disorders combined. Second, studies of the economic costs of major groups of mental disorders have shown that the anxiety disorders are far from trivial. Anxiety disorders produce higher costs to society than any other class of mental disorders. Most of this high cost is the result of lost productivity at work.

As a direct result of this new knowledge, research funded by the National Institutes of Health and by major pharmaceutical companies has increased. Today government and private research together devote hundreds of millions of dollars a year to the study of anxiety.

These dramatic changes offer new hope to people who suffer from anxiety problems as better treatments are being developed and brought into practice. An example of these promising developments is the explosive growth of the use of new medicines to treat anxiety. Another example is the greater appreciation for the specific and effective form of nonmedication therapy for anxiety problems. This form of treatment is called cognitive-behavioral treatment (CBT). The uses of better medicines and better psychological treatments are at the heart of this book.

All three of us have been at the center of these important new developments through our active work with the Anxiety Disorders Association of America (ADAA). ADAA has been the biggest factor in showing that the anxiety disorders are not only common and serious but, even more important, that they can be treated successfully. The ADAA has successfully linked research, practice, and consumer to the benefit of all three.

For more than two decades, we have worked with many pharmaceutical companies in developing new medicines and in finding new uses for some older medicines in the treatment of the anxiety disorders. Together we have conducted hundreds of sophisticated double-blind clinical trials of medicines in the treatment of the anxiety disorders. In this work we have been joined by researchers in all parts of the country and around the world as the anxiety disorders have become one of the most active areas of research in contemporary medicine. In our clinical practices we use these new pharmaceutical advances and the ever-improving cognitive-behavioral treatment to our patients.

In this chapter we look at the explosive growth in understanding of the biology of fear and anxiety. In Chapter 4 we look specifically at the new medicines used in the treatment of anxiety problems.

The Brain Biology of Fear

The brain is made up of more than 100 billion nerve cells connected to each other in a fabulously complex interactive network. Each nerve cell, or neuron, communicates with the many other neurons across tiny spaces, called synapses, between the connected neurons. Messages are carried from one neuron to others by a chemical messenger called a neurotransmitter. Brain biology can be looked at by focusing on the neuronal circuitry used to connect the various parts of the brain with each other and with the organs in the body that express the brain's activity, such as the muscles and hormone systems. In addition to studying the brain's circuitry, the biology of the brain can be understood by studying the neurotransmitters used to send signals from one neuron to the next.

Brain mechanisms of anxiety can be studied in the laboratory by measuring neurotransmitter levels in blood, urine, saliva, and spinal fluid; by assessing behavior and behavioral responses to pharmacologic challenges to specific neurochemical systems; and by measuring brain structures using neuronal imaging. Useful studies of anxiety have been conducted with both laboratory animals and human subjects.

The Fear Circuits

First let's look at the brain's circuitry that manages fear. From our five senses (sight, sound, smell, taste, and touch) come sensory impulses from all parts of our bodies into the nerve center in the midbrain called the thalamus. This is the brain's sensory clearinghouse. In the thalamus, sensory information of all kinds and from all sources that involve possible danger is split into two major pathways, the high road and the low road. The low road is the fast and automatic road for handling fear. It is designed to respond to possible danger practically instantaneously. Speed is important because signs of danger that can be life threatening can occur on a split-second basis. From the thalamus the sensory inputs travel via the low road to the amygdala and the hippocampus in the temporal lobe of the brain. These brain structures are part of the limbic system that manages memory and emotions. The hippocampus is especially important because it assigns context and emotional meaning to the constant flow of sensory inputs into the limbic system from the thalamus night and day. When the hippocampus identifies a familiar sensory pattern it assigns it a "safe" value if the person's past exposure to that pattern has been benign. When the hippocampus identifies an unfamiliar sensory pattern, or one that has been seen as dangerous in the past, it assigns a "dangerous" value to it. Context is important to the interpretation of sensory inputs over the low road. For example, a loud bang at a Fourth of July fireworks show is considered to be "safe" while a similar noise in the workplace or at home would usually be considered "dangerous." People with a damaged hippocampus often overgeneralize sensory inputs, treating even familiar sensory inputs as unfamiliar and therefore assigning them the emotional meaning of being dangerous.

From the hippocampus, the brain information judged to be dangerous travels to many centers, including the locus ceruleus (LC), the brain's alarm or panic center. This small but very important collection of nerve cells is located in the pons in the brainstem, right in the center of the base of the brain. After input from the hippocampus arrives in the LC, the danger signals in the brain are sent to sites of action to deal with the danger. These recipients of danger messages from the LC include the hormone center of the brain, the hypothalamus. There danger signals trigger the pituitary hormones associated with responses to stress. Signals go from the LC to many other parts of the brain, including the brain's parietal cortex, which controls the muscles needed for the fight-or-flight responses to danger. The low road brain circuitry functions without conscious thought. It is an emergency automatic pilot that manages immediate responses to danger. This is the primitive, basic brain system to manage fear and danger.

The second brain circuit that manages responses to danger—the high road—also starts with sensory inputs that flow from all parts of the body into the thalamus. However, unlike the low road, this brain circuit routes the signals from the thalamus to the cortex of the brain, the gray matter on the brain's surface. In particular, signals involving fear are carried to the medial prefrontal cortex of the brain. This is the gray matter on the outside of the brain toward the front of the head. This is the part of the brain needed for conscious thought, the formulation of ideas, and the attribution of meaning. The cortex is needed to provide complex analysis of a wide range of sensory inputs, including those that are sent from the thalamus relating to possible danger. The prefrontal cortex is where judgment is added to the mix of brain signals.

The cortex is the most highly developed and largest part of the human brain. An extensive brain cortex is distinctive in humans and closely related animals such as monkeys, although all mammals have some cerebral cortex in their brains. When the cortex is removed from laboratory animals, they lack judgment with respect to possible dangers. Strikingly, they exhibit more fear than when they have functioning cortex material. This experiment shows that the brain's cortex is involved in moderating as well as managing reactions to possible danger.

Both the high road and the low road circuits have important roles in the brain's responses to danger. Once danger is perceived by either road, the brain mobilizes the fight-or-flight response to stress. This involves changes in stress hormones, regulation of breathing and blood flow, and motor responses such as those needed to run away from the danger. These same fundamental brain mechanisms can be mobilized not only by actual dangers but by thoughts of danger that arise from specific cues that have been associated with past dangers. The brain learns from experiences. Past fear reactions are particularly powerful in shaping future behaviors. When an experience has been repeatedly associated with fear and danger, then even the anticipation of that experience, even the thought of it, triggers the cascade of brain changes associated with danger and stress.

When you take a child to a Fourth of July fireworks display for the first time, the child lacks an adequate context from past experience into which he or she can put what is about to happen. The bright lights and the incredibly loud explosions are, in themselves, terrifying to a young child. Before the sun sets and the fireworks display begins, loving adults (usually that means the child's parents) explain what is to come. The adults hold the child's hand or sit the child in their laps for reassurance. Using the words from the adults, the child's prefrontal cortex reframes the dramatic sensory inputs. From the words of the trusted adults the child's brain changes the sensory signal produced by the explosions in the sky from "dangerous" to "fun." The high road brain circuit receives the low road signal of danger because the sensory input from the fireworks is completely unfamiliar; therefore, it is automatically experienced as dangerous. Thanks to the adults' reassuring words, the high road has additional and vitally important information. The explanation from caring adults changes the meaning of the powerful sensory input. That is the effect of the brain's cortex, the effect of conscious thought that is provided by the high road.

The next time the child experiences Fourth of July fireworks, not only will the cortex offer reassurance but also, unlike the first time the child saw the flashes and heard the booms from the fireworks, the hippocampus will provide information about the context of these dramatic sensory inputs. This important information from the hippocampus on the second exposure will come from the brain's low road fear circuit. Like the information coming from the child's prefrontal cortex, this information will change the meaning of the sensory inputs from the thalamus, reversing the meaning and therefore the behavioral responses. The sensory input itself arriving into the thalamus, and sent out from there via both the high road and the low road, is not changed. But the meaning attributed to that sensory input is completely transformed by the information provided within the brain from both the high road and the low road as the experience of fireworks becomes familiar and well known to the child to be safe and fun.

In our example, even in the first exposure to the fireworks there was more going on in the child's brain than merely the verbal reassurance given by the adults. The adults held the child close when the fireworks display began. This gave context to the sensory inputs on the first exposure to the fireworks even though those extreme sensory inputs were utterly without precedent for the child and even though loud noises are one of the few innate fear-generating stimuli for all mammals regardless of their past experiences.

Now let's give this first exposure to fireworks another context. Assume that the adults did not help the child but were busy with their own interests as the time drew near for the fireworks display to begin. Since the adults had no fear of fireworks they simply assumed that the child would not fear them either. Or, even worse, the adults and older children the child revered might laugh at the young child's fear over such an innocent holiday display. Think about how the child would process this experience under those circumstances. Not only would the fireworks be terrifying but the child would feel alone and humiliated. Think of how that child would react to the next exposure to fireworks. In this version of the story, the inputs from both the high road and the low road would not be reassuring. In this scenario we have sensitization to fear reactions incorporated into the brain. In this scenario both the high road and the low road are primed for heightened fear reactions on future exposures that are judged to be similar and that may be generalized beyond just Fourth of July fireworks to include many other potentially frightening experiences.

Before leaving this holiday story, let us do some more changing, this time about the child. When it comes to fears, all three-year-olds are no more alike than are all parents. Some three-year-olds have fear mechanisms that are set on a hair trigger. It does not take much to scare these kids. A child like that might not be fully reassured in the dark as the fireworks are exploding overhead, even by the most considerate and nurturing adult.

Or the child could have been born with a fear mechanism that had a safety lock on the fear trigger. In other words, some children are all but impervious to fear. In these virtually fearless children the LC rarely fires off its signal of danger. In this scenario, even with careless, preoccupied parents this child would be untroubled by even the most dramatic fireworks display.

Here is yet one more observation about this common experience of fireworks: notice how closely related fear and excitement are in the brain. There is often only a slight shift in meaning between something that is terrifying and something that is a joy. The scariest rides at an amusement park have the longest lines of kids wanting to get on them!

Our point here is that no matter how automatic the brain's fear reactions are, when it comes to human experiences, they are not simple. One size does not fit all when it comes to understanding the anxious brain. There is a huge variability in fear reactions among different people—even within a single person at different times. One of the biggest factors governing the brain's fear responses is the meaning attributed to the potentially fear-generating experience. In other words, the cortex is king when it comes to the brain's management of fear.

It is important that you understand the two basic brain pathways for fear because they are both important in understanding anxiety. In this book we especially focus on the role of the cortex, which assigns meaning to sensory experiences, because that is where this book is able to have its greatest effects. The cortex is where all psychotherapy, including cognitive-behavioral treatment, has many of its effects.

Lest we overstate the role of the cortex in anxiety, recall once more our example of the child at the Fourth of July fireworks display. Not all of the reassuring magic was in the adults' words. The human touch was vitally important, as was the context of the child being with trusted adults who were supportive and understanding. Think how different that experience would have been for that child if the "trusted adults" had themselves been afraid of the fireworks or, making this more psychological, if one of the child's parents had been afraid of fireworks but was embarrassed by that fear and therefore had bundled the child off at the last minute saying, "I don't want him to be frightened so I am taking him home now."

In our initial story, sitting in an adult's lap was a big part of what made that fear-reducing experience work. Helpful also was the attention given by the adults, firmly and respectfully reassuring the child in advance to help him or her process the potentially terrifying and disturbing sensory experiences that were to come.

Think again about the experience of that child if the loving adults had not taken the child to the fireworks at all because "the fireworks are too frightening for a child of this age, so we will leave her at home tonight. We don't want her to have to endure that much stress at this age." If that had happened, the child would have learned nothing. In fact the child's fear on subsequent exposures to fireworks could have been magnified by the adult's view that the sounds and sights of fireworks were too stressful for the young child to be exposed to.

Here's yet another take on that fireworks experience. What if the child had been hurt or what if a person the child cared for had been hurt in an experience that the fireworks would remind the child of? Suppose the child's father had been shot on the front porch, or the child's mother had been injured in a noisy automobile accident. In these terrible cases the child's brain would have already been sensitized to loud noises as signals of real danger. Then the challenges on the Fourth of July for the child and for the adults would have been greater. Our advice would have been the same: Go to the fireworks and help the child manage his or her fears. But the problems faced by both child and adults would have been much more difficult in such situations.

There are many lessons in this exploration of brain biology for anxious people and for those who want to help an anxious person get well. Neither the high road nor the low road is simple or easily managed, even with greater understanding. However, having an understanding of how the brain handles fear helps us think more clearly and more constructively about the common experiences of fear in our lives.

The Neurotransmitters

Having looked at the brain circuitry, the way the brain's neurons are hooked together when it comes to the experience of fear, we need to shift to consider the chemicals by which the brain does its internal communicating. We will also look at how the brain communicates with the rest of the body about fear. Let's focus on the neurotransmitters that are involved in fear and anxiety. Fear can arise from an external threat. Fear can also arise from sensations originating within the body. A severe pain in the chest, for example, which may be interpreted as a heart attack, can lead to fear that is at least as intense as the fear produced by a criminal pointing a gun at your head.

To understand how the brain handles danger, whether the source of that danger is internal or external, you will need to understand these five chemically based brain systems: *the norepinephrine system, the serotonin system, the dopamine system, the corticotropin-releasing hormone system*, and *the benzodiazepine system*. These five chemical systems involve brain anatomy as described above, but instead of focusing on the physical linkages of the neurons, here we focus on the chemical messengers used by the brain to communicate within the brain and with the body as a whole. This chemical focus is important to understanding anxiety because one of the primary ways doctors relate to any illnesses is by using medicines that influence the chemicals inside the body.

Although today doctors do not do much to rearrange the brain's anatomy, they do many things that rearrange the brain's chemistry. Medicines do this without the need of brain surgery. Unlike surgery to rearrange the brain's anatomy, changes made by medicines are reversible. This means that if the patient and the doctor do not like the way a particular medicine works, then the medicine can be stopped and the patient's brain returns to its previous state. This fact is especially important to anxious patients who worry too much about bad outcomes and who often think too little about possible good outcomes, including good outcomes from medical treatments for anxiety. It is reassuring for an anxious patient taking medicine to know that if problems are caused by the use of the medicine, or if the results are less than hoped for, then the medicine can simply be stopped.

The Norepinephrine System

Epinephrine is produced in the two adrenal glands that sit like hats on top of the kidneys. Epinephrine, also called adrenaline, mobilizes the body for acute danger and stress. The epinephrine-related stress-management chemical in the brain is norepinephrine, or noradrenaline. This is the major chemical in the brain that deals specifically with fear. About 90 pecent of the brain's norepinephrine is found in the tiny locus ceruleus (LC), the brain's alarm center. The LC is connected to the neurons in all of the parts of the brain that manage emotions, including the medial prefrontal cortex, the amygdala, and the hippocampus.

When you are frightened, the brain's norepinephrine system swings into high gear, producing changes not only in the brain but throughout your body. For example, temperature, heart rate, and blood pressure all rise when you are frightened. Blood is taken out of the intestines and out of the skin and is put into the muscles to prepare for flight. That is why you turn "white as a sheet" and may feel the need to urinate or defecate when you are very frightened.

The Serotonin System

Serotonin is more widely dispersed in the brain as a neurotransmitter than norepinephrine, but it is also found in many of the same areas as norepinephrine, including the cortex, the amygdala, and the hippocampus. Serotonin receptors are correlated with anxiety. The brain has many distinct serotonin receptors, some of which increase anxiety and some of which decrease it. The complex serotonin system is the site of some of the most active research in the development of new antianxiety (and antidepressant) medicines. Laboratory animals exposed to stress show increased serotonin activity in their brains.

The Dopamine System

Dopamine is the neurotransmitter most involved in reward, sometimes called "pleasure," and in modulation of mood. Dopamine is closely related to the endorphins, the brain's own pleasure-producing chemicals, which use some of the same brain receptors as are used by opiate drugs such as heroin and morphine. Dopamine is thought to play an especially important role in social anxiety disorder, but because this neurotransmitter is so important in moods it probably has a role in all anxiety problems. Acute stress triggers widespread dopamine release in the brain.

The Corticotropin-Releasing Hormone (CRH) System

Stress, fear, and anxiety all trigger the CRH system located in the hypothalamus, the brain structure that lies below the thalamus. This collection of neurons is located immediately above the pituitary gland, the body's "master gland," which the hypothalamus controls. Studies have not shown elevated levels of CRH in the spinal fluid of patients with some anxiety disorders. However, because the CRH system is so closely related to stress and fear activation in the brain, and because abnormalities in CRH levels have been shown in posttraumatic stress disorder, it is likely that future research will learn more about the specific role of the CRH system in anxiety.

In response to danger, the hypothalamic-pituitary-adrenal axis swings into action with the release of CRH, which triggers the release of cortisol (a major stress-management hormone) and ACTH, which triggers the release of epinephrine and other hormones from the adrenal gland.

The Benzodiazepine System

Approximately 40 percent of the brain's more than 100 billion neurons use the neurotransmitter gamma-aminobutyric acid, or GABA. The highest concentration of GABA receptors in the brain is in the cortical gray matter, unlike norepinephrine receptors, which are primarily found in the more primitive brain stem. The GABA receptors are part of the benzodiazepine system, so called because this is the system that benzodiazepines influence. The benzodiazepines are a group of closely related medicines including Valium (diazepam), Xanax (alprazolam), and Klonopin (clonazepam). Introduced in the early 1960s, these medicines have proven to be uniquely helpful in the treatment of all of the many manifestations of anxiety, including all of the anxiety disorders. The benzodiazepines increase and prolong the effects of GABA, the brain's primary quieting neurotransmitter.

Because of this powerful antianxiety effect, researchers first identified the benzodiazepine receptor in the brain using this work to understand a great deal more about the biology of anxiety. GABA is the brain's specific antianxiety or antiworry neurotransmitter. Research has shown that people with panic disorder have a smaller number of benzodiazepine receptors than nonanxious people. Animals exposed to chronic stress show reduced benzodiazepine receptor binding, which is, in turn, associated with defects in memory. Chronically anxious animals show reduced ability to think. For example, chronically anxious laboratory rats lose their ability to escape from a maze.

Animals as Teachers about Human Anxiety

Life, often quite literally, depends on the avoidance of danger. This is true from the smallest one-celled organism to the human being. The three minimal requirements for an organism's "fear" are these: (1) a way to detect signals from the environment, (2) a way to identify which of those signals are associated with danger, and (3) a way of escaping from danger. One-celled bacteria, which evolved about 1 billion years ago, meet this three-part test. Bacteria typically have five to seven whiplike flagella that rotate in the same way that propellers work in a boat. Bacteria use their flagella to move in water toward food (such as sugar) and to move away from danger (such as a noxious chemical). Without any nervous tissue, the "learning" of bacteria is limited to simple habituation, with "memory" being restricted to about half a second.

Moving up the evolutionary ladder, mammals split off from their reptilian ancestors during the age of the dinosaurs, about 250 million years ago. One of the major differences between the mammalian brain and the reptilian brain is the much higher development of the limbic system in the brains of all mammals. This larger limbic system endows mammals with a range of distinctive behaviors. One of the most striking behaviors of mammals is separation anxiety, which is seen in all young mammals and in no reptiles. Infant mammals cry out for their mothers when they are left alone. This remarkable behavior is part of the highly social behavior of mammals. Mammals show intense social attachments—especially the attachments of mothers and infants, which is one of the hallmarks of mammalian behavior.

Infant laboratory rats and mice respond even to their first experienced separation from their mothers with loud calls in a characteristic ultrasonic frequency. In other words, there is no learning or conditioning required for this response. It is innate and universal in young mammals. Later research showed that this crying by the infant rodents was not necessarily a response to movement into a strange setting, to rough handling, or to loud noises. Simply removing the mother and the littermates produced long and loud crying. This experiment showed that it was the loss of social contact that triggered this separation distress. Isolated rat pups learned difficult mazes to regain contact with their mothers. They experienced even short periods of contact with their mothers as strongly reinforcing, and they experienced cues associated with separation from their mothers as strongly and enduringly aversive.

Rat pups learned less well when separated from their mothers except for learning threats of danger or negative cues. The pups were even more responsive to negative cues when separated from their mothers. Experiments with infant rats also showed that when rats reached the equivalence of adolescence, they lost their separation anxiety. Most strikingly, it has been found that medicines that reduce human anxiety also block the separation anxiety of young rat pups. When given Prozac or Valium, infant rats no longer cried out for their mothers when they were left alone. They just quietly (or nonanxiously) waited for their mothers to return.

Researchers investigated whether there were differences between individual rat pups in their sensitivity to separation anxiety. Within five generations of selective breeding, the scientists were able to breed strains of rats that consistently had either high sensitivity or low sensitivity to separation anxiety. This demonstrated clearly the genetic basis of the differences in this trait among rat pups. These researchers are now exploring the differences in the brain chemistry of the two strains of rats and are also looking for other differences in behavior between these two strains.

Much closer to the human brain than the rat's brain is the brain of monkeys, which have 90 to 99 percent of the same genes as humans. One group of researchers has found a group of wild rhesus moneys living on an island in the Caribbean in which about 20 percent of the monkeys have what appears to be a mild form of generalized anxiety. Infants in this group showed less exploratory behavior. As adolescents, when their mothers left them for hours or even for days during breeding season, these young monkeys showed greater agitation than their nonanxious peers under similar circumstances. When their mothers stayed away a long time, the anxious monkeys showed lethargy and assumed a fetal-like huddled posture associated with social withdrawal. The investigators took these behaviors to be the monkey equivalents of human depression.

The anxiety-prone monkeys had greatly increased sensitivity to inadequate mothering, as when they were experimentally reared with peers instead of with their mothers. This sort of motherless, but otherwise adequate, rearing made their anxiety symptoms worse. On the other hand, the physical, motor, and many social behaviors in these anxious moneys developed normally. The anxious young monkeys had a strong tendency toward anxious withdrawal and avoidance of novel experiences that increased as they became young adults. The anxious monkeys dropped to the bottom of the social hierarchies within the monkey colonies. Importantly, if these biologically anxious monkeys were raised as infants by unusually nurturtant and experienced mothers, then the expression of their anxious traits was entirely prevented.

These animal models of anxiety show that anxiety traits are heritable. The high levels of anxiety traits seen in these wild animal communities provide an opportunity for natural selection to act upon these traits. This suggests that in many environments there are selective advantages to at least modest levels of anxiety, especially when the population is subject to harsh and dangerous conditions. This animal research also underlines the importance of mothering in the expression of anxious traits. In the human context it offers real hope that early identification and intervention with anxious children can prevent the expression of many of the more maladaptive expressions of anxiety later in life.

The separation anxiety calling response of infant mammals is similar to the behaviors seen in very young birds. In the species where this behavior has been studied, the infant crying for the lost mother has shown to be remarkably similar to the phenomenon of agoraphobia in humans, which has been called "adult separation anxiety."

These are exciting times for everyone concerned with the problems of anxiety. Never before has so much attention been focused on anxiety and never before have there been so many good treatments for people with anxiety. It is impressive that so many talented people are today working hard to understand anxiety and to find new treatments for it. Even better, there is every reason to expect that the pace of discovery of new and better treatments for anxiety will increase in coming years with improved understanding of the biology of the anxious brain.

The picture of the anxious brain outlined in this chapter will be expanded in the discussion of medicines in Chapter 4. In that chapter we will zero in on the neurotransmitter systems that manage anxiety and see how medicines normalize the disturbed chemistry of the anxious brain. Most remarkably of all, in recent years scientists have learned that the anxious brain's chemistry can be changed not only by using medicines— by adding highly specific chemicals to the brain's environment—but also by changing thoughts and behaviors. It will come as no surprise that thoughts and behaviors reflect chemical events in the brain. Recognition that the anxious brain's disturbed chemistry can be normalized by specific changes in thinking and behaving is both new and gratifying. Healing strategies that do not involve medicines have been organized into the form of psychotherapy called cognitive-behavior treatment. The biology of the anxious brain is important for understanding not only how medicines work but also how CBT works.

CHAPTER 2

The Vocabulary of Anxiety

In Chapter 1 we outlined the biology of the anxious brain. The complexities of the brain are not easy to understand and they are certainly not easily recognized by an anxious person. In this chapter we break down the feelings experienced by the anxious person into the basic anxious states to make it easier to learn and to communicate about the complex experience of anxiety. It is important to learn the vocabulary of anxiety not only to think and talk about your own experiences with anxiety, but also to help you use information as new research is reported. The vocabulary of anxiety will help you understand how brain biology, medicines, and therapy all relate to your inner experiences of anxiety.

Worry along with tension and irritability are the central features of the six distinctive anxiety disorders: *agoraphobia/panic disorder (PD); specific phobia; social phobia; generalized anxiety disorder (GAD); obsessive-compulsive disorder (OCD);* and *posttraumatic stress disorder (PTSD)*. To understand these common and serious disorders, we need to have a vocabulary that lets us think constructively about what is happening in our minds and bodies.

First, we need to understand the terms *normal fear, normal anxiety,* and *pathological anxiety*. Then we need to understand the three types of pathological anxiety: *spontaneous panic, situational panic,* and *anticipatory anxiety*. Finally, we will discuss *avoidance*. Once we understand these terms, we can think more clearly about the anxiety disorders.

The vocabulary of anxiety disorders reflects the brain biology that underlies these disorders. This vocabulary also is essential to understanding these mysterious and powerful illnesses. The Anxiety Cure program relies on this vocabulary. The vocabulary also allows you to make the best use of the growing literature about recovery from anxiety.

What Is Normal Fear?

From time to time everyone has fear, the uncomfortable feelings of tension and worry that something bad may happen. These feelings of normal fear are healthy reactions to actual or possible danger. They reflect the fight-or-flight response triggered by two closely related chemicals, norepinephrine (also called noradrenaline), which is a brain neurotransmitter, and epinephrine (also called adrenaline), which is a messenger of danger from the adrenal gland that goes through the bloodstream to every cell in the body. The feelings of fear are the equivalent of having a fire in your home or a burglar alarm going off. Fear signals you to be alert, to look for danger. Physical expressions of fear are sweating, trembling, a tight chest, a lump in the throat, a gastrointestinal system shutdown, and tense muscles. The blood supply in your intestines shuts off, which may even lead to vomiting. Your blood, in stress, is sent to your muscles to prepare for fight or flight, for emergency action. Mental expressions of fear are having thoughts of danger that something terrible is about to happen. A fearful person whose fear reaction has been triggered is hypervigilant, on edge, keyed up, and ready for possible disaster.

The feelings of fear are understandable as the body's fight-or-flight mechanisms swing into action when the danger is real. Even if the fearful feelings are uncomfortable, they are not hard to understand. Moments of impending danger are moments when it makes sense to be keyed up and worried. Anticipation of possible danger is a necessary mental process. In fact, people who are not fearful at such times are in trouble, because they are not likely to take action to reduce their risk or to prepare for dangers that may be coming their way.

Fearful reactions are equally understandable in response to something that isn't directly happening to you. For example, you could get a phone call from the police telling you that someone close to you has been injured seriously in an automobile accident. There is no danger to the person being called; the danger is a thought or an idea and is not a threat to the anxious person's own body. The risk is of the loss of, or harm to, a loved one. The threat is the suffering not only of yourself but also of others you care about. In this case, the feelings of dread and terror associated with the adrenal glands pumping out spurts of epinephrine and the brain sending urgent messages by norepinephrine are normal. Danger is real in everyone's life. When accompanying danger, fear is healthy and should be seen as a friend.

What Is Normal Anxiety?

It is helpful to distinguish fear from anxiety, although both emotions use the same fight-or-flight mechanisms. *Fear is the experience of an immediate, real danger. Anxiety is the body's signal of possible future danger, a sort of emotional early warning system.* To think about primitive human experiences that triggered these physical and mental experiences, picture a tiger attacking a person holding a flimsy stick for protection. How do you suppose that stick-holding ancestor of ours felt at seeing that tiger poised to spring? Once having experienced and survived such an attack, how do you think our ancestors felt when they thought about the possibilities of such an attack in the future? It is not difficult to imagine panic and anticipatory anxiety in such a setting. A more contemporary example is understandable when you imagine your feeling if your car skidded uncontrollably on an icy street, spinning around and around toward parked cars. When the road iced up again, you would remember that incident and feel anxiety as a result of that experience. The memory of the earlier episode with your spinning car triggers anxiety when you drive on icy streets or even when you hear a weather forecast of possible icy roads. Anxiety is your mind identifying possible dangers and taking the necessary steps to prepare for those dangers.

When you felt your heart in your throat as your car spun out of control on the ice, you felt fear. When you felt your palms sweat and your heartbeat quicken as you looked out of your window the next winter at an icy street on which you were about to drive, you felt anxiety. Anxiety, like fear, is a healthy, normal emotion.

False Alarms: Pathological Anxiety

If you suffer from anxiety disorders you experience the feelings and thoughts that reflect the same basic fight-or-flight mechanisms mobilizing your mind and body for danger. But for you these feelings and thoughts are triggered when there is no generally understandable danger, or your thoughts and feelings are dramatically in excess of the feelings most people have in similar circumstances. This is what makes pathological anxiety. There is no tiger, no car spinning out of control, and no police officer on the phone with tragic news. If your heart sinks whenever you hear a siren or whenever your phone rings because it *might* be the police telling you that one of your loved ones has just been killed, that is pathological anxiety, and you probably have an anxiety disorder. Your body is responding to a false alarm.

If you experience panicky feelings when you leave home, drive on a highway, go to a shopping mall, or get on an elevator, then you probably have an anxiety disorder. When thinking about your fears, you are likely to overstate the risks. Ask yourself: "How do most healthy, sensible people react to this situation? Do they experience fear and anxiety or not?" If they do, that is normal fear. If they do not, that is probably pathological anxiety.

If your intense feelings of worry, which most other people do not experience, wake you up at night or come out of the blue at any time of the day, then you have an anxiety disorder. If you spend hours every day thinking about, fearing, and expecting these feelings, if you give up important activities in your life because of these feelings or because of the anticipation of having them, then you have an anxiety disorder. If you worry endlessly and senselessly about feelings in your body, fearing a dreaded illness even when your doctor says you are not ill, then you have an anxiety disorder.

Anxiety is experienced in your muscles as tension. Your muscles are set on edge for hours at a time. They feel stiff and tense. Muscle pain is a common outgrowth of the muscle tension. Irritability is a common symptom of anxiety. As your brain holds worry and fear for hours at a stretch, you feel exhausted and upset. Situations and events that would not otherwise bother you cause you to feel upset and irritable. Relaxation is hard to come by. Sleep is elusive. Especially harmed is the ability to fall asleep, as fear and anxiety come to dominate your life.

Having the feelings of anxiety is always extremely uncomfortable for the same reason that it is uncomfortable when a burglar alarm goes off. These are powerful signals that immediate action—fight or flight—is required. When anxious, your brain is hyperalert, and you search your environment and your thoughts for possible dangers. You find dangers where other people in the same situations do not find them, when other people who do not have anxiety disorders do not hear the burglar alarm that dominates your life night and day.

This is pathological anxiety. It is not the same as normal anxiety because it is not logical. Pathological anxiety is not a useful response that prepares a person for real danger. The unreasonable danger signal of pathological anxiety itself becomes a serious problem that results in major losses in the quality of your life. Imagine trying to live a normal life in your home if the burglar alarm went off without warning or reason *and* if no one else could see the flashing lights or hear the siren.

When you have anxious feelings and thoughts for no generally recognized reason, then you feel not only that you are in peril from a possible external danger but also that you are faced with an even more upsetting internal danger. It is easy to conclude that something is terribly wrong with you, with how your brain and your body are working. Is it any wonder that people with anxiety disorders often think that they are in danger of dying, going crazy, or losing control? Is it surprising that most people with anxiety disorders fear that they are suffering from life-threatening physical illnesses such as brain tumors and heart attacks?

Many people with anxiety disorders think that they have cancer or mysterious diseases that their doctors cannot find. When they go to their doctors to get these problems checked out, they are often told, "Nothing is wrong. It's just stress." Is it any wonder that such information is mystifying and troubling, especially if their lives are no different from those of other people who do not have this problem, and their stress is no different from the stress they had experienced before this anxiety disorder began? How can anything so real be "imaginary"? As we saw in Chapter 1, there is indeed something wrong with the brain of the person with an anxiety disorder. This disease is not imaginary or simply the result of stress.

Pathological anxiety is a false alarm that steals the body's healthy danger signals. It has physical manifestations—rapid heart rate, shallow breathing, tight chest, sweaty palms, distorted sight and hearing, and the feeling that you need to empty your bladder and bowels. That is the easy part! The really hard part of pathological anxiety is the thinking that goes along with these distressing feelings. *Discomfort* and *pain* are too mild. *Terror* and *dread* come closer. You think, for example, that you or a loved one are in immediate danger of death from an accident or incurable illness. You must act right now; there is not a moment to lose! Failure to act is intolerable and unimaginable. Everything else is gone from your mind as you devote all your thinking capacity to the urgent demands of the danger you feel and think. That danger, which seems more real than reality, is a false alarm.

Anxiety Is a Disease

A disease is a predictable pattern of problems, with physical components, that has a negative effect on the sufferer's life. Each disease has a range of severities and highly personal expressions. A disability results from a disease when it adversely affects one or more major life functions, such as work, social life, recreation, or physical activities. *The anxiety disorders are serious diseases, and they often cause serious disabilities.*

The feelings of pathological anxiety in the body often change, sometimes rapidly, so that just when you think that you finally understand them, there is a new symptom, an unfamiliar manifestation of the anxiety problem, to add new depth to your worry. The feelings of abnormal worry are terribly distressing. The natural, normal reactions to these feelings and thoughts of anxiety are to pull back, to stick close to home, to stay with safe and familiar people, and to stay near someone and someplace that can provide help if you need it on a moment's notice.

Is it any wonder that many people with anxiety disorders stay close to home and limit their activities, especially in unfamiliar places? This tendency on the part of people with anxiety disorders has often been misinterpreted as indicating that they are timid or dependent. Although some clinically anxious people are timid and dependent, most are not.

The anxiety disorders are not the result of a pathological dependency. You are not anxious because you are a dependent person. Rather, the pathological anxiety from which you suffer causes you to be fearful of being alone and of situations that may trigger panicky feelings. Similarly, you are not anxious because you lack self-confidence. Most people with anxiety disorders also develop, sooner or later, low self-esteem because they have so much difficulty doing ordinary things that nonanxious people do with little or no difficulty.

What Are Spontaneous Panic and Situational Panic?

Panic is a sudden burst of anxiety, a sharp surge of norepinephrine and epinephrine. This is the first fear produced by anxiety; it is the chemical signal that comes from your own brain to cause the physical sensations of anxiety. Panic frequently comes unbidden to dominate the thoughts and the behaviors of people with anxiety disorders. *Spontaneous panic* occurs when intense feelings and thoughts of panic come out of the blue, for no apparent reason. *Situational panic* occurs when panicky feelings and thoughts are closely tied to particular places or activities that repeatedly cause panic for an individual sufferer.

Agoraphobia/panic disorder usually starts with spontaneous panic and evolves to be mostly or even entirely situational panic, although the situations that trigger panic may be both many and varied. Being tired, stressed, or sick can make panic attacks more likely to occur. In specific phobia, the panic is limited to a particular situational panic, and the panic does not usually shift from one situation to another or involve multiple situations and/or activities, as it does for agoraphobia/panic disorder. Situational panic may arise when driving, flying, shopping, or riding in closed-in places such as elevators. For each person, the specific circumstances that trigger situational panic are usually consistent over the course of many years. People who are psychologically minded can sometimes recognize what particular disturbing thoughts brought on their spontaneous panicky episodes, but often there seems to be no way to understand what triggers them.

The most important fact to know about panic attacks, both spontaneous and situational, is that they will not harm your body. *Panic attacks do not cause heart attacks, strokes, or other serious physical problems.* In addition, panic attacks do not cause you to pass out, go crazy, or lose control of your body. A person having a panic attack can do anything a person not having a panic attack can do, including driving a car or giving a speech. Panic attacks cause terrible feelings—the worst possible feelings—but they do not cause loss of consciousness or loss of control of your body. You might feel as if you will pass out, go crazy, or lose control, but that will not happen. Panic is a normal reaction to danger and, as such, is itself not dangerous. Panic attacks are distressing but not dangerous. They are the body's normal alarm going off inappropriately. And then, because they are inappropriate, panic attacks trigger frightening self-doubt: "What is wrong with me?" This is not part of normal fear reactions.

What Is Anticipatory Anxiety?

The third common type of pathological anxiety, in addition to spontaneous panic and situational panic, is anticipatory anxiety. This is the fear of panic, and it often leads to avoidance or a phobia. Usually panic, often spontaneous panic, comes first in the course of the development of an anxiety disorder. Later in the development of the anxiety disorder, the sufferer comes to anticipate fearfully the reemergence of panic. The panic itself is called the "first fear," and the anticipated panic is called the "second fear." As it was described by Dr. Claire Weekes, the Australian physician who was a pioneer in the treatment of the anxiety disorders, the second fear usually dominates the anxious person's life within a few months of the onset of the illness and leads to the avoidance.

Avoidance Leads to Phobias

It is the avoidance, the "holes in the lives" of anxious people, that creates the disabilities in the anxiety disorders. A pattern of specific avoidance creates a phobia. Anxious people commonly avoid behaviors, situations, or activities that are otherwise a normal part of life. For example, some anxious people avoid elevators, shopping, or flying. Other anxious people avoid public speaking or crowded places. Phobic avoidance is caused by the brain's signals that there is grave danger in otherwise routine situations.

Elevator phobics are not so much avoiding elevators as they are avoiding their panicky feelings that are triggered by going into elevators. Although phobic people often speak of dangers in their phobic situations in their efforts to explain their behaviors to themselves and to others (for example, fearing airplane crashes or losing control of the car on an interstate highway), their fundamental fears are the dreadful feelings these experiences cause them.

To understand anxiety disorders, you must fix that understanding in your thoughts. The central problem is not fear of dying or getting stuck in an elevator. The central problem of all anxiety disorders is fear of the panic, fear of the anticipatory anxiety itself. The central problem is the unpleasant feelings (and thoughts) that are the anxiety disorder.

The serious problem facing the anxious person is found not outside but inside the anxious person. That is why it is not helpful to a flying phobic to explain rationally the low risks of flying or why it does not help the person who is phobic about crowds to say, "There is nothing to fear." There is something to fear, but it is not the airplane or the crowd. The basic problem is the inappropriate brain reactions taking place in the phobic person's brain. That fact explains why nonphobic people cannot understand the behavior of phobic people. Nonanxious people are not having the same experience in the airplane, in the elevator, or in the crowded supermarket because nonanxious people do not have severe alarm signals going off in their brains in these places. Because these inappropriate terror reactions occur over and over again in the same situations, phobic people become conditioned to this fear reaction and begin to suffer from anticipatory anxiety, the second fear. It and avoidance are the central features of this "what if" disease. The anxious person's brain is sensitized to these pathological reactions. That sensitization is the hallmark of the disease, its essential feature.

Understanding the Anxiety Dragon

Fear of fear is at the heart of the anxiety disorders, and it is like a dragon that attacks the suffering anxious person. Over the years we have learned a lot about this dragon and how he operates because we have seen so many people who have suffered terribly from his attacks. We have come to view the dragon as male, but you may view the dragon as either male or female. Or neuter! Or as something other than a dragon. Whatever works for you.

The Dragon Wants You!

The dragon wants you to believe that he can kill you or, perhaps even more frightening, that he can make you go crazy, cause you to pass out, or cause you to do something uncontrolled or embarrassing. He does this with an awesome display of feelings and by causing terrifying involuntary thoughts. When the dragon has you on the run, when he has scared you out of your wits, he offers you this deal: "Give up part of your life and I will give you some peace!" What does the dragon want you to give up? It might be public speaking, going to a shopping mall, or flying on an airplane. It might be driving on a highway, going somewhere that is unfamiliar, or talking with someone you fear will reject or judge you, including a boss or other person in authority. The dragon wants to take control of your life, piece by piece.

People with obsessive-compulsive disorder (OCD) see a somewhat different face of the dragon than do people who suffer from the other anxiety disorders. The dragon tells people with OCD that something dreadful will happen to them or to someone they care about if they do not behave in a certain way, such as washing their hands endlessly, checking something a thousand times, or repeating a senseless behavior or thought dozens of times in unusual, ritualized ways. These actions of a person with OCD are called compulsions. They are the equivalent of the phobias, which cause avoidance behaviors in many other anxious people. Once the dragon gets control of their lives, most phobic people eliminate certain normal behaviors from their lives (such as driving or shopping) as a result of anticipatory anxiety.

People with OCD, in contrast, have additional abnormal behaviors as a result of the dragon's influence on their lives. People who suffer from OCD do their best to hide their abnormal (dragon-driven) behaviors, just as phobic people do their best to hide their missing normal behaviors. For those with OCD, the abnormal behaviors are something added to their lives by fear; for other anxious people, phobias lead to the absence of normal behaviors from their lives. Both compulsions and phobias are the result of accepting the dragon's dreadful deals in the hope of lessening uncomfortable feelings. They are both ways of temporarily reducing panic and anxiety and lead to long-term restrictions in the lives of anxious people.

All anxiety disorders come down to the same thing. The dragon tells you, "Reshape your life the way I want you to and then I will give you a bit of peace, a bit of comfort. If, however, you do not comply right now, then I will cause your entire life to be filled with terror." The dragon does not countenance any delay in his gratification. He wants what he wants when he wants it. His approach is "Give me your life immediately—or else!"

The Dragon Is a Liar

Here are some things the dragon does not want you to know about him. He cannot do any of the things he tells you he can do. He cannot make you pass out or go crazy. He cannot cause you to have a brain tumor, a heart attack, or any other illness. He cannot make you have an automobile crash or do something uncontrolled. He cannot leave you stuck in the terror of a PTSD flashback. People suffering from anxiety disorders, or "dragon attacks," often doubt this because they have believed the dragon. They tell us just how close they have come to awful outcomes as a result of repeated dragon attacks. We have come to call the anxiety disorders the diseases of "this close," as people say, putting their fingers very close together, "I came 'this close' to passing out" or "I came 'this close' to having an accident." When someone tells us that they repeatedly came "this close" to something terrible happening, we know we are dealing with the work of the anxiety disorders dragon.

A woman who was simultaneously dying from metastatic breast cancer and suffering from agoraphobia said: "If I could be cured right now of one of these two diseases, I would choose to be cured of the agoraphobia because that disease ruins my life every single day. The cancer will kill me one day before too long, but until it does I can live a reasonably happy and full life. The agoraphobia wrecks my life all day, every day."

A sixty-five-year-old businessman who was a veteran of the Korean War developed agoraphobia at the age of thirty. He became virtually housebound, traveling only to and from his work. He insisted that his wife be with him whenever he went anywhere except to work or back home. He said: "It is incomprehensible to me that in the war, when I faced death, I felt only ordinary fear, which was not much of a problem for me. I parachuted into battle, and I was decorated for bravery several times. After the war, I traveled alone all over the world without fear. Now that I have this terrible agoraphobia, I cannot go to the supermarket and I cannot drive on the freeways. I cannot visit my brother in New York. I do not understand what has happened to me. My life now is just not my own, even though I have had agoraphobia for more than half of my life."

This man's humiliation from his anxiety disorder was tempered by the memory of his personal history of heroism: "If I had not had that war experience, I might have come to believe over all these years that I really was weak and a coward. But when I look at my medals and I recall my war years, I know for sure that I am not weak and that I am not a coward. I also know that this problem you call my agoraphobia is a whole lot tougher than most people who have not had it imagine that it is."

We tell these two stories to make it clear that we respect the dragon for what he can do. He can produce terrible, terrible feelings. We have learned that these feelings are all that the dragon can do; his other threats are empty.

Here are some other important things we have learned about the dragon:

1. He operates by blackmail. Although the dragon asks you to give up a part of your normal life in return for peace from his attacks, when you do give up the pieces of your life demanded by the dragon, as most anxious people eventually do, he will not give you peace. He will be back again year after year, like all successful blackmailers, asking for more and more of your life. The dragon has no pity and no honor. His goal is to make you his hostage. He does not want you to roam free in your life. He wants you to stay behind the bars he has constructed for you. "Stay here and you will be safe. Go outside these bars and you will feel my full wrath," the dragon shouts through his bared teeth and multicolored, fiery breath.

2. The dragon can eat only one food—your fear. Nothing else except your fear of him can sustain the ever-hungry dragon. The more you fear the dragon, the more you feed him and the bigger and more terrible he grows. Stop fearing the dragon and you stop feeding him. Without your fear, he withers away and eventually dies of neglect.

3. The dragon's greatest strength is his talent for disguise. Just when his attacks become familiar to you, just when you resolve not to fear him, the dragon changes costumes and comes at you with entirely new symptoms, often pretending to be yet another deadly physical disorder. People with OCD sometimes experience the dragon as threatening not only themselves but also others, especially the people whom they love the most. The dragon may have threatened you with a brain tumor at the start, but then he shifted to threaten an ulcer or heart disease. The anxious pain may at first have been mostly in your arms or your back, but then your stomach or your bowels become affected. The dragon will scare you about the medicine you take and the food you eat, convincing you that they are poison and that any unfamiliar symptoms are life threatening. There is no limit to the dragon's skill at disguise. One tell-tale feature that is usually part of the picture when the dragon is involved is the extreme worry produced by the dragon's pretending to be a physical disease.

4. When you start to get well, the dragon grows more and more desperate. As he senses your possible escape from his prison, he pulls out his last trick. It is one of his best. He lets you go for days, weeks, or even for years without any trouble. He encourages you to think that you have defeated him. You grow more and more confident about your achievements and secure in your new, fuller life, free of the dragon and your fear of him. You come to think that your panic is part of a distant and unpleasant past.

Then one day when you least expect it, sometimes when you are under stress and sometimes when you are under no stress at all, the dragon comes back with full force. Panic grips you once more. You suddenly remember, as if for the first time, how awful the experience of panic has been. You are confused and afraid. You feel weak and defeated. Then, facing a severe relapse, you confront the true test of your work to recover from your anxiety disorder.

The Wizard

The wizard, like the dragon, is another imaginary creature we have found helpful in explaining how to recover from an anxiety problem.

The dragon is our caricature of the severe fear response that character-izes panic. The wizard is the personification of the wise teacher who pro-motes acceptance with the practical knowledge that you need to tame the fear. The wizard, who knows all the dragon's tricks, is compassionate in helping you stay focused on your antifear techniques and live in the moment. The dragon trys to drag you down the path of "what if" thoughts. The wizard says to keep in the here and now, and to realize that right now you are okay. The wizard says you are fine, even when you have panic. Panic is unpleasant, but it is not dangerous. The dragon's urging you to perform compulsive behaviors, if you have OCD, can feel overwhelming. The wizard helps you resist giving in to the dragon. The wizard reminds you that giving in to the dragon makes your anxiety problem worse. The wizard helps you keep this truth in perspective, even as the dragon tells you that he is really going to ruin you this time.

Most people we work with get the hang of listening to the voice of the dragon right away. They struggle more to find the calm, patient, wise voice of the wizard. That makes sense, because you have had a long time to practice doing things the way the dragon wants you to do them, but you have spent only a little time learning the wizard's magic. Next time you have a panicky moment, stop and think about what the wizard would say to you. If you can't find your wizard's voice on your own, ask a friend to help you think about what this wise voice would say. But don't always rely on someone else to find the voice. You want to find your cure to defeat the dragon. To do this you must find the wizard's voice inside yourself every time the dragon reappears. This may sound impossibly hard. If it does, for now it is enough to know that the wizard's voice is possible to find, and that it will help you overcome the dragon every time he comes to torment you.

Taming the Dragon with the Wizard

Jerry, a patient who owned a delicatessen, said that for twenty years he had gone only between home and work and nowhere else. He came for help in desperation when his daughter was getting married. He feared being "trapped" at the wedding ceremony when he would have to walk down the aisle. He had been in psychotherapy for years but had not got-ten any better from his panic disorder and agoraphobia. He learned about the dragon and how he could find freedom by facing the dragon respectfully but without fear.

Accept the Dragon

My previous therapy, which I had over all these years, told me that I needed to understand why the dragon chose to attack me, of all people. I needed to know why he attacked me just exactly when and how he did. Every therapist I saw taught me techniques for protecting my life from the dragon, closing my house and sealing the doors and windows so that the dragon could not get to me. I learned complicated, detailed breathing and relaxation techniques to help me stay calm. I never could keep the dragon out of my life, but I dared not give up my ever more complex and frantic efforts to banish him.

You were the first to advise me to open the doors and windows of my life and to accept the dragon without fear and with no—absolutely no—defenses. You helped me learn to face the dragon calmly, with the voice of the wizard. When the dragon showed up before the wedding, I invited him in. I set a nice table for him and gave him good food and drink. Then I told him to enjoy himself and that although I would be back shortly, right now I needed to do some things outside of the house. I asked him to make himself at home and to know that I would be back to help him a little later on. Amazingly enough, the dragon seemed to be satisfied with that treatment. He got what he wanted, and I got my life back.

That is the way with this anxiety disease: it comes for no reason, and the sufferer is not responsible for having the disease. Nevertheless, a cure—knowing what is wrong and what to do about the problem—can only be earned one person at a time by that person's own hard work over a long period of time. A cure is regaining control of your life, not being free of panic or anxiety.

The first time you have a panic attack is always the worst, because that time you did not know what was happening to you. You were not only unprepared but you also had no way of knowing that even though these were bad feelings and bad thoughts, you would not die, go crazy, or lose control. The single most important part of getting well is knowing what you are up against, knowing what the dragon can and, even more important, cannot do. That knowledge comes only over time from experience and hard work.

Understand the Worry Machine

People with anxiety disorders suffer from anticipatory anxiety—the second fear. Because of the great importance of the anticipatory anxiety, we have labeled the anxiety disorders the malignant diseases of the "what-ifs." Anxiety disorder sufferers project themselves into the future and foresee disasters just around the corner. When they think about what might happen, they only think of bad outcomes, never good. It is as if they have worry machines in their brains that crank out nothing but worries—the "what-if" scenarios of troubles and disasters. The worry machines spin the precious gold of clinically anxious people's lives into straw.

A Positive Side to Worry

We have noticed one good result of these otherwise distressing workings of the worry machine. *When anxious people find themselves in genuinely dangerous situations, like a serious automobile accident or the major illness of a family member, they usually behave admirably.* They do not panic when confronted by real danger, even though many so-called normal people do. We have come to think of this as the result of the anxious person's always being in mental training for disaster. Disasters do not happen very often in anyone's life, but when they do happen to anxious people, they are the only people who are always prepared!

Practicing Problem Solving

Margaret was an artist whose husband was a physician. Margaret had generalized anxiety disorder (GAD) and used medication every day to help her manage her anxiety. She had been through a lot of psychoanalytic therapy many years ago, which she now thought had not helped her, but her more recent cognitive psychotherapy had helped her to accept her illness and regain better control of her life. Margaret was certain that her heightened sensitivity, stemming from her anxiety, was a big help in her art, as she was tuned in to intense feelings in visual ways that she compared to the power of a laser beam.

When their daughter, Becky, developed epilepsy at the age of seventeen, Margaret's husband had a hard time coping. He was worried about Becky and skeptical about her medical treatment. Margaret took over the management of Becky's care, doing what everyone agreed was a great job. Margaret put this all in perspective:

"My anxieties are hard to pin down. They come at me from every direction. When one leaves, another appears. With Becky's epilepsy, scary as it was for all of us, I knew what the problem was, and my usual systematic approach to life worked. I just took it step by step, and it all worked out. My irrational anxiety made this realistic problem seem easy. What amazed me was not that I handled Becky's problem reasonably well but that everyone else, especially my husband, was surprised and therefore quick to congratulate me. That shows me that they just do not know how hard the anxiety problem is to deal with compared to the problems that overwhelm most people in life."

What Does *Cure* Mean?

This book boldly uses the word *cure* in its title. *The Anxiety Cure* offers you a way to get well, to live a full and normal life without restriction from an anxiety disorder. This is possible—sometimes with and sometimes without medicines—despite the fact that the *anxiety disorders cannot be eliminated by any form of treatment*. A cure is keeping the dragon of worry from building a nest in your mind. Getting well—finding a real cure—means accepting that you have the anxiety disease and learning how to care for it in ways that take away most of the suffering and all of the disability that result from the anxiety disorders.

A "cure" is yours when you know what is wrong and what to do about it. This book helps you find your own path to a full life without being limited by an anxiety disorder.

We understand that some readers will be upset by our use of the word *cure* since, to them, a cure means eliminating the problem, rooting it out of their lives for good. Not only is that sort of cure impossible at this time, despite all of the knowledge now available about the anxiety disorders, but, as a practical matter, the search for that elusive goal also makes the anxiety problem worse.

The Universal Antidote

The universal antidote for all anxiety disorders is acceptance.

Acceptance as a cure for anxiety disorders means acceptance of the feelings and the thoughts that are automatically produced in the anxious, sensitized brain. But acceptance does not mean accepting the limitations in your life that anxiety is trying to force on you.

We have found that some people who are unable to think clearly or to benefit from treatment because of their anxiety disorders become able to make use of help once they find the right medicines to quiet their sensitized, overreactive nervous systems. If you are having trouble reading this book and even imagining regaining control of your life, you should consider seeing a doctor who specializes in using medicines to treat anxiety disorders. See Chapter 4 for more information about the medicines to consider. We have found that medicines do not conflict with or compete with effective therapy. For many anxious people, using effective medicines is the first step to making good use of therapy and other resources, including the Anxiety Cure program.

When you are anxious, it is hard to think clearly. You are afraid and confused because your mind is full of fear, which crowds out all other thoughts. Reading a book or even thinking about the steps needed to get well are impossible when you are intensely anxious. Wait until you feel somewhat calm and then get out *The Anxiety Cure* and begin to use it. If you get overly anxious while you are reading, put the book down for a while and do some simple everyday things to help take your mind off your scary thoughts and feelings. Washing the dishes or the car, vacuuming the rug, or preparing a meal might help. Doing nonstressful activities often reduces anxiety.

Despite emotional pain and the effort and time required, many anxious people are willing to make use of the tools that are available to retake control of their lives. This book is written for readers with anxiety problems who accept the reality of their illnesses and are willing to do the work necessary to get well. Anyone who promises you a way to overcome your anxiety disorder without work is not telling the truth.

Based on our experiences with other people suffering from anxiety disorders, we promise that if you use the techniques you will learn here, you will be able to turn the suffering of your anxiety disorder into a springboard for a better life.

CHAPTER 3

The Six Anxiety Disorders

Now that we have a basic understanding of brain biology and a standard vocabulary to think about anxiety disorders, we can use these words to identify six anxiety disorders. While anxious people are all unique, most suffer in ways that fit more or less clearly into one of these six specific descriptions.

Agoraphobia/Panic Disorder (PD)

This results in spontaneous panic attacks coupled with situational panic as well as pathological anxiety, with or without significant avoidance. The syndrome often begins with spontaneous panic and evolves over time to include fear of many experiences, most often driving, shopping, traveling to unfamiliar places, and being alone. Typically, agoraphobia shows up as a fear of being away from a safe person or a safe place.

Agoraphobia is the fear of being helpless and alone when perceiving great inner danger. This is why agoraphobia is called "adult separation anxiety." Often this is expressed as fear of dying, going crazy, or losing control of one's behavior and doing something either dangerous or embarrassing. Agoraphobia typically leads sufferers to stick close to safe (and familiar) people and places. At its worst, it can lead to the sufferer's being homebound—unable to leave home.

The Man with the Wild Hair: Agoraphobia

Sam was a twenty-five-year-old man who had his first panic attack after smoking marijuana with friends in high school. He did not connect the panic attack to his drug use, and he continued using marijuana and then cocaine frequently until he was twenty-one. At that point, he had a severe panic attack and was taken to the emergency room in an ambulance. He was told that nothing was wrong with him, which left him confused and

---

frightened. He began to avoid going out of the house alone in order to be near the phone if he had another panic attack and had to call for an ambulance. He stopped using drugs because he was frightened of being out of control in case a panic attack occurred and he could not summon help. He lost contact with his friends, and he relied on his girlfriend to do errands for him to places where he did not feel safe.

The more Sam avoided situations, the more fearful he became. He was able to go to his work as a road builder because he was outside, not closed in a room, and because there was always a team of workers who could help him if he had a panic attack. He developed a serious fear of sitting in a barber's chair, and he had a huge, bushy mound of hair and a long flowing beard when he finally sought help. He feared being trapped in the barber's chair. If he had a panic attack in the chair with his hair half cut, he would not be able to leave (fearing embarrassment), and he would not be able to stay (because he would be afraid he was dying).

Specific Phobia

A specific phobia is a particular form of situational panic such as fear of flying, fear of heights, fear of insects or snakes, or claustrophobia. Fear of vomiting or of medical procedures such as injections are common specific phobias. Specific phobias are usually situational panic of the experience or circumstance. These are called specific or single phobias to differentiate them from the more general agoraphobia. Sometimes what at first appear to be specific phobias are, at root, manifestations of agoraphobia showing up as multiple phobias, but many people suffer from single, discrete phobias without having either spontaneous panic or agoraphobia.

Fear of Snakes: Specific Phobia

Chantelle was a twenty-eight-year-old woman with a fear of snakes. Even the word *snake* in a newspaper or a fleeting picture of a snake on a TV show caused her to have a rush of fear. She feared walking on grass or going anywhere she might see a snake. Even though she rarely saw a snake, she lived in near-constant fear that a snake would materialize anyplace anytime. She avoided hiking and was severely limited by her phobia.

Chantelle worked as an office manager. When one of her coworkers inadvertently discovered her fear, he began to tease Chantelle about it, leaving the word *snake* or a picture of a snake in unlikely parts of her desk or on her e-mail. Chantelle knew she either had to seek help or find a new job when she realized she was fearful all of the time, which caused her to have trouble concentrating on her work.

Social Phobia

Social phobia is a pathological anxiety expressed specifically as fear of embarrassment, which may be limited to public speaking or it may be part of a global shyness that limits social experiences, including dating, marriage, and friendships. Agoraphobic people are usually afraid to be alone, being more comfortable with a safe person who could help them in an emergency. Social phobics are usually more comfortable alone. People are scary to them.

The Man Who Avoided Meetings: Social Phobia

Kenneth was a thirty-five-year-old middle manager in a fast-growing company. He liked his job, and he worked hard to get ahead. He had avoided public speaking, or even being called on, since he was in grade school. He knew his avoidance hindered his success in his job to a limited extent, and he also knew that to become a key player in his business, he was going to have to give frequent presentations effectively. None of his friends, family, or coworkers was aware of his public speaking phobia.

Although he was afraid of public speaking and avoided it, he was also pragmatic enough not to want a phobia to stand in the way of his success. He set about his Anxiety Cure, using the same methodical, thorough qualities that had placed him in a successful position in the first place.

Generalized Anxiety Disorder (GAD)

Generalized anxiety disorder is a general pathological anxiety, which includes the repeated experience of worry and tension that interferes with one's life and pleasure, but it is without panic attacks, phobic avoidance, or pathological shyness, as well as without obsessions and compulsions. This is both the base of all anxiety disorders (the worry, tension, and anxiety), and the residual category when the defining features of the anxiety disorders are absent. GAD is pure worry.

Worried All the Time: Generalized Anxiety Disorder

Blaine was an eleven-year-old who worried about how she would do on tests in school so much that it was hard to learn the material when she studied, hard to give clear answers in class when the teacher called on her, and hard to take tests because she was sure she was doing it all wrong. A few times she faked stomachaches in order to go to the school nurse instead of taking a test, but she found that this avoidance just made her anxiety worse. Her teacher could see that Blaine was nervous in class, but she chose to be unsympathetic in her responses to these worries, as a way to help Blaine toughen up.

Blaine's classmates were tired of her frequent calls in the evenings to check on homework assignments. Blaine's mother and grandmother, with whom she lived, were worried people themselves. These two women wanted to help Blaine so she would not grow up to be like them, worried about everything all the time. They tried to interest Blaine in the swim team, but Blaine complained every day about how many mistakes she made in practice. Every week she counted how many ribbons her best friend won at the swim meets and how few ribbons she won. This was more evidence for Blaine that she was a bad person.

Obsessive-Compulsive Disorder (OCD)

This anxiety syndrome is characterized by obsessions that are unwanted and intrusive thoughts, usually of a violent or sexual nature. These disturbing thoughts lead to intense pathological anxiety. People with OCD try to rid themselves of these hateful thoughts. The more they try to get the thoughts out of their minds, the more painful and persistent the thoughts become. One way that short-term relief from the anxiety caused by obsessive thoughts can be achieved is by engaging in compulsions, or ritual senseless behaviors such as repeating a word over and over, or actions such as hand washing, checking on something, or moving in a certain way. Your thoughts cannot harm you or other people, as many people with OCD fear. Thoughts are just that—thoughts. They do not cause things to happen in magical and scary ways. *OCD is a sort of virtual reality experience, as your anxiety convinces you that your thoughts are reality.*

The Safety Checker: Obsessive-Compulsive Disorder

Jenny was a sixty-five-year-old woman who had suffered from anxiety problems most of her life. She had used her husband as a safe person and had not had to limit her life much because of his help. However, her husband died the previous year, and Jenny became obsessed with checking to be sure that the doors and windows of her home were locked and that the stove was turned off. She performed other safety checks throughout the house for hours every day. She had to drop out of her bridge club because she spent so much time on this checking, and she was unable to travel with her senior travel group at church on the annual beach trip because she could not imagine being able to get out of her house.

Jenny had diabetes and heart problems. The doctor who monitored her health had recently made several changes in her medication. Jenny had to begin to talk to the doctor about the possible interactions of these medications with her anxiety problem before embarking on the Anxiety Cure. She chose to seek the help of a therapist because she knew that she was still grieving for her husband, and she did not want to burden her grown children or her friends with these concerns or with her obsessions and compulsions.

Posttraumatic Stress Disorder (PTSD)

Posttraumatic stress disorder is a pattern of anxiety that follows a severe stress, such as being in a war, being raped, or being in a terrible accident. PTSD includes flashback memories of the traumatic event that are so real that it feels as though the event is occurring all over again. These flashbacks often involve nightmares about the event. Situations may be avoided out of a desire to minimize triggering thoughts, such as the veteran who avoids going to the airport because the sounds of the airplanes at takeoff trigger flashbacks of being evacuated from a burning village. Not everyone who goes through a severe stress develops PTSD. While reliving a traumatic event is almost universal for everyone who goes through a horrible experience, these thoughts typically fade over the course of a few weeks or months after the trauma. The symptoms are usually minor and do not interfere with the person's life.

In contrast, PTSD is a persistent and severe disorder that significantly disrupts the sufferer's life for many years. The first fear, which is the traumatic event and the flashback reliving it, instead of fading in intensity over time, is reinforced by the second fear, the fear of the fear, which can be continuous. This leads to avoidance of triggering situations, which then increases the likelihood of having a fearful reaction when such situations are encountered.

Aftermath of War: Posttraumatic Stress Disorder

Consuela was a thirty-two-year-old immigrant to the United States. She moved here with her son in fear for their lives because their country in

Central America had erupted in war. She had watched her brothers' brutal, involuntary conscription into the guerrilla army and had never seen or heard of them again. Then her village was raided by the nationalist army, and she and her son hid in a tree while Consuela's mother and sister were tortured and killed because her family was identified as guerrilla sympathizers. Her house was burned down.

Four years after the violence, living in the States, she sought treatment, as she found that, despite having finally found a steady job with a hotel cleaning service, she could not escape the flashbacks of violence that plagued her. She noticed that her son, now sixteen, had seemed to adjust quickly to his new life, and while he remembered the horrifying scene at their village, he did not think about it often. Her flashbacks, in contrast, disrupted her sleep nightly and left her in tears whenever she saw a police officer or anyone else in uniform. She found herself increasingly isolated in her apartment by her fears.

All of the six anxiety disorders are built on the same underlying foundation of pathological anxiety and abnormal brain chemistry, including false alarms of terrible danger. Although most people with anxiety disorders suffer from one of these six syndromes, the boundaries between the individual anxiety disorders can be blurred. The pattern of anxiety symptoms occasionally changes over time so that a person who starts off with agoraphobia can later be seen to have a social phobia, or a person with panic disorder and agoraphobia may become primarily troubled by OCD symptoms. For most people, it is not difficult to determine which of these six syndromes of the anxiety disorders best fits their problems, and their diagnostic label does not change over time. To rise to the level of a formal diagnosis, the anxiety problem must be persistent (that is, it cannot simply be a short-term reaction to stress), and it must cause significant distress and/or disability in a major life area (such as family life, work, or recreation).

All of the anxiety disorders afflict the same sort of people (conscientious worriers), and the anxiety disorders generally respond to the same forms of both medication and nonmedication treatments. Although the differences among the particular anxiety disorders can be important for treatment, usually the similarities among the anxiety disorders are far more important. You will learn more about how to evaluate your own anxiety in the next chapter of this book.

CHAPTER 4

Medicines and Therapy

Having reviewed the brain-based nature of anxiety, it is no surprise that it is important to review medication and therapy. Once you understand that anxiety disorders are real illnesses—not just a figment of a weak personality or something that you can just ignore—you understand that medicines and therapy work to correct disordered brain functioning. Though we review the concepts here, we leave the detailed explanations of basic science to other authors. Most people who have an anxiety problem are relieved to know that what they suffer from is real and that scientists know how to go about solving these real problems in the brain.

No treatment is likely to entirely eliminate anxiety problems, but the treatments available today are not only far better than those available at any time in the past, they are very good indeed. The goal of treatment is to overcome all of the disability from anxiety problems and to overcome most, if not all, of the suffering caused by anxiety. This broadly defined goal for the treatment of anxiety can be called "full remission" or "recovery." That goal is within reach today for most people with anxiety problems, including those suffering from severe anxiety disorders.

One good way to approach the problem of anxiety is to learn about it. This is called "bibliotherapy" or "book-therapy." By reading this book you are engaged in bibliotherapy. Some years ago we saw a woman who wanted only one thing from us: "Tell me the name of my problem so I can find the help I need in the books I have available to me." We told her that she suffered from agoraphobia. "Thanks," she said, "I am a librarian at the Library of Congress, so now I will be able to solve my problem." We suggested some good books. She appreciated that help as well. A few months later when we called to check on her progress she reported that she was much better. "Until you told me what I had I did not know where to look for help. Once I had a name for my problem I could do my own research." This experience took place before the Internet was widely available. Today having the name for a problem is the key to the information not only in libraries but also on the Internet. Naming your problems makes information instantly available on a worldwide basis.

This same woman came to see us again twenty years later. She had recently developed tinnitus, a pathological, continuous, and disturbing ringing in her ears. She could see that her anxiety added greatly to the suffering she experienced from tinnitus so she wanted medical relief to reduce the anxiety component of her new disorder. Since some medicines can increase tinnitus, hers was not a simple problem. This clinical example makes the point that what is needed at one time is often different from what is needed at another time, even for a single patient. This story also makes clear that what is needed to deal with anxiety is often not simple.

In this chapter we focus on two broad forms of treatment for anxiety problems: medicines and therapy. We do not attempt to be encyclopedic about either area. Instead we present an overview of both areas, an overview that can be used as a starting point to find the best treatments for each individual anxiety problem. At the outset we want to emphasize that most people with anxiety problems benefit from more than one form of treatment. Combining different forms of treatment, either at the same time or one after the other, improves the outcome.

Medicines

Anxiety is the normal, healthy fear mechanism of the brain going off inappropriately. Anxiety is a false alarm of danger that is itself a source of pain and disability. In Chapter 1 we explored the brain circuitry of fear as well as the neurotransmitters used by the brain for one nerve cell, or neuron, to communicate with other neurons in the brain's fear circuits. In this section we explore the best ways to use specific medicines to quiet the overreactive brain's fear mechanisms by normalizing brain chemistry.

There are three broad types of antianxiety medicines to be considered: the antidepressant medicines, the benzodiazepines, and the heterogeneous mix of other antianxiety medicines. This third group comprises other medicines that have shown promise in the treatment of one or more of the anxiety disorders, including the mood stabilizers and the beta blockers.

The Antidepressants

The antidepressants are the first-line treatments for most of the anxiety disorders. This is true whether there is a depressive component to the anxiety problems or not. Roughly 20 percent of people with an anxiety disorder also suffer from depression. For these people the antidepressants are especially attractive because they treat both problems. When the antidepressants were first used to treat anxiety disorders, many experts thought that when anxiety and depression occurred in the same patient the anxiety was secondary to—and less important than—the depression. Subsequent research has shown that when the two go together, it is usually the anxiety that came first, not the depression. We now know that the antidepressants work well to treat anxiety disorders even if there is no depression. In other words, although these medicines are called antidepressants as a class, they are also effective antianxiety medicines.

The first antidepressants were discovered in the late 1950s as a result of a determined search for new antihistamines to treat allergies. The chemicals identified as potential antihistamines were tested on hospitalized mental patients, an easily available, large group of research subjects in the days when mental patients spent many years, often their lifetimes, hospitalized. That was a time before the current laws governing human subject research were in place. However unmodern that approach to research was, using hospitalized mental patients as the guinea pigs in these studies produced profoundly beneficial results for subsequent generations of psychiatric patients. These early pharmacological studies led to the accidental discovery that one of these chemicals, imipramine, not only worked as an antihistamine but also produced a remarkable reduction in depression in these patients. This effect of imipramine went far beyond the effectiveness of any treatment previously used for depression. The drug was introduced into medical practice under the brand name Tofranil.

Another chemical studied in hospitalized mental patients at that same time for its antihistaminic effects was chlorpromazine. It was found equally dramatic in reducing the severe psychotic symptoms in schizophrenia. It was introduced as the brand name Thorazine. Hard as it is to imagine today, when medical research is so much more complex and expensive, the doctors conducting these early studies were smart enough to recognize that these side effects of the chemicals they were studying had amazing clinical potentials that were completely unexpected. They had stumbled onto an entirely new way of treating two of the most serious and widespread mental illnesses in the world, depression and schizophrenia. While their use of these chemicals in this research population was accidental, the observations and conclusions they reached were far from accidental. They were brilliant. Subsequent research, which has been remarkable in both the treatment of depression and psychosis, has primarily made progress in reducing the side effects inherent in these earliest medicines rather than in improving their effectiveness. The original chemicals were considered "dirty" medicines because they had so many unpleasant and potentially dangerous side effects, such as weight gain and potentially serious heart effects, as well as their desired antihistaminic effects. This broad range of effects made these medicines very difficult for patients to take and that, in turn, led to frequent discontinuation of the medicines as well as unwillingness of many patients even to start taking them.

Modern antidepressants, while not more effective, are far easier to take and have far fewer dangerous side effects, making them "cleaner" pharmaceutical agents. The new antidepressants generally work on one or two specific neurotransmitters, mostly serotonin or norepinephrine, both of which imipramine affected. Researchers seeking effective new antidepressants that were free of the disturbing side effects of imipramine sought chemicals that affected one of these neurotransmitters "selectively." Rather than simultaneously hitting many brain chemicals, as imipramine does, these new antidepressants were precisely targeted at individual effects in the brain. Modern researchers knew where to aim their efforts because of the pioneering work that led to the discovery of imipramine.

In the earliest years of the study of imipramine, one of the world's most creative medical researchers, Donald Kline, discovered that imipramine blocked the panic attacks that lay at the heart of agoraphobia. It is humbling to realize that it was more than two decades after Dr. Kline's discovery before this groundbreaking research was incorporated into the routine practice of psychiatrists and other physicians who use medicines to treat anxiety.

There are many good antidepressants available today. To make it easier to understand the options available, we are separating them into two groups: the selective serotonin reuptake inhibitors (SSRIs) and the other antidepressants. There are now six SSRIs marketed in the United States. The success of these medicines will likely lead to an ever-increasing pace of new medicines entering this crowded category. The currently available SSRIs are: Prozac (fluoxetine), Zoloft (sertraline), Paxil (paroxetine),

Luvox (fluvoxamine), Celexa (citalopram), and Lexapro (escitalopram). These medicines each come in multiple dosages and many of them are now available in slow-release forms. Because of its very long persistence in the body, Prozac is now available in a once-a-week form.

All of these medicines work by blocking the reuptake of serotonin in the synapses in the brain and in other tissues that use serotonin as a neurotransmitter, including the gastrointestinal tract. This produces higher levels of serotonin in the synapses, normalizing the level of this neurotransmitter that is presumably lowered in depression and in most of the anxiety disorders. Although this change in the serotonin level in the brain's synapses occurs with the first dose of the medicine, the benefits from using these medicines begin only after several weeks of use. The benefits from the antidepressants are not maximal until four to ten weeks of regular use.

While this time lag for the onset of benefit for either depression or anxiety is something of a biological mystery, the current thinking is that the brain takes time to adjust to the presence of the increased levels of serotonin in the synapses. It is this adjustment of the brain to the raised serotonin levels that produces the benefit, and not the raised serotonin level in the synapses.

These medicines are generally taken once a day. Each of the SSRIs is a different chemical, and each of them has slightly different side effects. It is important to realize that none of them has been shown to be better than any of the others for all patients with anxiety. Each anxious person reacts differently to each medicine. For this reason doctors often try one medicine and then another, working with the patients, one medicine at a time, to find the best medicine for each individual patient. It is seldom necessary for patients to try all six of these SSRIs, however, because once a good medicine has been found for an individual patient there is no need to try additional medicines. Often the first medicine tried does the job with minimal problems. However, if the first medicine does not do the job, there are good alternatives to try.

The side effects from all of the antidepressants, not just the SSRIs, generally occur right away, usually with the first dose or two. These side effects are usually quite minor medically. If you have a side effect or think you may be having one, these concerns should be talked over with the prescribing physician. It is seldom necessary to stop taking one of these medicines because of side effects. Because most anxious people worry a lot, the side effects of medicines are high on most patients' list of worries. The therapeutic benefits of the antidepressants take weeks to kick in, but the side effects begin right away, are usually mild, and usually diminish or disappear entirely after a few weeks of daily dosing. The benefits typically do not diminish, even over long periods of continuous use.

The biggest problem doctors have using these medicines is getting patients to take a large enough dose for a long enough time to determine whether or not the medicine produces substantial benefits. Even when it does, there is another common problem. Many anxious patients feel guilty about taking medicines, believing that they should be able to handle their anxiety without resorting to the use of medicines. So when they feel better they often stop taking the medicine that got them better. All too often this leads to a return of the symptoms for which the medicine was taken. Our suggestion is that when you use any of these medicines you stay with them long enough to see if they will work. Any concerns should be worked through with the prescribing doctor.

"Compliant" is the word physicians use to describe patients who take their medicines reliably. Compliance is important when it comes to using medicines, including using antidepressants to treat anxiety problems. Skipping doses of antidepressants is not dangerous, but it lowers the chance of producing a significant benefit.

Patients taking antidepressants often ask about using alcohol. In general, alcohol is a depressant that increases anxiety. Although alcohol reduces anxiety in the first hour or so after its use, there is greatly increased anxiety when the body adjusts to the subsequent falling blood alcohol level. The net long-term effect of alcohol use is to raise both anxiety and depression. It is primarily for this reason that physicians recommend that patients using these medicines not drink, not because alcohol use is any more dangerous when a person is is using an antidepressant than it is when a person is not using one.

Typical mild side effects of the SSRIs are headaches, nausea, dry mouth, and tiredness. Most of these symptoms are mild and disappear with continued antidepressant dosing. On the other hand, two side effects, when they occur, often do not disappear with continued dosing: weight gain and sexual dysfunction. Mostly this means loss of sexual interest and reduced capacity to have an orgasm. Many patients taking antidepressants do not have these two problems. If you do have either of these problems, it is wise to talk with the prescribing physician to assess how important the problems are and to help manage them. Remember that if these problems do occur and if they are bothersome, they will stop when the medicine is stopped. In other words, they just happen when using the medicine and are entirely reversible on discontinuation of the medicine. It may be possible to lower the dose of the antidepressant or to make other changes in medication to take care of these problems. Management of side effects, including these two if they occur, should be worked out with your doctor, one-on-one.

The second group of antidepressants used in the treatment of anxiety disorders includes these four medicines: Wellbutrin (bupropion), Serzone (nefazodone), Effexor (venlafaxine), and Remeron (mirtazapine). They work in somewhat different ways from the SSRIs but they all affect the neurotransmitters in the brain and, like the SSRIs, they are usually taken once a day. Also like the SSRIs, these antidepressants must be taken for several weeks to produce benefits, and they all work for depression as well as for anxiety.

One clear difference between the SSRIs and the other antidepressants is that the SSRIs are the only antidepressants that have been shown to be effective in the treatment of obsessive-compulsive disorder (OCD). It may be that Wellbutrin is less effective in the treatment of panic disorder and agoraphobia than the other antidepressants, but we have worked with several patients with anxiety problems who have done well with Wellbutrin. So in a particular patient with panic disorder with or without agoraphobia, it may work well. Wellbutrin is also used to help people stop smoking. When used in this way it is called Zyban. Serzone has been used widely in the treatment of anxiety problems. Like Wellbutrin, Serzone is distinguished by the low risk of the sexual side effects that are seen in 40 percent or more of people taking many of the SSRIs. Effexor has been shown to be effective in the treatment of generalized anxiety disorder. Of the new antidepressants, Remeron has the biggest potential for weight gain and it is the most likely to produce sedation. Both of these side effects of Remeron are positive characteristics for some patients. For example, Remeron is a fine choice for older patients who need to gain weight and who suffer from troublesome insomnia. It is best taken about forty-five minutes before bedtime to maximize its useful sedating effects.

When used to treat anxiety, all of the antidepressants are started at low doses to reduce the likelihood of side effects and to make it easier for anxious patients to take the medicines long enough to get beneficial results; usually that means at least six weeks of daily dosing. If the result is not adequate after six to ten weeks, it is often desirable to increase the dose of the medicine or to add an augmenting medicine, which may be another antidepressant. Another alternative, when the initial results are inadequate, is to try a different antidepressant.

It is not possible to tell which antidepressant will work best for which patients. Since anxiety problems run in families, if a close relative has done well with a particular antianxiety medicine that drug may be a good one to try first. Although a decade ago it was a common experience for an expert in the treatment of anxiety to chose an initial antidepressant, today with far wider use of these medicines to treat anxiety, it is far more likely that when a person with anxiety sees a physician they have already tried one or more of these medicines. In this case the patient's own experience can be helpful in shaping the decision-making about which antidepressant to chose.

Three Problem Areas with the Antidepressants The antidepressants have many advantages over other medicines used to treat clinically significant anxiety. They are generally taken once a day, dosing is usually simple, and the newer ones do not require many dosage adjustments over time. The side effects of the antidepressants are generally mild, and they mostly diminish or disappear after a few weeks of continuing use. These medicines are not usually sedating and, unlike the benzodiazepines, they are not contraindicated for people with histories of addiction to alcohol and other drugs. The antidepressants remain effective over months and even years, usually at the same dose that was initially effective.

The first antidepressants, the tricyclic antidepressants such as Tofranil (imipramine) and Elavil (amitriptyline), had two side effects that were medically serious for some patients. First, they could be fatal when taken in an overdose. This was a particularly serious risk when patients taking them were depressed or had severe panic disorder. Second, the tricyclic antidepressants produced heart rhythm disturbances, especially in some elderly patients, that could be medically serious. Dose adjustments of the tricyclic antidepressants were frequent. Because of their many side effects many patients were reluctant to take them, and patients who did take them often stopped after a few weeks because of the side effects.

The newer antidepressants do not have any of the potential problems that had limited the usefulness of the tricyclic antidepressants. Nevertheless, there are three problems to be considered with the newer antidepressants. The first is that some side effects of these medicines do not go away with continued use. While these long-lasting side effects are not medically serious, in the sense that they are not life-threatening, they can be disturbing. Prime among these more troubling and enduring side effects are weight gain and sexual dysfunction. Many people using the newer antidepressants do not have either of these symptoms, but if these side effects do occur and if they are disturbing, they are unlikely to go away with long-term use of the medicine that is causing the side effects.

Second, it is not possible to tailor the dose of an antidepressant to the needs of anxious patients on a day-to-day basis. The dose of the antidepressants is usually held stable over weeks or even longer. Since the symptoms of anxiety tend to change rapidly, not only day to day, but often minute to minute, there is some advantage to being able to adjust the dose of an antianxiety medicine more rapidly. The long delay between dose change and changed effect—up to four weeks—makes this impossible for all of the antidepressants when used to treat either anxiety or depression.

Third, some of the antidepressants produce withdrawal symptoms when abruptly discontinued. This is disturbing to some patients. The antidepressants most likely to have this withdrawal problem are Effexor and Paxil. The one antidepressant that does not show withdrawal on abrupt discontinuation is Prozac, because of its very long persistence in the body.

The problem of withdrawal symptoms after abrupt discontinuation of an antidepressant is not medically serious. It is easily handled by gradual dose reduction over the course of several weeks once the medicines have been taken on a daily basis for many months. Having a withdrawal syndrome on abrupt discontinuation is a manifestation of physical dependence. It is not a manifestation of addiction, as will be described in the next section.

Benzodiazepines

These medicines, which we call "antiworry" pills, were introduced to treat anxiety in the early 1960s. Prior to that time the barbiturates were widely used to treat anxiety. These medicines, including Seconal (secobarbital), Nembutal (pentobarbital), and Amytal (amobarbital), produced many serious problems, including sedation at therapeutic doses, withdrawal on rapid discontinuation, abuse by alcoholics and drug addicts, as well as lethal outcomes when the barbiturates were used in suicide attempts.

Since they were introduced, the benzodiazepines have totally displaced the barbiturates and become a mainstay of medical treatment of significant anxiety. Compared to the antidepressants, the benzodiazepines have three potential drawbacks. First, they do not treat depression. Therefore, if a patient is both anxious and depressed, benzodiazepines alone are not likely to be effective. Second, the benzodiazepines are sometimes abused (meaning they may be taken dishonestly and at excessive doses) by anxious people who are also alcoholic or addicted to drugs such as marijuana, cocaine, and the opiates. Third, unlike most of the antidepressants, the benzodiazepines produce physical dependence. If, after use several times a day for many weeks, they are abruptly discontinued, patients may have withdrawal symptoms; these symptoms are heightened anxiety and insomnia.

We will discuss these three problems in more detail, but first we need to describe the distinct advantages of the benzodiazepines when it comes to the treatment of clinically significant anxiety. First, they reduce the anxiety component of all of the anxiety disorders, including specific phobias, such as animal phobias and claustrophobia. (The antidepressants do not work for specific phobias, but at least some of them do work for all of the other anxiety disorders.) Second, the benzodiazepines work right away with the first dose—it does not take two weeks or longer for the beneficial effects to take place. Finally, because anxiety problems are often episodic, it is possible to use the benzodiazepines just when they are needed. In other words, benzodiazepines are used the way people use aspirin for headaches, taking the medicine only when they have headaches. Even though as-needed dosing may be infrequent (just the way headaches may be painful but infrequent) many anxious people find it helpful to have a benzodiazepine available all the time just in case they should have an anxiety problem. Having this effective treatment easily available can even stop the progression of worry that leads to panic, since the anxious person knows that he or she can take a pill if it is needed.

The benzodiazepines generally produce their antianxiety effects within half an hour of taking a pill, and the benefit usually lasts four to eight hours. If anxiety is a round-the-clock problem, it is likely that the benzodiazepines will have to be used three or four times a day: often on arising, then again at noon, at dinnertime, and finally at bedtime. This dosing pattern is strikingly different from the single daily dose of antidepressants to treat anxiety. Taking a benzodiazepine three or four times a day seems like a lot to think about, but few anxious patients complain about this schedule because they get significant antianxiety benefits from each dose. That benefit makes the dosing easy to remember and not difficult. In contrast, taking an antidepressant produces no more immediate relief than does taking a daily vitamin pill, which makes it relatively hard to remember to take an antidepressant once a day.

Benzodiazepines need not necessarily be taken around the clock. For many people, even if they have significant anxiety every day, there are specific times of day that the anxiety is worst. Often the worst time is first thing in the morning or at bedtime. For these people taking a relatively short-acting benzodiazepine only once a day is usually sufficient. When the anxiety is associated only with certain activities, such as driving over a bridge or taking an elevator or giving a speech, it is possible to tailor the benzodiazepine use precisely to the time that it is needed. These people may take the benzodiazepine only once a month or even less often and still find it enormously effective.

Medications and Addiction When active alcoholics and drug addicts use the benzodiazepines, they typically use them at high and unstable doses. They generally do not find the benzodiazepines to be very helpful in reducing their anxiety, although they want to continue using the benzodiazepines. Even when addicts start out with low doses of benzodiazepines, over time they raise their doses, usually outside the recommended ranges used to treat anxiety.

In sharp contrast, nonaddicted anxious people who use the benzodiazepines find them extremely helpful and they typically use the benzodiazepines at low doses. Even if nonaddicted anxious people take a benzodiazepine every day for many years, they do not raise their doses. See Table 1 for a list of the most commonly used benzodiazepines and the doses that fall into the green light, yellow light, and red light dose zones. The green light zone is where more than 80 percent of nonaddicted anxious people start and end their use of benzodiazepines. They never take more. They neither need nor want more. They do not have to limit their use of benzodiazepines, and their physicians do not have to closely monitor their dose levels. The upper limit of the green light zone is half of the standard maximum antianxiety dose approved in the package insert for each benzodiazepine. The yellow light zone is from that level of dose up to the maximum recommended antianxiety dose. The red light zone is above the maximum recommended antianxiety dose. Some anxious people, especially early in the treatment of panic disorder, need to use a benzodiazepine in the red light zone. This high benzodiazepine dose level itself is not dangerous or even worrisome as long as the patient is not an alcoholic or a drug addict and as long as the prescribing physician is cognizant of the potential problems of using the benzodiazepine for alcoholics and drug addicts.

Back to the question of whether the benzodiazepines are addictive or not. They can be addictive for people who are currently addicted to alcohol or other drugs. Although it is less likely, the benzodiazepines can also be a problem for people with a personal history of addiction to alcohol and/or other drugs. If the benzodiazepines are addictive, these people will find that their use is not very effective and that they will need to continually raise their dose right through the top of the red light zone. In other words, even if the physicians do not detect the patients' preexisting addiction to alcohol or other drugs, the addiction problems will become evident through the high dose of the benzodiazepines with little antianxiety benefit.

There is a simple, one-word antidote to addiction: Honesty. For even people who have had a problem in the past with alcohol and other drugs to use benzodiazepines safely, it is essential that they be honest with their family members, their physicians and therapists, and their twelve-step sponsors. Being honest in this case means being honest about all use of alcohol and other drugs such as marijuana, cocaine, and heroin as well as about their use of all medicines with an addictive potential. This category includes controlled substances, such as narcotic pain medicines, stimulants, and depressants.

Table 1
Total 24-Hour Dose Zones for the Most Commonly Used Benzodiazepines

	Green Light Zone	Yellow Light Zone	Red Light Zone
Ativan (lorazepam)	Up to 5 mg/day	Greater than 5 mg up to 10 mg/day	Greater than 10 mg/day
Klonopin (clonazepam)	Up to 2mg/day	Greater than 2 mg and up to 4 mg/day	Greater than 4 mg/day
Valium (diazepam)	Up to 20 mg/day	Greater than 20 mg up to 40 mg/day	Greater than 40 mg/day
Xanax (alprazolam)	Up to 2 mg/day	Greater than 2 mg up to 4 mg/day	Greater than 4 mg/day
Xanax XR (alprazolam)	Up to 3 mg day	Greater than 3 mg up to 6 mg/day	Greater than 6 mg/day

If a particular person does not have a personal history of addiction to alcohol and other drugs, then using a benzodiazepine is not "addictive." None of us has seen even one patient who did not have a prior history of addiction who became addicted to a benzodiazepine.

For people with a personal history of addiction to alcohol and/or other drugs the best course of action usually is not to use a benzodiazepine to treat anxiety for the same reason these people are well advised not to try to become "social" or "moderate" drinkers of alcohol. That reason is that such attempts at controlled use often lead to new episodes of addiction that can be painful, prolonged, or even fatal. With so many other good medicines available to treat anxiety today, taking this risk is unwarranted.

On the other hand, for nonaddicted anxious people to take the benzodiazepines off their lists of therapeutic options because someone else may have problem with them is also unwise, because the benzodiazepines are often uniquely helpful for such people. Because of the common confusion over these issues, too many alcoholics and drug addicts do use benzodiazepines and too many nonaddicted people fear their use or feel guilty about using these remarkably safe medicines. Some nonaddicted benzodiazepine users even "admit" (wrongly) that they are "addicted" to these medicines. What they mean when they say this is that they feel the need to use the benzodiazepines.

To help sort this out we use the example of people who wear eyeglasses for severe myopia. They need their glasses to see. They use their glasses every waking moment of every day. They have no glasses-free days. Even people who are most horribly addicted to alcohol, heroin, or other drugs have some periods in their lives when they do not use these drugs. Many "glasses addicts" never have a day off from their habits of wearing eyeglasses.

So, are those people addicted to eyeglasses or not? They would surely show glasses-seeking behavior if their glasses were taken away from them. They would pay a high price to get their glasses back.

To answer the question of whether the glasses wearer is addicted or not, recall the two-part definition of addiction: first, continued use despite problems caused by that use, and, second, dishonesty. The glasses wearer shows neither of these two necessary traits to justify the label "addicted." There are no problems caused by the glasses and there is no dishonesty about their use. Presto, the eyeglass wearers are not addicted, although they show many of the superficial traits of addiction, such as using them everyday and showing glasses-seeking behavior when deprived of their glasses. Just as the everyday user of a benzodiazepine who has no continued use despite problems and no dishonesty is not addicted, even if that person "admits addiction" as a result of misunderstanding the nature of addiction.

We recommend that anyone concerned about their own use, or potential use, of a benzodiazepine, or the use of a benzodiazepine by a family member or friend, apply this two-part test to answer the question of whether that particular benzodiazepine user is addicted or not. We know some people are addicted to benzodiazepines. These people usually have major problems with alcohol and other drugs that preceded their benzodiazepine use. We are not saying that the benzodiazepines cannot be addictive. We are saying that they are not addictive for people who do not have prior histories of alcoholism or other drug dependence. Further, we are saying if a person does become addicted to a benzodiazepine, that addiction is easily recognized by the patient, by the patient's family, and by the patient's physician.

Even more important, we are saying that the vast majority of benzodiazepine users are not addicted to the benzodiazepine and never will be addicted to it. What this very large group of people mostly need is reassurance about their use of a thoroughly safe and effective medicine. They need ways to recognize problems of addiction should they occur. They also need ways to talk with their doctors and others about their benzodiazepine use so that these people, too, can be reassured.

The second problem with the benzodiazepines is physical dependence. When a benzodiazepine is taken several times a day every day for months at a time, the body becomes used to, or dependent on, the benzodiazepine. If the benzodiazepine use is stopped abruptly there is a sharp reversal of its effects. This usually produces a dramatic increase in anxiety and insomnia. These symptoms of withdrawal begin about twenty-four hours after the last dose and they peak in about two to three days. Withdrawal symptoms diminish thereafter and are usually over a week or two after the last benzodiazepine use.

However, like a myopic eyeglasses wearer who tries to "abruptly withdraw" from using glasses, the anxious person off the benzodiazepine is left with the underlying anxiety problem. In the context of abrupt discontinuation of the benzodiazepine, this anxiety problem can easily be misunderstood as a continuing withdrawal problem. The continuing problem, after two weeks off the benzodiazepine, needs to be clearly labeled as the underlying anxiety problem by the physician and the patient. Once that is done they are usually in a good position to manage the problems using other medicines and therapy if the decision has been made to discontinue the benzodiazepine use. In any event, this problem is not likely to be encountered if the dose is gradually reduced over the course of a few weeks if the benzodiazepine has been used for less than a year, or over up to three months if the benzodiazepine has been used every day for more than a year. Under those circumstances the patient and the doctor have to be highly motivated to stop the benzodiazepine and fully prepared for an upsurge in symptoms that is likely to follow. When that attitude is taken successful discontinuation of the benzodiazepine is usually accomplished.

The third problem with the benzodiazepines is sedation, a tendency to slow down reaction times and to make the user feel tired or groggy. This is a serious problem if the initial dose is large, because the patient's body is not used to the effects of the benzodiazepine. It is reasonable for physicians to start at lower doses and to caution their patients about possible sedation, especially when it comes to driving a car or doing other tasks when alertness is needed. However, once a steady and a reasonable benzodiazepine dose has been reached, the body becomes totally adjusted to it and there is no more sedation or impairment than in a person who is not taking a benzodiazepine. This is because tolerance of the sedation produced to benzodiazepine use develops rapidly and completely. On the other hand there is no tolerance to the antianxiety or antipanic effects of benzodiazepine use. For this reason there is no tendency for anxious people to raise their doses over time, even if they have used benzodiazepines daily for many, many years. If a person has used a benzodiazepine for a long time, the only way he or she can become sedated is to suddenly and substantially raise the benzodiazepine dose or by adding alcohol or some other sedating substance.

Most anxious people using benzodiazepines to treat anxiety use the medicines at low and stable doses. Many anxious patients do not even use them on an everyday basis. For this large majority of patients the only issue involving addiction or physical dependence or sedation is the worry that they may have about these widely publicized and poorly understood problems. For this large majority of patients we are attempting to provide not only information but reassurance. For the smaller number of benzodiazepine users for whom any of these three problems are more than irrational worries, we are attempting to provide not only understanding but solutions to these problems.

For people who are addicted to alcohol and/or other drugs as well as a benzodiazepine, we urge addiction treatment and the twelve-step programs. For people who are physically dependent on benzodiazepines, we suggest that this is no more of a serious problem than it is for patients taking antiepilepsy medicines or high blood pressure medicines. When it is time to stop the medicine, merely do so gradually and recognize that the symptoms that emerge are the symptoms of the underlying anxiety disorder that was, presumably, the reason for starting to take the benzodiazepine in the first place. For people who have sedation on one of the benzodiazepines, we suggest not adding other potentially sedating medicines and we suggest that they not suddenly raise their benzodiazepine dose. If they do feel sedated they should not to drive a car or engage in other hazardous activities. Just as alcohol use is undesirable for anxious patients taking an antidepressant because it blunts the beneficial antianxiety effects of the antidepressants, so we recommend that people taking a benzodiazepine to treat anxiety not drink. But when using a benzodiazepine there is additional good reason not to drink alcohol. The benzodiazepine adds significantly to the impairing effects of alcohol, making one drink of alcohol more like two or three in terms of impairment. The simplest and safest advice is don't drink alcohol if you are using any antianxiety medicine, especially if you are using a benzodiazepine.

Introduced in the 1960s, the original benzodiazepines are all off patent, meaning that generic, lower-cost versions are widely available. In 2003 a new formulation of Xanax (alprazolam) was introduced. It is called Xanax XR. This extended-release Xanax has important advantages compared to other benzodiazepines, because the slower release permits dosing once, or at most twice, a day compared to three or four times a day for the immediate-release benzodiazepines. Once-a-day dosing with Xanax XR also reduces "clock-watching," which may be a problem when using immediate-release benzodiazepines as patients carry on an inner dialog about when to take the next dose. The slower onset of effects with this new formulation means that even in the early dosing there is less sedation than with the immediate-release benzodiazepines. Finally there is less abuse potential for alcoholics and drug addicts with the XR formulation of Xanax, since the slow release makes this medicine less attractive to them than the immediate-release benzodiazepines.

The Other Medicines

BuSpar (buspirone) is a serotonin-related medicine that is not an antidepressant. Nevertheless, like the SSRIs, it has been shown to successfully treat generalized anxiety. BuSpar has not been successful in the treatment of obsessive-compulsive disorder or panic disorder although it is sometimes used as an augmenting medicine with other more specific medicines in all of the anxiety disorders, including obsessive-compulsive disorder and panic disorder. Like the antidepressants (but unlike the benzodiazepines), with BuSpar there is a delay of two weeks or longer after daily dosing begins before the antianxiety benefit occurs. BuSpar is usually taken two or three times a day, most often 15 mg twice a day. Because BuSpar produces upset stomach and other nonserious but distressing side effects, the dose often has to be started low and gradually raised to produce maximum benefits. Many physicians have had limited success for their patients with BuSpar so it is seldom a first-line treatment except for patients with a history of addiction to alcohol and other drugs, for whom the benzodiazepines are contraindicated. In these patients and in patients who choose not to use a benzodiazepine, BuSpar assumes a more prominent place among the therapeutic options for the medical treatment of anxiety.

Inderal (propranolol) is a medicine widely used to treat high blood pressure. Called a "beta blocker" because it blocks the beta norepinephrine receptors, Inderal is strikingly effective in the treatment of performance anxiety, including public speaking, acting, and singing on stage. This medicine dramatically reduces the racing heart, shaking hands, and quavering voice that accompany on-stage anxiety. Typically taken about an hour before a performance at doses of 20 to 40 mg, Inderal can be highly effective, with the benefit lasting six hours or more after taking the medicine. Its two possible side effects are sedation and low blood pressure. For this reason we suggest that its first use occur in a nonstressful setting so the anxious person can get used to the effects of the medicine before the stress of a performance. As effective as Inderal is for this one form of anxiety, it has not proven to be effective in the treatment of any of the other anxiety problems, presumably because these physical symptoms (racing heart, shaking hands, and quavering voice) are not the main problem in other anxiety problems and because Inderal reduces the bodily symptoms of anxiety without affecting the worry in the anxious brain itself.

A wide variety of other medicines have been shown to be effective in reducing anxiety, although they are all second- or third-line treatments compared to the newer antidepressants and the benzodiazepines. Included in this group are the antipsychotic medicines, such as Stelazine (trifluoperazine), which have been known for decades to have strong antianxiety effects. Because of the high rate of side effects, some of which are long-lasting even after the medicines have been discontinued, the early antipsychotics have rarely been used to treat anxiety. The newer generation of antipsychotics, with their dramatically lower side effect profiles, are sometimes used today although usually as augmenting agents for one or more of the first-line treatments even for patients who have not exhibited signs of psychosis.

Similarly, the mood stabilizers or the antiepilepsy medicines, including Depakene (valproic acid) and Neurontin (gabapentin), have shown some promise in the treatment of anxiety. Among the first antidepressants, the monoamine oxidize inhibitors (MAOIs), such as Parnate (tranylcypromine) and Nardil (phenelzine), have powerful antianxiety effects. Because of their potentially serious side effects of high blood pressure and the necessity of food restrictions, these medicines are seldom used today to treat anxiety problems.

The antidepressant medicines have assumed prominence as the first-line treatments for most of the anxiety disorders because of their effectiveness and their favorable side effect profiles. The only anxiety disorder that has not responded to one or more of the antidepressants is single phobia, such as isolated airplane or animal phobia, or claustrophobia. For these problems, the benzodiazepines are the treatment of choice if a medicine is to be used. For OCD the SSRIs are the treatment of choice; the other antidepressants are less likely to be helpful, although the tricyclic antidepressant Anafranil (clomipramine) is highly effective against OCD, presumably because of its serotonin effects.

The benzodiazepines are a second mainstay in the treatment of all forms of anxiety problems, used either every day or on an as needed basis. While there are concerns about the use of these medicines, those concerns usually can be managed successfully. The fact that the benzodiazepines work rapidly and powerfully to quiet the anxious brain makes them attractive either as the primary therapy or as agents to augment one of the antidepressants.

One interesting strategy for the use of a benzodiazepine along with an antidepressant is to use them together at the outset of the treatment of panic disorder or other anxiety problem. The benzodiazepine can be combined with an antidepressant from the first day of treatment. Because the benzodiazepine works immediately, there is immediate relief. Then, as the antidepressant kicks in over a period of three to six weeks, the benzodiazepine dose is reduced gradually to zero after eight to ten weeks. The antidepressant is continued for many months, perhaps for a lifetime. The benzodiazepine is used after the first few weeks only for short periods of heightened distress. This approach maximizes the benefits of both major classes of antianxiety medicines while minimizing their disadvantages.

The calculation of the best mix of benefits and side effects can only be done one patient at a time. For some patients the antidepressants are essentially without side effects and the benefits from their use are enormous. For these patients the antidepressants are the treatment of choice for most anxiety problems, often for months or years at a time, even over the entire lifetime.

For other patients the side effects of the antidepressants, even after trying many of them, are disturbing. For these patients the relatively benign side effect profile of the benzodiazepines makes them the choice as the core medication. For other patients, those who do not need any medicine on an ongoing basis but need help only for particular brief upsurges in anxiety, the as-needed dosing of a benzodiazepine is just right.

Most commonly, especially if the anxiety problem is severe and enduring, anxious patients do best with a combination of antidepressants and benzodiazepines, often over long periods of time. For other patients who have found problems with both the antidepressants and the benzodiazepines, or whose therapeutic results have been inadequate, augmentation with additional medicines or the use of novel antianxiety agents can make a great choice.

The bottom line in choosing medicines to treat anxiety is that today you and your physician have a large number of safe and effective medicines to choose from. The fact that anxiety problems are typically long-lasting, often for a lifetime, means that there is plenty of time for you to work together with your physician to find the right medicine or combination of medicines. There is no rush to find the perfect medicine to treat anxiety as there is in the treatment of an acute illness. You and your doctor have plenty of time to work through many good options to find the treatment that maximizes the benefits and minimizes the problems for you.

Therapy

Complex as finding the best medicine is, finding the best therapy can be even more so. In thinking about therapy we consider two broad areas: cognitive-behavioral treatment (CBT) and traditional psychotherapy.

Cognitive-Behavioral Treatment

One of the great discoveries of the past two decades, fully the equal of the phenomenal growth in the options for medicines to treat anxiety, has been the development of effective and specific treatments called cognitive-behavioral treatments. The "cognitive" part of the treatment involves new thinking about the anxious symptoms. What you think about your anxious symptoms has a great deal to do with the nature and the severity of your anxiety. An essential feature of the anxiety problem is the worry about the symptoms. The more serious the anxiety symptoms are judged to be, the more upsetting they are, the more frequently they occur, and the longer they last. Conversely, the less importance assigned to the symptoms of anxiety, the less often they come, the shorter they stay, and the less severe they are. The simple cognitive mantra is that the anxious symptoms are "distressing but not dangerous." When the symptoms are defined as "dangerous," the vicious cycle of anxiety is not only set in motion, it is self-sustaining.

In Chapter 1 we described the way context, past experiences, and the human touch powerfully influence the experience of anxiety. CBT takes advantage of brain biology using thoughts and behavior to quiet sensitized and overreactive fear mechanisms in the brain. CBT normalizes brain functioning by gradually reducing the false alarms of danger that characterize anxiety problems. If you recall our discussion of a child facing Fourth of July fireworks for the first time, or after the child had been sensitized to a fear reaction to loud noises, then you have a head start in understanding how CBT works.

The first great, modern guru in the field of anxiety problems was the Australian general practioner Claire Weekes, who was in her eighties when she visited the United States for the last time. In her books she never mentioned that she suffered from agoraphobia with panic attacks, although her extraordinary ability to describe the often bizarre and counterintuitive symptoms of this disorder was surely a hint about her personal familiarity with them. Dr. Weekes admitted privately that she had "what you call panic attacks." When asked about them she responded with vehemence that she did not consider that to be a subject worth talking about since the symptoms, even though they still woke her at night from time to time, were utterly unimportant to her. What we call a panic attack was nothing more than a "few normal chemicals temporarily out of place" in her brain.

This is the ultimate in cognitive restricting of panic attacks. By this thinking, Dr. Weekes took away the power of her temporarily disordered brain chemistry to affect her life in any way whatsoever. This view did not come easily or quickly to Dr. Weekes. In fact it took her years to grasp this perspective on panic and anxiety. Once she got it, however, she was able to help literally millions of others use this strategy to overcome their own anxiety problems.

The behavioral component of CBT is as simple to understand as is the cognitive component. Anxiety is so unpleasant that the natural reaction to it is to avoid whatever seems to cause it. Avoidance of anxiety-causing experiences is fully natural and completely understandable. It is also dead wrong. Avoidance is what creates the disability from anxiety problems.

The only way to get well from an anxiety problem is to "impersonate a normal person"—to act normally even with desperately painful, abnormal (anxious) feelings. Getting well means moving toward your fears rather than away from them. CBT has nothing to do with how the anxiety problem started or the complex psychological thoughts and feelings—let alone the unconscious thoughts—underlying the anxiety problem. Getting well by using CBT has everything to do with changing thoughts and behaviors in a highly structured way.

CBT typically occurs once a week in individual or group sessions for a relatively short period of time, perhaps three to twenty weeks. The CBT therapist is the guide and the coach. In CBT you keep a journal of your thoughts and behaviors involving anxiety, using a structured approach. This book grew out of our experiences with CBT as a manual to use in our own clinical work. In pursuing CBT you have some good days and some bad days as you progress toward recovery. Your level of success literally depends on your level of effort. If you work hard and spend time on your practice sessions, you will move forward fast and far. Holding back, procrastinating, or avoiding the hard work that CBT requires will lead to little or no benefit from this form of therapy.

Psychotherapy

More traditional therapy, in contrast to CBT, focuses on the individual and his or her unique life story. In psychotherapy, you sit down for regular sessions with a therapist to talk about how you are, how you think and feel, how your anxiety problem developed, and what sort of relationships you are in. There is a lot of satisfaction in being able to tell your life story to someone who is interested and sympathetic. Not only can the therapist give you suggestions for how to improve your life, but just the act of telling your story from start to the present, and thinking out loud about your hopes and fears for the future, can lead to having a better understanding of your anxiety problems. Therapy can lead to new ideas for how to live a better life. Anxiety problems that have persisted for many years often cause problems in relationships and with self-esteem. These issues can be addressed in psychotherapy over time. Unlike CBT therapy, which is usually fairly brief and highly structured, psychotherapy can go on for many years. There is an endless supply of new material as your life literally unfolds day by day. Psychotherapy can be done in an individual, family, or group format. It can involve one or more therapists. Sometimes psychiatrists handle both medicines and therapy, but increasingly psychiatrists handle medicines and social workers and psychologists handle the therapy. Two of this book's authors are psychiatrists who treasure the opportunity not only to handle medicines but also to work with our patients in therapy. On the other hand, all three of us also work comfortably with patients who see other therapists and physicians at the same time we work with them.

We have found that most people with anxiety problems benefit from CBT and almost as many benefit from psychotherapy. As with medicines, anxiety problems are seldom best dealt with using a single approach. Combining multiple approaches is far more likely to produce the maximum benefits. That usually includes using both medicines and therapy—usually more than one medicine and often more than one form of therapy.

Deciding Whether to Use Medicines or Therapy or Both

Many people with anxiety problems need neither medicines nor therapy. They need to know what their problem is and what they can to do about it. This book, and other materials and experiences, provides a road map to recovery. For many anxious people what is needed is an understanding of how anxiety works in the brain and what sort of care their anxious brains need.

In contrast, some people suffering from anxiety benefit enormously from both medicines and therapy. When the anxiety problem causes significant disability and distress it is usually time to try both methods of treatment. What constitutes "significant" disability and distress must of course be determined by each individual. If you consider your problems to have reached this level of significance we recommend at least one attempt with an antidepressant, probably an SSRI, at a reasonable dose for at least six weeks. In addition, if you do not have a history of alcohol or drug abuse you probably should try at least ten doses of a benzodiazepine to see what that class of medicines offers for you.

On the nonmedication side of treatment, we suggest at least ten sessions of cognitive-behavioral treatment. If you are psychologically minded, interested in the inner workings of your mind, and willing to devote the time and money needed to explore these realms with the help of a mental health professional, we suggest at least ten sessions of psychotherapy as a trial for what this approach to anxiety has to offer.

Recognizing that anxiety problems are likely to be long-term problems with a waxing and waning course, there is plenty of time to work through these basic options. Once this initial exploration is complete, you have an opportunity to explore in greater depth the options that appear to be the most promising. Finding and using help is likely to be a lifelong adventure, one we encourage you to approach with optimism and determination.

We often hear anxious people say "I don't need medicines" or "I don't need therapy." The question is not "need," as it is usually possible to limp along with an anxiety problem by limiting your life—by taking out parts of your life that are given over to the anxiety dragon. Sometimes these are fairly small parts of one's life, as typically occurs with an isolated snake phobia. More often the forgone pieces of life are not small at all—for example, flying in a commercial airplane for work and pleasure or shopping at a crowded mall or taking a promotion at work that may involve public speaking.

We encourage you to resist the understandable temptation to give up parts of your life to the dragon. The appropriate question is not whether you can get by without medicines and/or therapy but whether these treatments can significantly improve the quality of your life. If either medicines or therapy or both can do that, then it is a fool's bargain to get by without that help.

Finding a Prescribing Physician or a Therapist

With respect to the use of medicines to treat anxiety, many anxious patients do well on the first medicines they try, usually an antidepressant with or without a benzodiazepine. Virtually all physicians are now trained in the use of both of these classes of medicines in the treatment of anxiety, so virtually any physician can be a candidate to handle medicines for uncomplicated anxiety problems. On the other hand, if a person suffering from anxiety has had a poor response to one or more medicines, or if the anxiety problem is complex, it may be wiser to seek out a psychiatrist who is trained in the treatment of anxiety problems and the many other problems that often accompany anxiety. Even within this group of psychiatrists, some do better with some patients than others so it may desirable to try more than one psychiatrist if the initial experience is not satisfactory.

When it comes to finding a therapist, the same advice applies. Many therapists are now comfortable with and competent to handle anxiety problems. If your initial therapy experience is not satisfactory, however, it is often desirable to find someone who has made a specialty of the treatment of anxiety problems. This is not easy to figure out, however, since almost all therapists will claim expertise in this area. They do this because there are so many people with anxiety problems.

One good way to find an expert in either medicines or therapy is to contact the Anxiety Disorders Association of American (ADAA), which can be found on the Internet at www.adaa.org or telephoned at 240-485-1001. ADAA will provide you with the names and phone numbers of clinicians in your area who have expressed a special interest in the treatment of anxiety disorders. You may find help by calling your local psychological association, social work association, psychiatric association, or the department of psychiatry at your nearest medical school. You may also find expert help from friends and family members with similar problems who have found someone helpful. If you do find a doctor who is good with anxiety, it is likely that this doctor will be able to help you find a good therapist. And a good therapist will probably know of several physicians who have shown an aptitude for the treatment of anxiety problems.

Once you have found a physician or a therapist we suggest that you stick with that person long enough to see what he or she has to offer. All too often anxious people drop out of treatment before they have given medicines or therapy a chance to work. We have also seen the reverse: anxious people who, out of loyalty or fear of someone new, stick too long with a doctor or a therapist who is not helping them get well. If you don't have confidence in the health care workers you have chosen or if you do not get good results after a few months, it may make sense to try someone new. Most doctors and therapists are used to people shopping around to find the best fit for their needs. They are comfortable when their clients (which is what social workers and psychologists call their customers) or their patients (which is what doctors call their customers) tell them that they would like to try someone else for a while but may be back in the future.

In additon to working with physicians and therapists in practice, there is another option that has become more widely available throughout the country over the past two decades: the opportunity to participate in a clinical trial of a new medicine or a new use of an established medicine in the treatment of anxiety disorders. Clinical trials are research studies that typically last for eight to twelve weeks but may last for a year or longer. Volunteers for these studies begin with a formal evaluation to see if they qualify for the particular studies being conducted. There is no charge to the patient and clinical trials do not require insurance coverage. In many clinical trials some volunteers may receive a placebo, or sugar pill, thus serving as a control for the study. Neither the doctors nor the participants typically know who is receiving active medicine and who is receiving a placebo.

At the outset of a clinical trial study you receive a consent document that describes the study in detail, including all problems that are thought likely arise. Participation in a clinical trial is entirely voluntary, so you can withdraw at any time. The biggest problem in many clinical trials is that a large percentage of the people receiving placebos get better. This is called a "placebo reseponse." By participating in clinical trials, you receive careful diagnosis and extensive laboratory work and are closely monitored over the course of the study. You have the opportunity in this way to help evaluate new treatments and to contribute to the improvement of the care of anxious people everywhere.

To find out more about clinical trials locally and whether you may qualify for a study, check the health section of your newspaper, call your local medical school, respond to advertisements commonly put on the radio, or log on to one of the national Web sites listing clinical trial opportunities: www.clinicaltrials.gov and www.clinicaltrials.org. While clinical trials are relatively short experiences, they give participants a chance to learn more about their conditions and a chance to try medicines. Clinical trial staff often have suggestions about further care at the end of the study.

PART TWO

The Anxiety Cure: Eight Steps to Getting Well

Here you will find a practical guide for using the principles contained in Part One and for achieving the goal of living a full, normal life without restrictions as a result of anxiety. Do each step once and then go back to specific steps as you need them later on. Every step will take each individual anxious person a different amount of time. Some people can do all eight steps in eight weeks, but for others, each step will take several weeks. Throughout, we refer to the steps as each taking a week in order to establish a practical time frame. If you find too much is expected at a given step and/or if you decide to take more time, simply translate the weekly goals into a time frame that works for you.

The key to getting well is to be accountable to your support person about the work you are doing and the progress you are making every single week. It is important to do each step, but it is also important to make progress, moving from step to step. Here is a list of the topics covered in the eight steps:

Step 1: Become a Student of Your Anxiety
Step 2: Use Wizard Wisdom to Tame the Dragon
Step 3: Practice—Put Yourself in Your Discomfort Zone
Step 4: Use Support People—Relate to Others about Your Anxiety
Step 5: Evaluate Stress and Other Biological Causes of Anxiety
Step 6: Evaluate Your Need for Medicines and Therapy
Step 7: Structure Your Life without Anxiety
Step 8: Plan for Lifelong Recovery

In each step you will find new ways to think about your anxiety and new ways to overcome the limitations it puts on you. At the end of each step is a homework assignment. These assignments build on the topic in the step. Through your structured writing in a journal, they will help you write your own self-help book specifically tailored to your unique anxiety disorder. The reading, writing, talking, and practicing we outline will take some time every day. You may initially feel overwhelmed by what we recommend.

Remember: You are already spending far more time with your anxiety disorder than any program could demand. The time you spend worrying about your symptoms is wasted. The time you spend on the Anxiety Cure is invested in a better future for you, your friends, and your family. You may be dealing with anxiety in some way every hour of your waking life if your anxiety is severe—avoidance, worry, excuses, and guilt all take their toll. If you follow every step we suggest in the Anxiety Cure, you will ultimately spend far less time on your anxiety than you spend now. That is our goal together—to help you get yourself out of the prison of your anxiety.

Many people feel tremendous relief to have a constructive way to direct their anxious thoughts. Far from being burdensome, it could be exactly what you have been looking for: answers to questions that trouble you and, at long last, solutions to problems.

You will find in the following chart a list of all the homework assignments, step by step. Notice that each assignment asks you to do something a little different. Importantly, each step (after the third week) asks you to do one important activity: Practice! *Practice is the most important element of the cure for anxiety disorders.* If you do nothing else, set goals each week and practice once a day or at least once each week. Even without all the other assignments, you will find that you slowly improve. You will learn that practice is not the same as testing. To avoid this common error, be sure to read Step 3 carefully before setting goals and starting to practice.

Some readers will eagerly use all the forms and make daily records. Others will do none of the paperwork we suggest. We want you to make this your own program. Take what helps you and leave the rest behind. But by all means regularly practice by putting yourself voluntarily in situations that produce fear and panic. You get well only by working, over and over, in your anxiety discomfort zone. If you do this, you are sure to get better.

Each step of the Anxiety Cure refers you to further readings from recommended books we have used to supplement our program. Use these books, which are available at most bookstores and libraries, as you go through the eight steps. The books we suggest do not all agree with one another or with every element of the Anxiety Cure, although these books are highly regarded by us and have been useful to many anxious people. We are open to alternative paths to recovery, and we encourage you to be open to many alternatives—just so you find the ones that work best for you.

Look for Tips to Help with Anxious Moments

Throughout the eight steps, you will find highlighted tips to help you through anxious moments. Some of them are concrete things to do; others are ideas to hold in your mind when you feel your level of anxiety rise. We have included techniques that come from our clinical practices. Not all of these tips will work for any one person. For example, some people find cold drinks helpful in reducing anxiety, others find warm drinks calming, and some people do not benefit from drinking any kind of liquid when they are anxious.

Try the tips that make sense for you, and be sure to record in your journal what you try and how it works. You or your support person may come up with other tips that you find helpful, and you should record these in your personal journal also. Think of these tips for dealing with anxiety as tools, and keep them in your journal as if they were in a toolbox, so that you can pull them out to use whenever you need a tune-up to cope with your anxiety.

Schedule for the Anxiety Cure Homework

Assignment				STEP				
	1	2	3	4	5	6	7	8
Read This Step	x	x	x	x	x	x	x	x
Read Additional Specified Assignments	x	x	x	x	x	x	x	x
Anxiety Inventory	x							
Specific Anxiety Disorder Inventory	x							
Anxiety History	x							
Daily Anxiety Cure Journal	x	x						
Goal Setting	x							
Personal Progress Log		x		x		x		x
Weekly Practice Worksheet			x	x	x	x	x	x
Practice			x	x	x	x	x	x
Recruit Support Person				x				
Meet with Support Person				x	x	x	x	x
Share "Dear Friend" Letter				x				
Evaluate Stress, Exercise, and Caffeine					x			
Practice Breathing and Relaxing					x			
Review Medication Use						x		
"Structure of Your Life" Evaluation							x	
"How My Time Is Spent" Evaluation							x	
Review Need for a Group								x

CHAPTER 5

Step 1

Become a Student of Your Anxiety

Notice that this step will not ask you to make changes in your behaviors and thoughts but will ask you to begin to notice these behaviors and thoughts and how they are caused and affected by anxiety. Remember that anxiety is caused by the first fear, the powerful physical symptoms, as well as the second fear, the fear of the symptoms. You will further explore the relationship between the first and the second fears in this step. Only by studying your current behaviors, physical symptoms, anxious thoughts, and fear levels will you know where to start making changes to take back your life from the anxiety dragon. Changes can wait. Now just observe and learn. This is the first lesson of the wizard. The dragon wants you to be scared without knowing why. The wizard reminds you to become a student of your anxiety.

Study the dragon of anxiety, which has you on the run. You are likely to be not only scared out of your wits, but also unable to look at the monster that is driving you crazy and ruining your life. To get well you need to stop running. Turn and face your tormentor. Check out his face and his claws. Look at his teeth and feel his fiery breath. This is what it means to become a student of your anxiety. This first step in the Anxiety Cure is about getting organized to do the work that you need to do to get better.

Use Your Journal

The best way to get organized about your anxiety disorder and to stay organized over time is to keep a journal. Without this permanent record, it is hard to make progress and even harder to acknowledge the progress that has been made. For your journal, use a loose-leaf notebook, a binder, or any other blank booklet that you can carry easily. This is not a journal in which the profound or the monumental need be recorded. Rather, it is your personal workbook, which you create as you cure your anxiety disorder. You will continue the journal by writing an anxiety history and a list of goals, and then use it daily to record your practice. This will help you keep a concrete record of your successes and your setbacks. Date all of your entries so you can keep track of changes over time.

Your journal is the place to note the tips you would like to try or those that have been beneficial to you. If you are in therapy, have your therapist help you set up reasonable, concrete, and small goals for yourself based on your work together. This will give you another way to make therapy more effective. Throughout the eight steps of the Anxiety Cure, we will give you suggestions about how to use your journal. Try these ideas as you adapt your journal to the format that is most helpful to you.

Evaluate Your Own Level of Anxiety

The following Anxiety Inventory and Specific Anxiety Disorder Inventory will help you determine if you are suffering from an anxiety disorder and, if so, which one. You may choose to write the answers to these questions on a separate piece of paper—or on a photocopy of the page—rather than writing in this book. You will find that your score on these tests will fluctuate over time, so it is important to date any tests that you take so you can mark your future progress.

After you have taken the Anxiety Inventory, add your score and record it in the top right-hand corner of your evaluation. You can find where your score puts you compared to others with anxiety.

0–16   May be anxious but unlikely to have an anxiety disorder
17–32   Likely to have an anxiety disorder
33+   Among the most anxious of people with anxiety disorders

Where your score puts you on this chart is likely to confirm your suspicions about yourself rather than be a surprise to you. To learn more about what specific area may be a problem for you, take the Specific Anxiety Disorder Inventory, answering yes or no to each question.

Anxiety Inventory

Please circle the response that best describes you. Feel free to change the wording of a particular question to fit your situation. Please answer all questions.

0 = does not describe me   2 = describes me mostly
1 = describes me somewhat   3 = describes me completely

1. I am a tense person.	0 1 2 3
2. I worry more than most people do.	0 1 2 3
3. I have a hard time relaxing.	0 1 2 3
4. I have unexpected panic attacks.	0 1 2 3
5. I avoid particular situations, things, or places because of extreme fear.	0 1 2 3
6. When I am anxious, I have physical symptoms.	0 1 2 3
7. I find excuses not to do things because of my anxiety.	0 1 2 3
8. I am embarrassed by the things I can/cannot do because of anxiety.	0 1 2 3
9. I have horrible thoughts that I cannot stop.	0 1 2 3
10. I have to do things over and over because of fear or worry.	0 1 2 3
11. I am usually shy and uncomfortable when other people are not.	0 1 2 3
12. My work suffers/I cannot work because of my anxiety.	0 1 2 3
13. Family/friends notice that I am anxious.	0 1 2 3
14. Family/friends find my anxiety upsetting.	0 1 2 3
15. I depend on family/friends to do things because of my anxiety.	0 1 2 3
16. I have lost contact with family/friends because of my anxiety.	0 1 2 3

Specific Anxiety Disorder Inventory

1. **Agoraphobia/Panic Disorder**
   Agoraphobia
   I have extreme anxiety (fear/worry) or panic
   attacks when I am (or even think about being)
   away from a safe person or a safe place.　　Yes_____　　No_____
   Panic Disorder
   I suffer from sudden flashes of panic out of the
   blue, for no reason (spontaneous panic).　　Yes_____　　No_____

2. **Specific Phobia**
   I have extreme anxiety (fear/worry) or panic
   attacks when I am (or even think about being)
   in specific situations, such as closed places, high
   places, flying, or about specific things, such as
   animals, birds, or insects.　　Yes_____　　No_____

3. **Social Phobia**
   I have an extreme anxiety (fear/worry) of
   public speaking that leads to avoidance.　　Yes_____　　No_____

   I am shy and uncomfortable in social
   situations that most people are not troubled
   by (e.g., talking in a group or with someone
   in authority).　　Yes_____　　No_____

4. **Generalized Anxiety Disorder (GAD)**
   I am a worrier whose anxiety (fear/worry) has
   risen and fallen over many years, if not my
   entire lifetime, causing me substantial distress.
   I do not have the defining characteristics of the
   other major anxiety disorders.　　Yes_____　　No_____

5. **Obsessive-Compulsive Disorder (OCD)**
   I have intrusive, repugnant, unwanted thoughts
   that I cannot get rid of (obsessions), and I
   engage in ritualized behaviors to reduce my
   fears of these thoughts (compulsions, such as
   hand washing or checking).　　Yes_____　　No_____

6. **Posttraumatic Stress Disorder (PTSD)**
   Following a severe trauma in my life, I
   developed nightmares and flashbacks in which
   I relive the trauma.　　Yes_____　　No_____

Many people suffer from more than one anxiety disorder, as their excessive worry shows up in a variety of ways. If you answered yes to more than one diagnosis, rank those that apply to you, starting with number 1 (the most severe). The usual custom is to assign the diagnostic label for the anxiety disorder that is most severe when more than one diagnostic label applies to a person. Keep in mind that your distress merits a diagnosis of an anxiety disorder only if the problem causes serious and prolonged distress and/or disability.

Six Tips for Using Your Mouth to Help You

1. Sip ice water.
2. Drink a soda.
3. Fix a cup of herbal tea or warm milk.
4. Suck hard candy.
5. Chew gum.
6. Whistle or sing.

The Anxiety Cure is useful for people who fall anywhere along this continuum, from mildly anxious to severely impaired. Only a psychiatrist or a therapist trained in anxiety disorders can diagnose you formally as having one or more anxiety disorders. Though it can be useful to know that you have a specific anxiety diagnosis, it is not necessary in order to begin the work of getting well.

Document Your Personal Anxiety History

This documentation will help you now and in the future, should the anxiety problem ever return. You will be able to use this as a reference point to tell if you become better or worse than you are now. Answer the following questions in your journal:

1. How old were you when your anxiety disorder started?
2. What were your first symptoms of anxiety?
3. How and when did your anxiety disorder first seriously interfere with your life?
4. When was your anxiety disorder at its worst? What were your major problems then?
5. What treatments have you tried? Include therapists' and/or physicians' names and dates seen, medications, dosages taken, and results of treatments.

6. What have you found most helpful in the past in dealing with your anxiety disorder?
7. Add any other comments, remembering that you will reread this history months, and even years, from now.

Chart Your Anxiety

Every day this week, write down in your journal the characteristics of anxiety as you experience them, separating the event, the physical symptoms, the thoughts, and the level of fear that characterize your own personal torture.

Use the Anxiety Cure Daily Journal form found at the end of each step as your guide in making your own journal, or make many copies of this form, always leaving one copy blank so you can make new copies for future use. In the journal, describe where in your body you feel anxiety and precisely what those feelings are. Use words to describe these experiences. Notice carefully exactly when the anxiety is worse and when it is not so bad. *Notice precisely what makes your anxiety level go up and what makes it go down.* Are you surprised that your fear level can change so quickly? Are you surprised that it goes down if you just wait and let it run its course over a few minutes? This step is meant to get you in the habit of noticing the details of your anxiety: where, when, and how anxiety appears. It is your baseline.

Label your level of fear from 0 (meaning no fear at all) to 10 (meaning the worst, the most intense panic/fear you have ever experienced). You will probably notice that your fear of the fear (the second fear) makes the first fear grow larger, and that your activities and immediate involvement with other people make the fear grow smaller.

Fear Level Scale

0 = no fear at all; completely relaxed
10 = the worst fear you have ever had; pure panic

This is a standard way to evaluate fear. Begin labeling your fear levels as they change from hour to hour and from day to day. Keeping track of your fear level will give you a reference for change over time and will help you explain your state of fear to anyone you talk to, from friends and family to therapists and doctors.

Touching someone else's hand often makes the fear level fall, as does carefully describing your fear in words to another person. When you are afraid, it is often helpful to tell another person what you are feeling and what you want that person to do to help you find that calm voice of the wizard to describe your fear. The simple but difficult act of thinking of answers to those questions will bring your level of fear down as your mind jumps free of the dragon's grip and functions more normally.

Dan's Journal

Dan was a forty-five-year-old man who lived alone. A year ago his prosperous business restoring art went bankrupt with no warning. Dan went from being comfortably middle class to being on the verge of homelessness. He began working at night as a clerk in a copy center to pay his bills. He believed that he had lost his business because his lifelong problems with anxiety and depression had finally become so severe that his worry and the resulting preoccupation led him to treat his customers badly when he failed to deliver their art on schedule. Dan abandoned his friends when he went bankrupt because he was feeling too depressed, anxious, and humiliated to face them.

Dan had no idea how to reclaim his life when he began the Anxiety Cure. Writing his anxiety history, he realized that he had been anxious and, because of his anxiety, depressed his entire life. Nevertheless, he had managed to function despite these problems until the previous year. He also realized as a result of writing his history in his journal that the recent worsening of his problems had started soon after the death of a close friend. When he took the Anxiety Inventory, his score was high, which confirmed his own sense that he was suffering terribly. He began to record his daily anxiety levels and found that he was never below a 4. With these objective measures of the severity of his current problems in mind, Dan wisely decided to find a psychiatrist and evaluate the possible role of medicine before continuing with the rest of the eight steps.

Set Goals

List your major goals in your journal and put them in order, starting with the easiest to the hardest. Make the hardest goal the one that, if you could do it, you would know that you were functioning as a fully normal person without restrictions on your life because of anxiety or panic. Use the following to guide you in making your list in your journal:

1. List four goals that you think will be fairly easy to achieve.
2. List four goals that you think will be fairly hard to achieve.
3. List four goals that you think will be very hard (or impossible) to achieve.
4. List the one goal that you think will be the hardest of all for you to achieve.

Record your goals in three sections, from the easiest to the hardest, with that final, hardest-of-all goal highlighted at the bottom of the page.

Tips for Friends and Family

This is the week for you to get organized. You may want to start your own journal, documenting difficulties caused by the anxiety problems as they arise. Your journal is a place for you to record the frustrations you feel over the anxiety problem, since most friends and family are often unhappy and feel anger about the impact of this problem on their lives. Think about what you have tried in the past to help your anxious person. Have you forced him or her to do something? Have you acted as if nothing was wrong? Have you covered for your anxious person to a boss or a child? Write down all of your failed attempts to help.

Also document the books about anxiety problems you have read or the professionals or groups from whom you have sought help. Have any helped you? What has been helpful? What has not been helpful? Continue or begin this type of outreach by doing the reading assignment suggested at the end of each step and recording your thoughts about what you have read. Also write down when you have tried these suggestions and what the good and bad results have been.

Homework for Step 1

1. Read Part One of *The Anxiety Cure* if you have not already done so.
2. Read Step 1.
3. Take the Anxiety Inventory and the Specific Anxiety Disorder Inventory.
4. Record your anxiety history.
5. Record your anxiety levels daily as described in the Anxiety Cure Daily Journal.
6. List your goals in your journal.

Readings for Step 1

1. Davidson, R. T., and H. Dreher. *The Anxiety Book.*
2. Markway, B. G., C. N. Carmin, C. A. Pollard, and T. Flynn. *Dying of Embarrassment—Help for Social Anxiety & Phobia.*
   Section II: "Preparing for Recovery"

Anxiety Cure Daily Journal

Date	Situation/Event	Physical Symptoms	Thoughts	Fear Level*	Comments

*Rate 0–10

CHAPTER 6

Step 2

Use Wizard Wisdom to Tame the Dragon

Anxiety disorders are disorders of ideas and actions. If you blindfold someone who is phobic about bridges and then drive him or her over a bridge, there is no panic. It is the link between the idea (the cognitive function) and the action (the behavior) that creates the heightened anxiety and panic. In this step, you will learn the wizard techniques that will break this link by reducing the way your automatic thoughts and behaviors feed your fear. Notice that we are not asking you to change what you are doing in this step. We are not asking you to begin to practice yet, nor are you going to begin working toward your goals. Rather, you are going to build on what you learned in the last step, your baseline week of anxiety observation. This week you will use the new ideas you are learning to change your thinking and actions about your daily activities as they exist now.

The Three Cycles of Anxiety

Three cycles illustrate how anxiety is sustained and how new, wizard-aided behavior works to break the escalation in fear. The first two cycles are probably quite familiar to you, especially when you consider what you already learned about your own anxiety in Step 1. As you read about Cycles I and II, think about how they apply to you.

Dragon Cycle I is the anxiety cycle associated with avoiding possible anxiety-generating behaviors, such as shopping, traveling, or leaving the house without checking to be sure the stove is turned off. Anticipatory anxiety leads to avoidance, which in turn feeds self-doubt and self-criticism. This is the vicious cycle of the anxiety disorders experienced by most anxious people before treatment, when their lives and self-images are

Dragon Cycle I
DON'T DO IT

Think of Anxiety-Generating Situation
"What-If" Thinking
Anticipatory Anxiety Rises

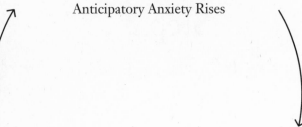

Dragon Grows
Decreased Self-Esteem

Listen to Dragon
Avoid Anxiety-Generating Situation
Anxiety Falls

dominated by fear and avoidance. Fear causes avoidance, avoidance causes fear. This cycle is called the "Don't Do It" cycle of anxiety.

Dragon Cycle II is the "Do It and Flee" cycle of anxiety. This is similar to the first cycle, but instead of avoiding the anxiety-generating trigger behavior, the anxious person enters the situation, feels increased anxiety, and fears it with a mind full of "what-if" thoughts. Dragon Cycle II also perpetuates the self-defeating cycle of avoidance and eroded self-esteem.

Instead of these cycles, which lead to increased anxiety, we are going to help you create for yourself a suit of armor against dragon attacks by using the wizard antianxiety techniques. The wizard makes an especially effective defense because, like the dragon, it is in your own head, so you can customize the help to fit you just right. Remember that the dragon is produced by your own thoughts and actions, and no amount of reassurance from others is going to change the way the dragon attacks you. Remember also that the only food the dragon can eat is your fear. You let the dragon grow by feeding him with your fear.

Dragon Cycle II
DO IT AND FLEE

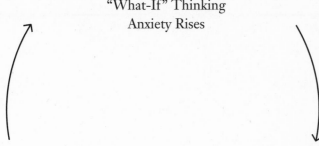

Enter Anxiety-Generating Situation
"What-If" Thinking
Anxiety Rises

Listen to Dragon
Escape Discomfort Zone
Anxiety Falls

Dragon Gains Power
Decreased Self-Esteem

Think of all the people—friends and family, doctors, emergency room workers, and others—who have told you that everything in your body is all right. Your only thought was that if they understood how bad you felt, they would not be so sure. The wizard can help you by specifically defeating this type of negative internal dialogue. Only when you make your own cognitive and behavioral changes will the dragon stop being a threat to your quality of life.

Wizard Wisdom

1. *Allow* anxious thoughts and feelings to reappear, and do not fight them.
2. *Recognize* that these thoughts and feelings are not dangerous but are normal bodily reactions.
3. *Function* in your discomfort zone and notice your achievements.
4. *Move on* to new goals.

The Wizard Cycle, Cycle III, is about using wizard wisdom to say "So What If?" to the dragon. Use the first two parts of your Wizard Wis-

Wizard Cycle III
SO WHAT IF?

Enter Anxiety-Generating Situation
"So What If" Thinking
Anxiety Rises

Dragon Shrinks
Increased Self-Esteem
and Less Anxiety on Subsequent
Exposures to This Situation

Listen to Wizard
Stay in Discomfort Zone
Anxiety Falls

dom—*allow* and *recognize*—to get into the anxiety-producing situation. This helps to overcome the anticipatory anxiety, which is defeating in Cycle I. Then *function* in your discomfort zone as the anxiety increases. This leads to increased self-confidence, which in turn diminishes both anticipatory anxiety and the likelihood of panic. Use *function* to break the second cycle of fear and flight.

Cycle III is named by the wizard "So What If?" Many anxious people call this approach "I Don't Care" or "Letting Go." It is effective when facing anxiety-triggering experiences. Instead of answering the "what if" anxiety-generated question by avoiding or running away from the panicky feeling, the stance in Cycle III is a calmly assertive "so what" to the dragon's threats. So what if you have anxious feelings? Anxious feelings eventually fade. So what if you have a panic attack? The panic will not hurt you.

Peace Lies on the Other Side of Panic

Go through your panic and find the peace you seek—a peace based on pride resulting from your hard work.

Say to yourself, "I don't care." Instead of trying (and always failing) to control your panic and anxiety, let go, let the feelings come and go. Since the dragon feeds on your fears, this approach starves the dragon and keeps your anxiety from growing in a vicious cycle of fear and avoidance. Self-esteem rises in Cycle III. It falls in Cycles I and II.

Touching Anxiety—Four Tips for Comforting Yourself

1. Hold your pet.
2. Hold a smooth stone in your hand.
3. Hug a stuffed animal.
4. Squeeze a friend's hand.

Wizard Wisdom

It is important to clearly understand the way Wizard Wisdom works in order to begin using these techniques in your anxiety cure. In Cycle III, you saw how the Wizard Wisdom can help you move forward toward your anxiety cure. Now we will break apart the five parts and examine each one in detail.

1. Allow anxious thoughts and feelings to reappear. You know from the study of your anxiety problem, which you did in Step 1, that before you began the Anxiety Cure you were experiencing anxiety frequently even though you were likely to have been avoiding and fleeing from anxious situations, as in Cycles I and II above. No matter how many changes you made in trying to avoid anxiety, you were still cowering from the dragon. To take back your life from the dragon, you must end your flight from the fear. Whether you avoid or do not avoid, you will feel crippling anxiety until you can permit these disturbing feelings to do what they want to, without your fighting or fleeing from the anxiety-generating experience.

When you use the first Wizard Wisdom points, a change in your thinking about anxious thoughts will occur; you will simply know that at times you will have anxious feelings and thoughts. This change helps begin to break the connection between the biological fact that your sensitized nervous system causes you to have anxious feelings and your pattern of trying to avoid situations in a self-defeating effort to minimize the anxiety. Expect to have anxious thoughts and feelings in your life. Some will be minor, and some will be major, but both exist. Do not feed the dragon with your secondary fear of the fear. Anxiety is normal for an anxious person.

2. Recognize that these thoughts and feelings are not dangerous but are normal bodily reactions. If you have had multiple medical evaluations for these problems, then you know from your doctors that there is nothing physically wrong other than the anxiety disorder itself. The feelings of anxiety are real and they are physical. They are distressing, but they are not dangerous. This is another change in your thinking about the feelings and thoughts that anxiety provokes. Your body is simply misinterpreting anxious feelings as an alarm that danger is occurring when, in fact, there is nothing dangerous going on. Your anxious feelings and thoughts are painful, but they are harmless *false alarms* from your sensitized, overreactive alarm mechanisms.

Remember that if you were in a dangerous situation, you would know that it was appropriate to have these thoughts and feelings. As with the first of the Wizard Wisdom points, you know from your work on Step 1 that avoidance does not prevent anxious thoughts and feelings. In fact, over time, avoidance makes your anxiety disorder worse. You have suffered from this anxiety disorder for a long time without having bad physical consequences, such as a stroke or a heart attack, and the worst anxiety is behind you.

3. Function in your discomfort zone and notice your achievement. Recall that anxiety is measured on a 0–10 scale, with 0 representing no anxiety and 10 representing the worst anxiety you have ever had. Your discomfort zone is the block of numbers representing heightened anxiety levels within which you can more or less get on with your life. For most people that means numbers between about 4 and 8. Below 4 and you have only slightly anxious thoughts and physical symptoms. Above 8 it is hard for most anxious people to focus on anything but their fear. We will talk more about levels 8 and above in Step 3. For now, think about this middle range of anxiety as *your discomfort zone*. You are clearly aware of your anxious thoughts and feelings, and it is easy to add frightening thoughts and push the fear up to a 9 or 10 level. Try, though, simply to do what you can in your discomfort zone in a low-key, steady, and unspectacular way. Do not flee the anxious situation. Give yourself lots of credit for this hard work in your discomfort zone. No one likes the discomfort zone, and by voluntarily entering it, you are beginning to break your "Don't Do It" and "Do It and Flee" cycles.

4. Move on to new goals. Once you have been practicing Wizard Wisdom points 1, 2, and 3, you will have begun to experience increased self-esteem and decreased anticipatory anxiety as a result of breaking the anxiety cycle. This self-confidence will lead you on to tackle other goals, goals that you once believed to be out of your reach. In the next step, "Practice—Put Yourself in Your Discomfort Zone," we will describe further how to choose appropriate goals. For now, it is important to remember that the ultimate sign of progress is taking back your life from anxiety. You have the right to choose for yourself what you do with your life. No longer let the dragon control all of your choices. This is the final marker of progress—you set your goals without interference from the anxiety disorder. Build on your successes. Look for the next challenge.

Incorporate New Attitudes

To make the four Wizard Wisdom points your own, copy them into your journal. Keep them nearby, so when anxiety strikes, you can look them up easily. Make notes in your journal about how long it takes before your anxiety level begins to go down, even if you do nothing but wait. It is important to begin now these cognitive, thought-based changes about how you look at your anxiety symptoms.

Change your relationship to the dragon and the worry machine. Regain control of your life. Get out of the dragon's dungeon by accepting the distressing feelings and by not adding frightening thoughts to the painful, but not dangerous, feelings of anxiety. Remember that these experiences are the normal workings of your healthy fight-or-flight responses, which are triggered inappropriately. Your body and your mind will let you do what you choose to do, even with panic and anxiety.

Track Your Progress

Keeping track of your progress is another way for you to take charge of your anxiety. Look at the Personal Progress Log at the end of this step. We suggest that from now on you evaluate your overall anxiety every week as compared to how you felt the week you started the Anxiety Cure. Last week you wrote about the anxieties you felt at that time. Now you have a permanent record of how you were doing when you began this program. Even years from now you can compare yourself to how you were last week. This documented starting point is important in many ways. Seeing improvement, or the lack of improvement, or backsliding in numbers is a helpful way to quantify your emotional state. Use the Personal Progress Log as it is or copy it into your journal. We have suggested some questions to evaluate your progress, but you will come up with others that are specific to you.

There will be ups and downs in your progress from week to week, month to month, and even year to year. Even if you have steady improvement over a long period of time, you most certainly will have a bad week occasionally. Do not get discouraged by day-to-day fluctuations or even a week or two of setbacks. What you want is overall improvement over the long haul. If you stick with the Anxiety Cure, that is likely to happen faster and better than you can believe right now. If, however, improvement does not occur and if, even more dramatically, you see yourself becoming worse over the course of months of steady work, this is a clear sign to reevaluate this situation with your support person and consult a therapist or physician.

Six Tips to Distract Yourself from Feeding the Dragon

1. Look at a favorite cartoon book.
2. Go for a short walk, preferably with someone else.
3. Watch a videotape of a favorite movie or sports event.
4. Call a friend who likes to talk.
5. Carry a tape player and listen to a relaxation tape or music.
6. Look at a photo of a favorite place or a favorite person.

Peace lies on the other side of anxiety. Only by voluntarily going through anxiety can sufferers find peace from anxiety, release from the dragon's grip. This is what practice means, and what you will be working toward in Step 3.

Tips for Friends and Family

The easiest thing to give to an anxious person is reassurance: "You will not have a heart attack," "You do not have cancer," "You cannot get AIDS from using a public telephone," "Your plane will not crash," and so on. Reassurance is like avoidance; it buys peace from the dragon for the moment, but it strengthens the anxiety in the long run as the anxious person comes to depend more and more on the reassurance. All friends and family, as well as all physicians and other health care professionals, get caught in the reassurance trap. If anxiety disorders were rational, then a single episode of reassurance would be sufficient.

Reassurance for an anxious person is similar in one important way to giving heroin to a heroin addict. It brings a sense of peace right after it is given. The problem with this approach comes later, when the reassurance (or the dose of heroin) deepens the dependence so that the sufferers who have chosen those seductive solutions find that their lives are ever more dominated by their diseases. Reassurance, like avoidance, is a trap.

So how do you know when you should give reassurance to your anxious person? Ask yourself this: if I, as a nonanxious person, were in this situation, would I need reassurance? If the answer to this question is an honest yes, then go ahead and be reassuring. If the answer is no, as it usually is with an anxious person, help that person use Wizard Wisdom to find his or her own reassurance through doing the activity. This success will be much stronger than any reassurance you could give. This approach leads to freedom and release from prison, for you and your anxious person.

In this step, we ask you to stop continuing to give the reassurance to your anxious person. Instead, gently return to the techniques of Wizard Wisdom and remind your anxious person that external reassurance has never worked before. Stopping reassurance can work only when it is combined with real compassion and respect for how hard it is for the anxious person to face his or her fears and do the things that are necessary—working in the discomfort zone—to get well.

Remember that in this step, we are not systematically practicing anxious situations, but rather we are applying Wizard Wisdom to life as it is now. The next step will be to practice systematically, and that will be covered in Step 3.

Homework for Step 2

1. Read Step 2.
2. Continue to record answers to the Anxiety Cure Daily Journal.
3. Fill out your Personal Progress Log.

Readings for Step 2

1. Burns, D. D. *The Feeling Good Handbook*.
    Part One: "Understanding Your Moods"
2. Wilson, R. R. *Don't Panic—Taking Control of Anxiety Attacks*, rev. ed.
    Chapter 13: "How to Inoculate Yourself against Panic: The Eight Attitudes of Recovery"

Personal Progress Log

Use this progress log to rate your progress weekly. Compare your anxiety each week to how you were the week you started the Anxiety Cure. Always date your log so you can watch for changes over time. The blank spaces can be used to list your own standards for judging your improvement. Rate each item, using the Rating Scale listed below.

Today's Date: _____

Date I Started to Use the Anxiety Cure: _____

Signs of Progress	My Rating
1. I enjoy life more	
2. I am less anxious	
3. My anxiety interferes less with my life	
4. I feel more in control of my life	
5.	
6.	

Rating Scale:

−3 Much worse
−2 Worse
−1 A little worse
 0 No change/the same as the week I started the Anxiety Cure
+1 A little better
+2 Better
+3 Much better

CHAPTER 7

Step 3

Practice—Put Yourself in Your Discomfort Zone

In Step 1 you started your journal and listed your goals. In Step 2 you learned to use Wizard Wisdom to protect yourself against the dragon. Now with this step we get down to the heart of the Anxiety Cure program. You need to commit yourself to active practice, putting yourself in your discomfort zone for preferably thirty to sixty minutes each day. That means voluntarily and routinely putting yourself in anxiety-provoking situations.

Practice in Your Discomfort Zone

Recall from your work in Step 2 that anxiety is measured on a scale of 0 to 10, and your discomfort zone is from about 4 to 8. These numbers typically represent the heightened anxiety levels within which you can function even though you feel more or less discomfort. Remember that it is important to work voluntarily in your discomfort zone in order to reclaim your life from the dragon of anxiety. Remember also that you are changing the faulty wiring in your brain by not responding to the false alarm that is being sounded. If you work at lower levels of anxiety, say at 3 and below, you will usually have only modestly anxious thoughts and physical symptoms. Most people with severe anxiety function at this level of anxiety on a daily basis, even when they are avoiding their anxiety-provoking situations, so it will usually be necessary to move your work higher up into the discomfort zone in order to see meaningful improvement.

Improvement comes when you voluntarily enter your personal discomfort zone. All anxious people have times when the dragon pins them down, producing anxiety levels of 4 and higher involuntarily, even when they do not voluntarily choose to enter anxiety-provoking situations. This discomfort, then, is the same as the discomfort of being in the situation voluntarily. The big difference is that involuntary exposure to high levels (when you avoid and when you flee) actually increases your sensitization. *Only repeated, voluntary exposure will cause your levels to fall over time.* Only active practice will *de*sensitize your nervous system.

While you are working in your discomfort zone, adding frightening thoughts is likely to cause your anxiety level to jump to a 9 or 10 level. Instead of adding frightening thoughts, simply do what you can in your discomfort zone. Apply the Nike slogan "Just Do It." Little steps will get you to your goals—all of them, even the hardest. Give yourself lots of credit for this hard work, especially for taking repeated small steps. By staying voluntarily in your anxiety-provoking situation, you are beginning to break the "Don't Do It" and the "Do It and Flee" cycles you saw in Step 2.

The dragon will try to surprise you. He will give you a hard time at a level 3 or 4 sometimes—jumping to a level 8 or 10 without warning or reason. At other times you will do something you are sure will produce a level 10 and you will have no anxiety at all. That is the unpredictability that is standard operating procedure for the anxiety dragon. Just accept his unpredictability and do your practice tasks whether the anxiety level is low or high. Give yourself credit for your efforts regardless of the dragon's behavior, regardless of the level you experience.

Functioning with High Levels of Anxiety

Most people find that an anxiety level above 8 makes it hard to focus on anything but their anxiety. This makes it difficult to use calming techniques such as you learned with Wizard Wisdom, the tips throughout these steps, and the deep breathing practice you will learn in Step 5. It is likely that you will have times during your practice sessions when your anxiety level becomes higher than you had anticipated. It is wise to prepare ahead of time and write a plan for yourself about what to do when experiencing high levels of anxiety. This plan will help you avoid adding frightening thoughts to your anxiety during practice, making it less likely that you will need your plan. Mark your plan in your journal with a paper clip, since you will need to find it quickly if your anxiety gets too distressing.

The most important thought to keep in mind at an anxiety level of 8 and above is: this is unpleasant, but not dangerous. The feelings at this high level of anxiety are so overwhelming that it is easy to respond to the false alarm your body is sounding by concluding that real danger is at hand. Remind yourself that nothing dangerous is happening. Would a nonanxious person experience fear in this situation? Look around you. Are other people scared now? It is your body's false alarm to a common situation that is causing your anxiety to get so high. Nothing is actually wrong. Panic is a false alarm, a few chemicals out of place in your sensitized brain.

Use Outs

At high levels of anxiety it is important to keep in mind that it is wise to have an out. This is true because panic is fed by these two mistaken ideas: you are trapped and you are alone. An out is any way to change your feelings about the anxiety-provoking situation so your high anxiety can return to the more manageable discomfort zone, going from a level 10 to a level 6 or so. An out is different from running away from a situation. Fleeing anxiety never works because the dragon feeds on his victory. You are, in a sense, reinforcing your faulty beliefs when you flee high anxiety. When you flee and your anxiety level falls, you conclude that you must flee to regain your composure, to drop that terribly high level of anxiety. That is exactly what the dragon wants you to think and what he wants you to do (avoid or flee). With active, voluntary, repeated practice, you will learn that your anxiety level will fall if you stay in your anxiety-provoking situations. That is exactly what we want you to learn and what the possessive dragon hopes you never learn.

By taking an out, in contrast, you contract with yourself to take a break and return to the situation in a more manageable way in the near future. Best of all, most of the time when you have an out, a good out, you are so reassured by not feeling either alone or trapped that you do not need to leave the panic-causing situation at all. If you do take an out, return to the situation as soon as possible. It is like the old proverb: get right back on the horse that threw you. The longer you wait to return, the harder it will be to get on that horse again.

Set Goals

Write down some fairly modest goals to work on for this week, and think of some ways to practice them. Look at the goal sheet you wrote in your journal in Step 1 to think of where to begin, but do not pick something too hard this week. Begin with the easiest goals. Remember, persistence is the key to long-term success, not fast starts!

Planning Your Outs

John is a twenty-two-year-old graduate student with social phobia. Prior to working on finding a cure for his social phobia, John went out for pizza after class with a small group with whom he was assigned to do a project. He was frightened by the prospect of eating in this social setting, but the group was planning the required project during lunch, so he felt there was no way out of the frightening situation.

As he entered the restaurant, his anxiety was a 7. He was so anxious he could not understand any of the plans that were being discussed, and he could not eat. Suddenly, his anxiety soared to a 9. John jumped up, grabbed his books, and fled the restaurant without a word to his startled classmates. This was not an out; this was terror-driven flight.

John almost dropped out of graduate school over this humiliating crisis. Fortunately, however, he sought help and began to work voluntarily in his discomfort zone. He planned carefully for his next social encounter, a date with a woman in his program. She had asked him to go to dinner, but after thinking it over, John suggested an alternate plan of seeing a popular movie and having coffee afterward. This, he thought, would be less intense for him (i.e., he would feel less threatened) than would a long period of face-to-face conversation in a formal restaurant. During the movie he began to feel his level of anxiety rising. He quietly leaned over to his date and told her he was going to get a soda and asked if she would like anything. When he was in the lobby of the darkened theater, he pulled from his pocket a piece of paper with antianxiety tips and reminded himself to steer clear of avoidance and "what-if" thoughts. He used several techniques that he found helpful. He returned to his seat with his cold drink and was actually able to enjoy the rest of the movie because he felt so successful about his use of the out.

Once John began to use planned outs, he found that he had much better control of his social interactions, and in turn, these successes led him to feel confident enough to face even more challenging social situations.

Imagery Practice

To achieve the goal of working in your discomfort zone, it may only be necessary at first to spend time thinking about the place or situation that makes you anxious. That is fine. If going to a place or being in an anxiety-provoking situation would push your anxiety level above the discomfort zone, simply set your goal as something that is manageable. Many people find that imagery practice is useful because it allows you to control the intensity of the anxiety level. Most anxious people have overactive imaginations, which is part of what causes "what if" fears to grow so large. Imagery practice capitalizes on this imagination. For example, a woman who was afraid of flying sat in a chair, closed her eyes, and imagined that she was on a flight. She felt the chilled cabin air, smelled the coffee brewing, and heard the captain announce how high the plane was flying. Her anxiety quickly soared to a level 7, despite the fact that she was still sitting in her living room!

Be sure to use your senses during your practice to heighten the awareness of reality. Imagine the taste, feeling, sight, sound, and smell of your anxiety-provoking situation. During this imagery practice, if your anxiety gets to be higher than your discomfort zone, it is easy to give yourself an out—just open your eyes! During your out, remember that nothing dangerous is happening to you. You are in a safe place, and the events are all in your mind. Once your anxiety level is again at a manageable level, close your eyes and pick up your practice where you left off.

Imagery practice is especially useful for people with fears that are difficult to practice regularly, such as flying, fears of specific bridges that are far away, and public speaking. Imagery practice is also useful with OCD. To work on obsessive thoughts, allow yourself to imagine in detail the images that you are afraid of. Let your imagination go, and as your anxiety level rises, remind yourself that this is a false alarm—not real—and not even really happening.

You can assist yourself with imagery practice by first writing a script of your anxious situation and then reading the script into a tape recorder. To practice, simply listen to the recording. You can also use this technique for OCD, by counting or using phrases that are "stuck" in your mind or your recording. You will find that it does not take too many times listening to that same tape to become bored with the repetition of the same fears and that your mind begins to wander. When this happens, you have desensitized yourself to that fear, and it is time to record another fear on tape or to be in the actual setting.

The ultimate goal of the Anxiety Cure is not to desensitize you to any particular situations or experiences, but to help you to desensitize yourself to the painful feelings that are the heart of the anxiety disorders.

Six Good Thoughts for When Your Anxiety Is High

1. Remember that anxiety is unpleasant but not dangerous.
2. Think of panic as a false alarm.
3. Take a few deep breaths.
4. Think of outs.
5. Remember that you are not trapped and you are not alone.
6. Plan to return to the anxiety-provoking situation when the anxiety is more manageable.

Testing versus Practicing

Some people have pointed out that if all it took to get well was to have panic on a regular basis, they would have been well long ago. Correct! The trick to getting well from this disease is to have panic voluntarily, to let the dragon come without resisting him. That changes "testing" into "practicing" and lets you develop a solid and realistic sense of confidence and mastery.

Testing sets you up for failure. Sooner or later you will fail one of your "tests" and your self-esteem will shrivel.

Voluntary, *Repeated*, and *Regular* are the Key Words

Feel good when you complete a practice step with high levels of fear, not when you complete the task with no levels of fear. Practice with high levels of fear takes courage and hard work, for which you deserve praise from yourself and others. Practice with no fear levels at all is easy and is much less deserving of praise.

Feeling good about those practice experiences that provide low levels of fear and feeling bad about those practice experiences that produce high levels is rooted in the old way of thinking about getting well. It equates getting well with not having any painful, anxious feelings. This new way of thinking about getting well sets you on a path to working toward having a full normal life, *with or without* your painful, anxious feelings. The new way puts you in control. The old way leaves the dragon in control of your life and your self-esteem.

Testing may work for a while, but it always fails. Set up a test, and sooner or later you will fail. But when you practice, you always succeed.

This is how it works, because testing is based on the idea that you will do something as a test to see if you can do it without fear and with low levels of anxiety. When the dragon strikes, as he surely will, you chalk it up as a failed test. With practice, you work regularly and moderately in your discomfort zone. You do your practice whether or not the dragon shows up. You always win when you practice. You win if the dragon shows up (because you do what you have set out to do) and you win if he does not show up. When you test, the dragon controls the game. When you practice, *you* are in control, and the dragon loses all of his power over you.

Tips for Friends and Family

It is finally time for you to begin changing the way you interact with your anxious person so that you no longer reinforce the anxiety problem. With this step your anxious person begins to practice regularly in anxiety-provoking situations. Now it is time for you to gently and respectfully begin allowing your anxious person to experience the situations that you have been helping him or her avoid. Do not metaphorically dump your anxious person into deep water to learn to swim under the threat of drowning. You need to make the transition into deep water gradually. Start in the shallow end. Start with short episodes of having your anxious person put his or her head under the water voluntarily, briefly at first.

If you have been doing the driving for your anxious person because of a driving phobia, plan to start allowing your anxious person to drive for short distances at times when it does not interfere with work. If you have been touching only those dishes in the kitchen that your anxious person with OCD says are safe, use a few of the "unsafe" dishes at each meal. Remind your anxious person during this transition that you are no longer supporting the anxiety disorder because you care about him or her. Supporting the anxiety disorder reinforces the belief that the dragon is right. It is time for you to show your anxious person that the dragon is not right. There is a healthier way to do things. Give outs, and always praise your anxious person for hard work done. You cannot go too slowly—easy does it. Being persistent is what works, not taking big steps. Going too fast risks discouragement and quitting the effort. Just like starting an exercise program, if you do too much too fast, you may get injured and quit altogether. Better to take it easy and build up slowly so that control and confidence can grow slowly.

Homework for Step 3

1. Read Step 3.
2. Practice in your discomfort zone daily, preferably for thirty to sixty minutes.
3. Select and record a goal for this week's practice.
4. Record your practice on the Weekly Practice Worksheet.

Reading for Step 3

1. Ross, J. *Triumph over Fear—A Book of Help and Hope for People with Anxiety, Panic Attacks, and Phobias.*
    Part Three: "Recovery from Panic Disorder and Phobia: A Self-Help Program"

The Anxiety Cure Weekly Practice Worksheet

Your Goal for This Week: _____

Each day record the minutes of practice and the expected and actual levels of fear or panic. Record your general level of satisfaction with your life for that day, from 0 (completely unsatisfied) to 10 (completely satisfied).

Date	Practice Activity	Maximum Expected Level*	Actual Duration (Min.)	Maximum Actual Level*	Satisfaction Level*	Comments

*Rate 0–10.

CHAPTER 8

Step 4

Use Support People—Relate to Others about Your Anxiety

When it comes to recovery from anxiety disorders,

**You alone can do it,
But you cannot do it alone.**

You can get an anxiety disorder on your own, but you are not likely to get well alone. Getting well from an anxiety disorder usually takes the help of others. The first step is facing that *you* have the problem. You need to face that vital fact without embarrassment or shame and without denial. That is not easy because of the societal stigma that anxiety is the result of weakness, poor coping skills, or laziness.

Be Honest about Your Anxiety

If you have been following the Anxiety Cure step by step, or if you have read any other part of this book, you know that we do not believe that weakness, poor coping skills, or laziness are the causes of anxiety. Rather, this is a biological and conditioned response of your nerves to inappropriate signals of anxiety when no danger exists.

Do you believe you have a clear understanding of your own anxiety problem? It is important that you do before you try to explain the problem to others. If you are feeling unsure at this point, back up and review Chapter 1. For most people, this will not be necessary, but if you are a highly anxious person, you may find that your thoughts about your own suffering are chaotic because of your anxiety. This may make it hard to focus on the information you have read about anxiety. If this is true for you, either continue with this step, being careful to find a trusted person to be your support person with whom you can learn this information together, or seek professional help from a therapist or psychiatrist.

Honesty is a good place to start—honesty with yourself and with those who care about you when it comes to your thoughts and feelings. Even if people do not understand your symptoms, if they care about you, you are better off to be open with them in most cases. Please realize that this does not necessarily apply to people in your place of work or others who are in authority over you. We are only talking here about people who truly care about you, such as friends and family. For more ideas about honesty at work, see Chapter 18.

Honesty is an important starting point precisely because it is so easy to be dishonest with yourself and with friends and family when you have an anxiety disorder. Most people with anxiety see these types of dishonest communications as "little white lies," but they are untruths nonetheless, and they always worsen your anxiety problem, lower your self-esteem, and reduce your ability to get well.

Everything Is Contaminated!

Joy was a thirty-five-year-old woman with severe OCD. She had particular trouble with the laundry and felt that she had to wash the clothes "just right" to make them safe for her family to wear. She spent three or four hours a day doing the laundry, and yet each family member only had a few pieces of clothing that Joy would let them wear. All of the clothes looked worn and faded because of the many times they had been laundered. To keep her husband and five-year-old son from wearing other clothes, which she considered to be "contaminated," Joy would explain that the other clothes were torn and needed mending, or that the water in the apartment had been shut off during the day for repair work, which prevented her from doing the wash, or that she had run out of laundry detergent. No one else was allowed to touch the dirty laundry. Joy became fiercely angry with her husband when he attempted to do a load of wash himself, telling him that he was too dirty from his construction job to go into the laundry area.

Joy's husband sought help because he could not understand what was wrong with his wife. Her lies had him completely confused. He had been embarrassed once during a conversation with a neighbor when he commented about the chronic problems with the water being turned off in the building, only to have the neighbor reply that the water had never been turned off.

Joy could not explain her OCD to herself and was frightened to tell her husband the thoughts she knew were unreasonable about the laundry. Her anxiety dragon told her that if she did not do the laundry "just right," her family would become sick and die. In her mind, she was trapped between giving in to the OCD and keeping the people she loved safe, even though they were angry with her, or ignoring the OCD and risking losing them to illness from the germs she believed were on the clothes.

Our secrets keep us sick. By not admitting the problem to herself or her husband, Joy prevented herself from finding help. Only honesty about the OCD that was driving the lies could explain to Joy's husband what was happening. Once Joy was not secretive about her anxiety problem, they could find help together.

It is important to be direct about telling friends and family what is wrong with you and what they can do to help you regain control of your life over the anxiety disorder. We have included a sample Letter to a Friend at the end of this step. Make copies of it to give to people you want to understand more about your anxiety disorder. It is not a short or a simple letter because it is not easy to explain the anxiety experience. You can also use the letter as a starting point to write your own Letter to a Friend, which can be a more personal description about your experiences and which more fully explains what you want from the person to whom you are giving it.

The only way to overcome any disability, including an anxiety disorder, is to work harder than people who do not have this disability. There never was any other way and there never will be any other way that works over the long haul. The bonus of facing your anxiety disease and working hard to conquer it is that when you have admitted the problem with your anxiety disorder, you can start building your self-esteem on a solid foundation. Confronting any problem and working hard to get well builds self-esteem. Other people can understand your effort and can help you along the way, if you will take the time and be unselfconscious enough to let them know what the problem is and what they need to do to help you.

Choosing Your Support Person

Once you have been open and honest about your situation to people who care about you, you can enlist other people in helping you get well. Although many people will help you as you continue with your recovery, it is useful to have one particular person to work with on a regular basis. This support person will assist you in evaluating your anxiety, choosing goals, practicing, and being accountable for your actions. This final role is especially important as you recover because it is easy to let yourself fall back into the pattern of dishonesty with yourself over small things. Do yo really want to skip the museum tour on a family vacation or are you afraid you will not be able to see an exit sign at all times? Did you not volunteer for an extra assignment at work because you are too busy already or because you did not want to have to present the information to a group of people?

When considering how you function at work or in other situations where you do not choose to be completely honest about your anxiety, it will be important to have your support person help you evaluate your actions. Think of your support person as an extension of the healthy part of your brain—someone to help you gain perspective on the thoughts and feelings that bombard you when anxiety is high.

Perhaps your choice of a support person is obvious. Perhaps it is not so clear. Begin by making a list in your journal of all the possibilities for support people. Next to each name write down the advantages and disadvantages of working with that person. If you have social phobia or are withdrawn from people because of your anxiety, you may have no one to choose from, or your list may be of people who all seem not quite right for one reason or another. Clearly, one of your goals will be increasing your social contacts, and reaching out for help to someone whom you do not know well can be a good way to begin to get to know a person better. You may find it helpful to go to an anxiety support group to meet others with similar problems, and pick someone who you think would be a good support person from the people at the meeting. If you are truly feeling stuck with this step, it is probably wise to find a therapist to be your support person for now. Eventually you will get to your goal of having a nontherapist friend as a support person, but for now it is simply important to have someone to help you get started on your work.

Once you know who you want to have as your support person, your path is relatively clear: ask the person to read the section for support people in Chapter 17, and then let you know if he or she is willing to volunteer for this role. Once you have found a support person, set up a regular weekly meeting time so that the two of you can practice together and review the practice you have recorded in your journal. Allow your support person to give you praise and to help you through anxious moments.

Let your support person praise you, and accept the praise without hiding behind an apology such as "I should have done more" or "That was nothing. When I tried to do something really hard, I failed" or "Normal people do that stuff with no effort. Why should I get praise for doing such a simple, ordinary thing?" Those are self-defeating and hurtful thoughts produced by your worry machine. Such thoughts undermine your self-esteem and mock your hard work. Instead, just say to your support person, "You are right. It was hard for me, and I am proud I did my practice and grateful to you for sharing this experience with me."

With a good support person, you can accomplish more goals faster than you believed to be possible. Keep up the work between practice sessions by repeating the work on your own. For example, if you have a fear of elevators, practice at a mall with your support person one week. At the end of your practice, set up a meeting for the following week at a tall building for longer elevator rides. During the week return to the mall and practice on the same elevator on your own.

Some anxious people never get around to practicing. While unfortunate, this is also uncommon. Many more anxious people practice, but they fault themselves for not doing more. We recommend practice once a week with your support person and for thirty to sixty minutes each day on your own. That is a high standard. But give yourself some slack. Take some days off, take some weeks off, but always come back. The more you practice (the longer and more frequent your practice), the faster you will get well. But slow will get you to the same place as fast. Set your pace but do not quit. Keep at it, and your results will be far beyond your best hopes.

Tips for Friends and Family

Whether you are a designated support person or not, there are plenty of opportunities for you to help your anxious person relate better to others. Review the list of people with whom it is better to be open and honest about the anxiety and the people with whom it is simply better to learn how to relate without explanation about anxiety. If you have friends and family in common, talk about these specific people and review the pluses and minuses of honesty.

It is also useful to talk over how your anxious person handles specific interactions, such as talking to a boss at work or returning items to a store. You will find that anxiety often leads anxious people to have difficulty with these types of situations. Practice role-playing particular situations with your anxious person by first acting as the anxious person and having your anxious person pretend to be the boss or sales clerk or whatever the specific situation suggests. In these roles have a dialogue that your anxious person has feared. Then switch roles and do the same role-playing again. After you have done both roles, talk over how each of you felt during the roles. You may need to repeat the same situation several times before your anxious person feels confident about being able to handle it in real life.

Homework for Step 4

1. Read Step 4.
2. Select and record a goal for this week's practice.
3. Practice in your discomfort zone daily and record this practice on your Weekly Practice Worksheet.
4. Recruit your support person.
5. Meet with your support person to practice together.
6. Fill out your Personal Progress Log.
7. Discuss with your support person the potential people to be honest with about your anxiety disorder.
8. Talk to people about your anxiety disorder, if this is what you decide to do.

Readings for Step 4

1. Ross, J. *Triumph over Fear—A Book of Help and Hope for People with Anxiety, Panic Attacks, and Phobias.*
    Chapter 13: "Sylvia: The Impact on the Family"
2. Schwartz, J. M. with B. Beyette. *Brain Lock—Free Yourself from Obsessive-Compulsive Behavior.*
    Chapter 6: "OCD as a Family Disorder"
3. Wilson, R. R. *Don't Panic—Taking Control of Anxiety Attacks*, rev. ed.
    Chapter 20: "The Fear of Being Seen: How to Face Social Anxieties"

Five Venting Strategies

1. Cry into your pillow.
2. Pound your pillow.
3. Curse and pound the steering wheel in your car—with the windows closed.

> 4. Talk to your support person.
> 5. Go for a walk, a run, or a bike ride.

Sample Letter to a Friend

Dear Friend:

Although at first it may be hard for you to understand, I want you to know that I have an anxiety disorder. It is characterized by feelings of panic and fear in situations where other people do not have those feelings. It is embarrassing to admit that in situations where other people are calm, I experience dizziness, sweating, breathlessness, the "shakes," and other alarming body sensations. All anxiety disorders are forms of claustrophobia. The experience of feeling trapped and alone with unbearable feelings is at the heart of panic.

An anxiety disorder can cause these physical responses—the same responses as those suffered by people who are facing imminent peril—when an anxious person is in a seemingly safe situation, such as driving a car, going to a shopping mall, getting on an elevator, or flying in an airplane. Panic is a false alarm. Because the anxious person is not in imminent external danger when the alarm sounds, these reactions are irrational, and anxious people recognize that they are irrational. Everyone sometimes experiences feelings of anxiety, but those universal, normal feelings are not related to the intense and ovewhelming feelings those of us with an anxiety disorder experience when we are in panic-generating situations.

Recently, there have been important scientific discoveries in the understanding of anxiety disorders. These disorders are not related to laziness or insanity, they do not lead to bizarre or dangerous behavior, and they do not lead to physical illness such as heart attacks or strokes. Anxiety disorders often run in families, affecting about 20 percent of women and 8 percent of men in their lifetimes. An anxiety disorder usually waxes and wanes over a lifetime. The good news is that anxiety disorders can be successfully treated.

It will be easier for me to get well if you understand what I am facing and how I am coping with it. I am learning specific techniques to enter and remain in the situations that produce feelings of panic and dread. It takes courage to do that because the feelings and thoughts are all-consuming and extremely painful. As you can imagine, it is unnerving to feel that you cannot trust your own body in many everyday situations.

That is why anxiety disorders often lead to avoidance of the situations and experiences that trigger these reactions and why they lead to a loss of self-esteem and a desire to hide the problem. I know other people cannot see the danger and do not understand my reactions. They cannot see my inner terror. That fact makes me feel even more strange and hopeless. Think about what it would be like trying to explain the color red to a person who was born blind. In the end, that is the problem I have in explaining to you the inner experience of my anxiety disorder.

It will help me if you ask me what I am feeling and what you can do to help in any of these situations. It is always the right thing to give me "outs" from any circumstance in which I feel trapped. Paradoxically, knowing that I have an out helps me to stay in the difficult situation. It also helps if you acknowledge my accomplishments and give me praise and support for my efforts to practice my antipanic techniques. I know it may seem ridiculous to you—as it does to me sometimes—to praise me for doing something that for most people is perfectly easy, but believe me, it is not easy for anyone with an anxiety disorder to do this practice.

If you would like to know more about my anxiety disorder, please ask me. I appreciate your efforts to understand my problem. Thank you for your concern. It means a lot to me that you have taken the time to read this letter and to think about how you can help me.

Regards,

[Your Name]

CHAPTER 9

Step 5

Evaluate Stress and Other Biological Causes of Anxiety

In this step you will evaluate possible external causes of anxiety. By external causes, we mean events that happen in your life and outside of your brain. This contrasts with the main sustaining force of your anxiety, which is the fear of having the anxious and panicky feelings again—having the dragon arise within your brain. It is important to evaluate external causes in your anxiety cure, as there may be simple changes you can make, such as cutting down on caffeine, that will make the work of finding a cure much easier. Some of the external causes of anxiety we cover here may not apply to you at all. If this is the case, simply skip over this section and move on to the next one. We suggest that you document this skip in your journal, however, and review your decision in the future with your support person, since it is possible to be so close to the problem yourself that you do not realize that the piece you skipped over is a place to begin future work.

Medicines and Drugs

Some medicines and drugs cause significant increases in anxiety for susceptible people. Remember that anxiety disorders are triggered in genetically susceptible people by events that may or may not be clear at the time. People who do not have this hard-wired susceptibility can use medicines that potentially cause anxiety and never have a problem. People with anxiety, however, should be wary of medicine that lists anxiety, agitation, insomnia, or tremors as possible side effects. Be sure to discuss your anxiety disorder with any doctor who prescribes medicines for you

120

for other reasons. Read package inserts from over-the-counter medicines carefully. While we believe that no one should use street drugs, anxious people have an especially powerful reason not to use them, as many people report their first panic attack occurred following use of marijuana, cocaine, and other nonmedical drugs.

The following is a list of medicines that may cause increased anxiety. This list is a good place to start, but it barely scratches the surface of substances that cause anxiety. If you have any questions about a specific medicine you are taking, check with your doctor or a pharmacist.

Potential Anxiety-Causing Medicines

Caffeine—in some headache remedies, coffee, tea, colas, chocolate
Pseudoephedrine—in cold medicines, decongestants, appetite suppressants
Epinephrine—in novocaine, EpiPens
Nicotine—in patches and gums used to curb smoking
Theophylline/prednisone—and other asthma and allergy medicines

---

Note in your journal what medicines or vitamins you are taking now and if you believe that any changes are warranted. Call doctors or pharmacists for more information if necessary. Be sure to review this list with your support person.

You do not know for sure whether any of these substances or medicines contribute to your anxiety, and neither does your doctor or pharmacist. They can give you useful advice, but in the end, the best way to figure out whether any particular substance is contributing to your anxiety is to try a period of time—usually a week or so—off of the medicine to see if that significantly reduces your anxiety. Then, if you are still in doubt, start taking the medicine again. Did you see a change or not? Recording your levels of anxiety and panic in your journal before, during, and after these trials will help you work through what can be a difficult decision-making process. Just as you would work with a person who has an allergy to a food or other substance, you can use the scientific method to reach your conclusions. You can conduct a personal experiment to decide whether your life is improved by avoiding a substance or medicine that is sometimes known to cause anxiety.

When it comes to prescription medicines, the *Physicians' Desk Reference* (*PDR*) lists virtually all possible side effects for virtually all medicines.

These exhaustive lists are almost certain to contain "insomnia," "anxiety," and "agitation" for any medicine you look up in the *PDR*. But we do not want you to avoid medicines that can help you simply because they may have one of these possible side effects. That is one more way to let the dragon run your life. We want you to consider the question of medicines causing anxiety and to work with your prescribing physicians to sort this out, one medicine at a time. Many medicines, such as antidepressants used to reduce anxiety, can add to anxiety in the first few days or weeks, but in the long run they reduce anxiety and insomnia. We want you to think of the long term in such situations and not to be turned away from medicines that can help because of anticipatory anxiety about possible side effects.

Do not stop taking any prescribed medicine out of concern over anxiety without talking with your prescribing physician. We cannot know all the facts of your particular case. Only your own doctor can. Sometimes it is hazardous to your health to simply stop a medicine to see if it is part of your problem with anxiety. When it comes to either starting a new medicine or stopping an old medicine, we want you to work closely with your doctors so that your decisions about the use of particular medicines are right for you.

Stress and Anxiety

Stress and anxiety are not synonymous, but they are linked through your brain. Stress is externally located, while anxiety is an internal state. Change causes stress. Anxiety is a feeling usually associated with tension, worry, and irritability. It is not easy to distinguish between stress and anxiety because many people erroneously use the two words interchangeably. Early on in the process of your anxiety cure, you also may have difficulty separating stress from anxiety. This is especially true if you have a high level of anxiety.

Most people with anxiety find that reducing social commitments and work obligations does not diminish anxiety and, in fact, may increase anxiety. You may find, for example, that weekends and vacations are especially anxious times for you. For many anxious people, social and work commitments actually liberate them from anxiety. These obligations are *not* sources of stress. This is exactly the opposite of the conventional thought that working causes anxiety.

To feel anxious—to feed the anxiety dragon—you have to focus on your own fear. When you are busy meeting obligations in your life, you have less time to focus on your fear. This reduces your anxiety. When you relax, when external demands are lowered, you have more opportunities to focus on your inner experiences, and for many anxious people, that means you focus on your fear and panic, which makes the anxious feelings worse. This becomes a vicious cycle as more fear leads to more focus on the fear, which in turn leads to more fear.

We do not believe that reducing life's external stress will, on its own, either cure or even reduce your anxiety. Rather, in this step you will evaluate the interaction between stress and anxiety. Make a list in your journal of sources of external stress that occur in your life now. Some of these will be things you cannot change, such as the stress of having a parent who is ill and in need of extra assistance. Other situations will be within your control, especially as you begin to recover from your anxiety disorder.

Family Stress

Jenny, a thirty-two-year-old woman, suffered from severe agoraphobia when she first began working on a list of stresses in her life. She lived at home with her father and her sister, who was twelve years younger than Jenny. Her mother had abandoned the family when the sister was, as an infant, found to be disabled. Jenny became a caregiver at an early age. The year her mother left was the first time Jenny had a panic attack.

Her father now drove Jenny to and from work. Because of her agoraphobic fears, the drive was so hard for Jenny that she would wear a Walkman and listen to gospel music because she was sure they would have an accident and be killed during the short journey. Other than that drive to and from work, which she felt forced to make because her father and sister counted on her income, Jenny did not leave her house.

When she first evaluated stress in her life, Jenny regarded her relationship with her father to be a problem because her father told her that she was too dependent. Her relationship with her sister was stressful because Jenny resented her sister's need for Jenny's income. Jenny thought that she had no personal life and that she was missing any opportunity to date, marry, and have a family of her own. Her job, which was the same one she had held since she graduated from high school, had become boring.

All of these negative thoughts were a big problem because Jenny had too much free time to worry about her anxiety symptoms. She felt trapped in the job, but she did not believe she had the skills to do anything better. Because of her phobia about driving, she could not imagine how she could work at a different location. Most days she rated her average level of anxiety at about 7 or 8. Her stress list read as follows:

Jenny's Initial Stress List

1. My father wants me to drive, and I can't!! I am afraid he will make me lose my job one day because he will refuse to drive me anymore.
2. My sister. I know it is selfish, but I am tired of taking care of her and having my pay go to support her.
3. No social life.
4. Being trapped in a dead-end job.
5. Being lonely and isolated in my home.

One year later, Jenny's list of stresses looked considerably different. She had worked hard at the Anxiety Cure assignments and had finished a semester at a community college. Her grades were so good that she won a scholarship to study at a local university. She had bought a car and was practicing for her driver's license. Jenny regularly attended church. She had a new job, which she had found through one of her college professors. Her new life was hardly stress free! Yet her anxiety level was quite low, usually no higher than a level 3.

Jenny described an especially busy week in which she had ongoing problems with her sister, taken a college final exam, interviewed for a new job, and had a date with a man she met at church. Yet Jenny noted that the final three stresses on her list were positive changes because they brought enrichment to her once terribly limited life.

Jenny's Stress List—One Year Later

1. My sister. I still wish I did not have to care for her both financially and physically.
2. My final exam. I am so proud that I finished this course. I hope I can show on the exam how much I learned.
3. My job interview. This sounds like a wonderful job; I hope I get it.
4. Going on a date. I am so excited! He is a really nice guy, and he seems to like me.

As you see from Jenny's first stress list, her anxiety caused all of her stresses except her problem with her sister. Jenny's progress in treating her anxiety disorder resulted in external stress changing from having negative to positive effects on her life, which resulted in lowering her anxiety symptoms.

Remember that people are like the bones and muscles that support us. Our bones and muscles need to be used to keep them strong. In space, which is without gravity, the bones of astronauts rapidly become brittle because they do not have the stress of working against gravity to keep them strong. People need positive stress to grow and to learn new things. External life stress is not negative; it is what we do with it that makes it negative or positive.

Notice in Jenny's example that there is no way to solve her stress about her sister. Social services possibilities had been explored to the fullest and private respite care alternatives had been used. Still Jenny felt overworked. Even so, she did not want to institutionalize her disabled sister, which was the only other alternative left to her. Jenny joined a support group for caregivers and felt at least a bit better understood in her long-term dedication to her sister.

How Is Your Thyroid Functioning?

Jenny's example brings us to another important cause of anxiety that is not related to the fear of the feeling of fear brought on by the dragon. It is, however, internal to the brain, but not in any conscious way. Jenny found out early in her anxiety cure that she had a thyroid deficiency. She had not had a medical examination for years when she first began her treatment for anxiety. She noted that her menstrual cycle was unusual. She scheduled a gynecological appointment and made sure her doctor knew that anxiety was a problem for her.

Routine blood work confirmed the doctor's guess that her thyroid was not functioning properly. She was referred to an endocrinologist who stabilized her on Synthroid, and Jenny found that she had a dramatic reduction in her spontaneous panic attacks. Review the box at the end of this section for symptoms of thyroid problems. If you have any questions about whether or not this is a part of your anxiety problem, ask for a thyroid screening by your primary care doctor, a gynecologist, or an endocrinologist. Very few clinically anxious people find that they have a thyroid problem, but it is worth checking because it is so easily solved with supplementation and can make such a dramatic improvement in anxiety levels.

Some other medical disorders can cause symptoms of anxiety. It is a good idea to see your doctor to check out your medical status. Most people with anxiety disorders, even after many years of suffering from panic and other symptoms of anxiety, are remarkably healthy. Most people have seen many physicians about their symptoms before they conclude that their problems are the result of an anxiety disorder.

Common Indications of Thyroid Disorders	
Hypothyroidism	*Hyperthyroidism*
Tiredness/fatigue	Nervousness
Forgetfulness	Difficulty sleeping
Dry, coarse hair	Bulging eyes, unblinking stare
Loss of eyebrow hair	Goiter
Puffy face and eyes	Rapid heartbeat
Goiter	Increased sweating
Slow heartbeat	Unexplained weight loss
Cold intolerance	Light menstrual periods
Weight gain	Frequent bowel movements
Heavy menstrual periods	Warm, moist palms
Constipation	Fine tremor of fingers
Brittle nails	Irritability

Breathe the Anxiety Away

Tension is both a mental and a muscular expression of anxiety. Once present in your body, tension signals your brain that you are anxious. This pattern of anxiety—where increased muscular tension leads to an increased perception of anxiety—can be maintained perpetually. This cause-and-effect relationship explains the chronic headaches, jaw pain, muscle stiffness, and general aches and pains so commonly experienced by people with anxiety disorders. One of the first places to try to break free of anxiety is to learn consciously to relax your body, which in turn will signal your brain that you are relaxed, that there is nothing to fear.

Some people scoff at the idea that changing the way you breathe can significantly lower your anxiety level. It is true that breathing practice certainly will not solve all your anxiety problems, and it may not even make much of a difference in your anxiety. Breathing practice does help many people, however, and it is so simple that it is worth trying.

Begin to calm your anxious breathing by taking a few nice, easy breaths, moving your abdomen up and down as you breathe. You may find it helpful to lie on your back on the floor or your bed to practice this simple breathing technique: place one hand on your stomach and a second hand on your chest. Feel your hand on your stomach move up and down when you breathe deeply. Feel how far into your abdomen you can swell with air when you relax your shoulders and allow yourself to breathe fully.

This focus on the simple, natural body movements associated with deep breathing helps to quiet anxiety. It helps you to think about your body as your friend, not as an enemy. It is important to understand that your brain will get all the air it needs no matter how scared and upset you become. Many anxious people fear that they will suffocate or not be able to get the air they need. This never happens, period. *You will get all the air you need.* If your brain's mechanisms that control breathing required you to be calm or to work hard at breathing correctly, all the anxious people in the world would have died of asphyxiation long ago!

Anxious, irregular breathing will move plenty of air so that your lungs keep your blood full of oxygen. That is not the problem with anxious breathing, although fear of not getting enough air is often a symptom of anxiety. The problem with anxious breathing is that it adds to tension and fear. It signals danger to your sensitized brain. This triggers the false alarm of panic and the more chronic danger signal of anxiety. Anxious breathing both results from and causes anxiety, but it does not cause low oxygen levels.

A Wonderful Antifear Strategy

Now try a paradoxical intention exercise: breathe as abnormally as you can. Hyperventilate as much as you can to see if you can make yourself panic or pass out. Alternately, hold your breath for as long as you can. Most people with anxiety are surprised at how hard it is to do these exercises for more than a few seconds. In fact, what makes breathing normally so hard for anxious people is trying so hard to do what is best done with no effort—by letting go. Breathing is natural and unconscious, like walking. If you try to walk carefully, you are likely to trip over your own feet.

Even during the worst anxiety, your body is not poised on the brink of disaster with respect to breathing. Learn to trust your tense and anxious body; it will get you through what you need to go through. In the words of Dr. Claire Weekes, "Jelly legs will carry you." We could add, "*Abnormal breathing will still get you all the air you need.*"

Record your deep breathing and paradoxical breathing practices in your journal. Include the length of time you hyperventilated and held your breath, and record any changes in your anxiety level during these exercises. Try taking three deep breaths when you are anxious.

As you do, remind yourself: "*My breathing is good enough.*" This positive thought will encourage you to continue and will begin to take the place of the negative thoughts that you have been bombarding yourself with and that only make your breathing more difficult.

Relaxation Practice

Deep breathing practice can be effectively combined with relaxation and guided imagery practice. Relaxation is relatively easy for most anxious people because part of their anxiety stems from an overactive (fear-generating) imagination. In doing this exercise, you will be harnessing this imagination and using it to help yourself, rather than allowing it to be destructive, as it has been in the past.

Relaxation reduces distress for many people, including people who are suffering from chronic pain and people undergoing cancer treatment. Anxious people also benefit from learning relaxation techniques, although many find sustained concentration difficult early in their cure because they feel too anxious to concentrate on anything but their fear. We have purposely kept this exercise short so you will not have to concentrate for too long. The goal of practicing relaxation is to be able to summon a physical and a mental feeling of peace and calm whenever you need it during the day. Try each of the several relaxation exercises we suggest.

Script for Relaxation Exercise

*Read this—or your own version—slowly and
calmly into a tape recorder. Pause for five to
thirty seconds at each*.*

Begin to relax by finding a comfortable position. Settle yourself, finding relaxing places for your arms, your hands, and your feet. * Close your eyes gently. * Now that you are settled, take three calming, deep breaths. Feel your stomach expand with each breath. Feel the tension leave your body each time you exhale. Think the word *calm* each time you exhale. * Continue to breathe deeply and slowly as you relax by focusing on letting tension drift out of your body. Do not fight tension. Instead, let it slide away.

Scan your body, and when you find places where you are tense, focus your attention on that area. Hold your focused attention on an area of tension while you breathe deeply. Imagine that tense place becoming warm, loose, and relaxed. * It is as though you are shining a spotlight over your whole body. You are illuminating each place that is tense. When you find a tense area, hold the light on that place. As the light rests on that tense area, you feel the warmth from the light entering your skin, warming your muscles, relaxing that part of you. *

Now direct your attention to your head, and feel the muscles in your scalp and face become soft and relaxed. * Feel the skin around your eyes and mouth become smooth as you relax. Focus especially on the muscles in your jaw. Feel the muscles release the tension they have been holding. Feel the warmth of your illumination lengthen and relax the muscles. Perhaps your mouth will open slightly with this relaxation. * Continue to breathe slowly and deeply.

Direct your attention to your neck and shoulders, feeling the tense, tight muscles gradually relaxing and become smooth and warm. * Allow the warmth and calm to travel down your arms, around your elbows, and down your forearms. Feel your arms settle down as they become heavy, warm, and relaxed. Let your wrists and hands become limp and relaxed, feeling the tension drain out of your hands. *

Take another deep breath and bring your attention to your stomach and back. Think of your back. Let it relax, slowly. Follow the relaxation down your abdomen, feeling the muscles and inner organs relax and calm. * Feel your hips settle with relaxation. Let your thighs and knees relax. Feel your lower legs and calves relax and become warm and heavy. Feel the tension from your body flow out your feet, and feel your feet become warm and relaxed. *

Savor the feeling of being completely relaxed and loose. * Let your body learn how it feels to be warm and calm. * Now that you know this feeling, it can be yours anytime you want. Simply recall the words *relaxed* and *calm*, and breathe easily, slowly, and deeply. Peace will return to you. * *

Now it is time to begin to focus on the world outside your body again. You may feel like shifting in your seat. Blink and open your eyes. Think about how good it feels to be alert and yet relaxed and calm. Give yourself praise for taking the time to do this relaxation exercise. You deserve to feel this calm and relaxed. Take this peace with you as you rejoin your day.

Exercise Helps Every Body

Most anxious people need to learn, or relearn, to trust their bodies. One good way to do that is to start a regular program of aerobic exercising. Aerobic means any activity, even if it is not intense, that is rhythmic and continuous and raises your heart rate to your target heart rate (THR) zone. Most anxiety, and especially panic attacks, is associated with a feeling of rapid heart rate, but this usually is less than 100 beats per minute even during a level 10 panic. Learn how to check your pulse when you are anxious and when exercising. Learn what your resting pulse is. For many people, their resting pulse is between about 70 and 80 beats per minute. Aerobic exercise, depending on your age, brings it up to between about 110 and 140 beats per minute. It surprises many anxious people who worry about their heart rates that when they exercise, even moderately, their pulse is higher than it is during a panic attack. Panic does not hurt your heart, it just gives it a minor workout. Exercise regularly and moderately to help both your mind and your body.

You can feel your pulse on the inside of your wrist at the base of your thumb. You can also feel it in your neck on either side of your windpipe (trachea). Push your fingers into your neck and count the beats for 10 seconds. Multiply that number times six to get your heart rate (beats per minute). In general, exercise so that your THR is between 70 percent and 85 percent of your maximum heart rate, which is your age subracted from 220. For most people, this means a pulse rate above about 100 and under about 140.

For most people, the best aerobic exercise is walking, which can often be done with someone else, making it more fun. Aerobic exercise need not be difficult or strenuous. But the activity does need to be regular and sustained. The simple goal for healthy aerobic exercise is to exercise for thirty minutes four times a week, but start out with five minutes two to three times a week. This simple exercise routine will not only help your mind, it will also help your body, too. If you have heart disease, if you are over forty and in poor health, or if you have any doubts about exercising, you should check with your doctor before starting a program of exercise.

In your journal write your current level of exercise and your ideal weekly exercise routine. Record your total minutes of aerobic exercise each day and add up the daily numbers each week. Your goal is 120 minutes, or more, each week. Begin to think how you could move toward that goal. If you need to see a physician prior to exercising, schedule that appointment. Otherwise, begin with some simple, easy-does-it exercise. If you have concerns about your ability to engage in moderate aerobic activity, check with your physician before you start to exercise.

Yoga, Tai Chi, and Other Good Options

Some anxious people find great benefit in a program of yoga or tai chi. If you are attracted to either approach, you will find many useful books and videotapes at libraries and bookstores. Some public television stations broadcast yoga or tai chi classes in the early morning. These programs can be taped to play at your convenience and are an excellent way to try a new approach for free.

You will also find many professional programs ready to help you. Many anxious people do not significantly benefit from either biofeedback or formal meditation—both of which require much effort and time—but some do. Try several approaches for yourself if you are interested.

Two Tips for Staying in the Here and Now

1. Splash cold water on your face.
2. Put a rubber band around your wrist and snap yourself lightly.

Food and Anxiety

Examining the role of food and eating in an anxiety disorder is another area that may or may not be helpful to you. Some people find that eating sugar or chocolate, or skipping meals, triggers panic attacks. Unless you have a food allergy or a problem with blood sugar, it is probably sufficient to do some detective work on this connection by yourself. Try keeping a list of all flare-ups of your anxiety symptoms, whether panic attacks or obsessive-compulsive disorder symptoms, and then trace back what you have or have not eaten over the previous few hours. If you believe you have found a link, make a change in the direction that you predict will reduce your anxiety problem. See over the course of several days if this link continues to hold true. If you feel better, try a planned return to the problem-provoking food or eating pattern to see if the anxiety problem worsens. Many changes along this line are possible, and while most people with anxiety find no difference in anxiety levels from eating particular foods, others feel that they do. Caffeine is a special case, as discussed earlier. Many, but not all, anxious people find that caffeine in foods and beverages is a trigger for anxiety.

Tips for Friends and Family

Many of the tips for handling external causes of anxiety mentioned in this step are useful for people other than just the person with an anxiety disorder. Consider making some changes in your own life to support the changes your anxious person is making. For example, why not set up a schedule of walking together? Perhaps you also would like to try tai chi, and the two of you could sign up to take a class together one evening a week. Another possibility is for you to evaluate your eating and set a goal for change, whether it is to lose weight or to cut out caffeine. Whatever you do, be sure to encourage each other's success at sticking to your goals and following through on your commitments.

Homework for Step 5

1. Read Step 5.
2. Select and record a goal for this week's practice.
3. Practice in your discomfort zone daily and record this practice on your Weekly Practice Worksheet.
4. Meet once to practice with your support person and to review your journal.
5. Fill in your Personal Progress Log.
6. Evaluate stress, exercise, and caffeine in your life.

Readings for Step 5

1. Norden, M. J. *Beyond Prozac—Brain-Toxic Lifestyles, Natural Antidotes & New Generation Antidepressants.*
   Part II: "Natural Prozac"
2. Wilson, R. R. *Don't Panic—Taking Control of Anxiety Attacks*, rev. ed.
   Chapter 10: "The Calming Response"
   Chapter 11: "The Breath of Life"

CHAPTER 10

Step 6

Evaluate Your Need for Medicines and Therapy

It is important, as you continue to do the work of practicing daily in your discomfort zone, that you evaluate your need for medicine and therapy with your support person. You may have found at this point, for example, that you need more help from your support person than he or she feels can be offered. Or you may be proceeding well with your practice but finding that there are other problem areas of your life that the anxiety has masked. These are signs that you would benefit from having a therapist. Similarly, you may have found that even after using many different techniques to deal with your panicky feelings, you are still routinely having high levels of chronic anxiety or spontaneous panic attacks. These are indications that medicines may be particularly useful to you to give your brain a break from the biologically caused panic feelings. Once you have a supportive therapist or helpful medicine, you may find that you are able to make great strides in overcoming your anxiety.

Many anxious people feel guilty about taking medicines or seeing a therapist. They may reject medicines or therapy without even trying them. That is usually a mistake. If you can live a full normal life with your anxiety disorder without undue discomfort and without using medicines or seeing a therapist, then you do not need to use these resources. But if your discomfort is substantial, and if you find your life is limited by your panic and anxiety, then consider using medicines or seeing a therapist to help you reach your goals. We encourage clinically anxious people to try medicines and therapy to see if they produce significant benefit. If you do use them and they do not benefit you, at least you have tried, and you will know what medicines and therapy can and cannot do for you.

As described in Chapter 4, there are three types of medicines useful in the treatment of anxiety disorders: the antidepressants, the benzodiazepines, and other medicines such as the beta blockers and BuSpar. Prozac, Zoloft, and Paxil are the most widely used antidepressants, and Xanax and Klonopin are the most widely used benzodiazepines today. The beta blockers, including Inderal, are used in the treatment of public speaking phobia.

In general, it is wise not to drink alcohol within at least twenty-four hours of taking any medicine for anxiety. The effects of alcohol can be magnified by simultaneous use of these medicines, which is especially dangerous when driving or doing anything else that requires you to be fully alert. Alcohol also negates the positive effects of antianxiety medicine. See the tables at the end of this step for a listing of the most widely used medicines to treat anxiety and the typical maximum daily doses of each.

One of our patients, who had been through countless years of intensive therapy for agoraphobia when she started the Anxiety Cure, found that using very small doses of Valium for acute anxiety when she needed it, combined with the shift in thinking and behavior that she learned from this program, were just what she needed to help her be able to go with her husband to Europe for a family vacation. This was all the more remarkable to her because she had never been so far from home, and a few months before this trip she had been nearly housebound from her disorder, despite her best previous efforts to overcome it. Here is a letter she wrote describing her joy while taking a trip that had terrified her before she took to the air and crossed the Atlantic Ocean:

> I wanted to drop you a note to let you know how well I'm doing! You definitely were a *much* better predictor of how things would go than I was. As usual, my anticipatory anxiety was way out of range with the reality of things.
>
> I did take much more Valium than before (2.5 mg about every four hours, with a total of about 15 mg over the course of the day) on the day of the flight. I felt almost completely free of anxiety, and the flight was fine.
>
> Since I've been in London, I've been able to do everything—including very crowded buses, subways, sightseeing, restaurants, etc., feeling quite comfortable. Again, as you predicted, I've been doing well on about 2.5 mg two or three times a day.
>
> I can hardly believe I'm here in Europe—leaving for Paris Monday morning. This is not only a wonderful family trip that we'll always remember, but also a great lesson in what I can do. I am so relieved that I

am actually *enjoying* myself (also, as you predicted), not just getting through each day painfully. That is a great gift for me.

Thank you! It helped me so much to see you right before I left. And guess what? I'm not even walking around "ga-ga" from the medication. I believe I appear to be a normal person.

The usual maximum dose of Valium for anxiety is 40 mg a day. This woman did not take more than 15 mg a day, and most days she was using 5 to 7.5 mg. She used small doses of Valium and had a good response. This is typical of anxious people. She was concerned about her use of Valium and had been afraid she would be a zombie if she took more than a tiny dose. Those concerns and fears are also characteristic of how anxious people often feel about the use of all medicines. Valium helped her use cognitive and behavior techniques. The medicine helped her escape from her phobia prison and enjoy her life.

Feeling Guilty for Taking Medicines?

Many anxious people do. They feel that using medicines is a sign of weakness or failure, but they do not have such feelings about using medicines for most nonmental diseases. Both medicines and therapy are ways of coping with many serious but solvable mental problems, including the anxiety disorders. They are complementary, not competitive. Using either medicines or therapy is not a sign of weakness. Both are signs of strength, of doing what it takes to live a full, normal, and reasonably comfortable life. Using medicines does not interfere with effective use of nonmedicine therapies for anxiety disorders. The opposite is more often the case. Only when medicines have quieted the overreactive, clinically anxious brain can the anxious person make the best use of psychotherapy and of practice as outlined in this book.

The Problem of Addiction to Medicines

Is an anxious person addicted to a medicine? Addiction is characterized by two features: loss of control and denial. If the anxious person lies about the use of alcohol and other drugs, obtains drugs from more than one physician without telling all the physicians the truth about the use of medicines, and/or uses the medicines despite obvious harm that is caused by the use of that drug, then that is addiction.

In contrast, if the anxious person uses medicines that produce benefit instead of harm and if that use is entirely honest and openly described to all physicians (and family members), then that is not addiction. The same thing is true for therapy. If the anxious person tells the truth about seeing a therapist, and if that relationship is helpful, then it is not an "addiction." These simple distinctions are often not made, which leaves many anxious people who use medicines feeling guilty, as though they were "addicted" to their medicines. Equally bad is the fear of addiction, which inappropriately leads many anxious people not to use medicines that could genuinely benefit them. For more about anxiety and addiction, see Chapter 16.

When to Take and When to Stop Taking Medicines for Anxiety

Anxiety problems usually come and go repeatedly over the lifetime of an anxious person. That means that they are worse at some times and better, or even absent entirely, at other times. Medicines can quiet down the panic dragon and let the sensitized nervous system heal. On the other hand, antianxiety medicines work only while they are taken. When they are stopped, they no longer help. Since the anxiety disorders are usually chronic and often lifelong, it is not surprising that many anxious people find that medicines are necessary for them to lead more normal lives for long periods of time and even for their lifetimes.

While there can be no simple rules for every anxious person, below are some guidelines for your own personal needs for medicine for your anxiety disorder.

Should I Take Medicines Now? *Use medicines when you find your quality of life is diminished by anxiety.* If you are doing well without medicines and if you are getting help from nonpharmacological forms of treatment, then you do not need medicines. But if you use nonmedicine treatments and find that you are still suffering from your anxiety, it is usually wise to give medicines a try. If the first medicine you try does not help, or if it has side effects that are bothersome to you, try another medicine. There are many good choices, and no one can say which is best for any particular person until several have been tried. However, if after trying several you find that medicines do not help you or if the side effects continue to be more bothersome than the anxiety, then you may be better off not taking medicines. This is not common in the treatment of anxiety disorders, but it sometimes happens.

When Do I Stop Taking Medicine?   After six to twelve months or so of successful medical treatment, you can try a period with no medicine. Do not stop medicines abruptly, since that may produce heightened anxiety as your brain is jolted by the sudden loss of the medicine. Work with your doctor and/or therapist to establish whether you still need the medicine. Then gradually reduce your dose over the course of one to two months. It will probably take two months or so for you to be off medicines entirely to know whether you need them or not, because the symptoms of your anxiety disorder may not come back immediately when you stop the medicine. On the other hand, when you stop a benzodiazepine, you may have a temporary upsurge of anxiety when you get close to or actually reach the zero dose. Often this rebound anxiety will pass after a few weeks. For these reasons, it takes several months of being medicine-free to know for certain whether you continue to need medicines or not. If, when you try this gradual dose-reduction experiment, you find that your anxiety gets so much worse that the possible gains of being medicine-free are more than overbalanced by the increased distress you feel, then it is usually desirable to go back to your regular dose of the medicine for an additional six to twelve months and then consider trying another discontinuation experiment.

How Do I Stop Taking Medicine?   If you have trouble thinking about how to stop taking medicines, talk with your doctor to work out a plan of discontinuation. The most likely explanation of the difficulty is the recurrence of your underlying anxiety disorder.

It is desirable to discontinue medicines gradually so that your nervous system has a chance to get used to a lower level of medicines over a longer period of time. Two months of gradual dose reduction to reach zero dose is about average, but even six months is reasonable if you have been using medicines every day for a year or longer.

How Much Medicine Should I Take?   Many anxious people take too little medicine to get the full benefits. Talk over your dose with your doctor. It is often desirable to use higher doses early in treatment to quiet your oversensitized nervous system and to explore the maximum potential of the medicine. After a few months of a good result, it is sometimes possible to lower the dose by half or more without losing the therapeutic benefits. Lowering the dose can also reduce whatever side effects you may be experiencing. In general, do not use doses above the listed maximum doses unless you discuss this with your physician. In some cases higher doses are desirable and safe.

With respect to the benzodiazepines, such as Xanax and Valium, concerns over taking too much are common. In general, the treatment of panic may require doses higher than the listed maximums to control the panic initially. Usually this is not the case because most often panic is controlled at lower doses. Even when higher doses are needed at first, the dose can usually be reduced to levels below the listed maximum doses after a few months of successful treatment.

We use a green light, yellow light, and red light system for benzodiazepine doses for anxiety (see Table 1 on page 65). The green light zone is half the maximum dose or less. The green light zone for Xanax and for Klonopin is 2 mg or less a day; for Valium it is 20 mg or less a day. The yellow light zone is between one-half and the full maximum dose. For Xanax the yellow light zone is doses above 2 mg and at or below 4 mg a day. The red light zone is above the maximum listed dose. Most anxious patients, even those with panic attacks, do well at doses in the green light zone. Doses above the maximum (in the red light zone) are rarely needed except for short periods of time for the treatment of panic disorder/agoraphobia. If you find yourself in the yellow or red light zones, discuss this with your physician. Sometimes alcoholics and people addicted to drugs who are prescribed benzodiazepines for anxiety move into the red light zone because of their unique tendency to addiction.

The typical anxious person using a benzodiazepine will find no need to raise his or her dose above the green light zone, no matter how long the medicine is used. The benzodiazepines do not lose their effectiveness over time (that is, there is no tolerance to the antianxiety or antipanic effects of these medicines).

We have seen many anxious patients who are inappropriately worried about their benzodiazepine use. They then take terribly small doses and find that their response is inadequate. They complain to their doctors that they are addicted (because they feel a need to use more of the benzodiazepine). These people are never suffering from addiction. They are suffering from inadequate doses of the antianxiety medicine. If this description fits you, try slowly raising your benzodiazepine dose higher in the green light zone, and see if you can find a dose where you are more comfortable with significantly less panic and less anxiety. Most anxious patients who do not have preexisting problems with addiction to alcohol or other drugs find this modest dose escalation in the green light zone works well for them.

Will I Need Medicine Again?   Even after you have been medicine-free for a period of weeks, months, or even years, you may have an upsurge of anxiety problems in the future that is so severe that it would make sense to use medicines again for a period of time. Often when a relapse occurs, patients wait too long to restart medicines. This can make the relapse both more severe and more prolonged than it would have been if medicines had been started earlier. In general, if an upsurge of anxiety symptoms is severe and if it lasts more than a week or so, it is desirable to restart medicines and to continue them for at least a month after the upsurge of symptoms has abated.

Do I Have to Take Medicine?   It is desirable not to use medicines at all if you can do well without them. On the other hand, *if you find that the quality of your life is degraded by the anxiety problem and if medicines help you by improving the quality of your life, then you are generally wise to use the medicines.* This advice is no different from that given for the treatment of depression or other mental disorders. It is also no different from advice given for any other diseases, from arthritis and diabetes to high blood pressure and ulcers. The important thing is to remember that the anxiety disorders are just as real and just as serious as these diseases and that you are no more guilty or weak if you need medicines for anxiety than you are if you need medicines for these other diseases. The medicines used to treat anxiety are generally safe, even when taken every day for many years. It is important that your prescribing physician have all the facts about your use of all medicines and your use of any other substances that can affect your brain, including alcohol and illegal drugs. If you are not telling your doctor the complete truth about your use of medicines or drugs, then you are at risk for serious problems.

How Do I Find a Therapist or Psychiatrist?

There are many ways to find a therapist or a psychiatrist. If you know someone else who can give you a referral, that is an excellent way to find a good mental health provider. Often, however, people are reluctant to talk about these problems, so you might have no idea which of your friends has found a good therapist or psychiatrist. You can ask your family doctor for a referral. You can also call the Anxiety Disorders Association of America (ADAA), a nonprofit organization. There is more information about ADAA listed in Resources, in the back of this book; or look online at www.adaa.org. The ADAA keeps a national list of therapists and psychiatrists who are experienced in treating people with anxiety disorders. Another good source of referrals is anxiety self-help groups in your area. Even if you are unable or unwilling to go to the group, you can often call the group leader and ask him or her for recommendations. People in self-help groups are a wonderful source of information about locally available resources, since members of these groups have been through many of the same things that you are facing. You can also call the National Self-Help Clearinghouse, listed in the Resources, for a list of groups in your area.

Dealing with Managed Care

The ongoing evolution in managed care leaves you with another factor to consider when you work out your own care for your anxiety disorder. You need to think about how your health insurance coverage can meet your needs within the financial constraints your managed care or indemnity plan and your budget create.

We suggest that most people first try to work within their managed care network to find the best care they can. More and more first-class health care providers are joining managed care networks. That may mean your educating your network providers so that they can better understand anxiety disorders and the ways to treat them with medicines and with cognitive behavioral treatments. You can use *The Anxiety Cure* as a test in your educational efforts. Recall from the Introduction that Bob first learned about this new form of treatment for agoraphobics from a patient of his who brought him an article about new treatments from *Glamour* magazine. Even highly educated professionals are often educated by their patients. Do not be shy in your efforts and do be persistent—as Bob's patient was in 1977.

If you cannot get the help you need inside your managed care network, then we suggest that you become an educated consumer outside your network, seeing just how many of these costs can be covered by your health insurance. We do not work in any managed care network. Many other doctors and therapists work outside networks. Many of our patients find that our costs are relatively modest when budgeted over a year and when compared to the value of the changes they are able to make in their lives. You will need to work this out for yourself with the providers in your area.

Unlike the costs of open heart surgery or the inpatient costs of managing many chronic illnesses, the costs of outpatient care for anxiety disorders can often be budgeted successfully by people who are by no means rich, since these treatments are relatively affordable, even without the help of health insurance. For many anxious patients, the fact that managed care plans are increasingly providing options for partial payment outside the network is a big plus, since many patients know about some good providers outside their managed care networks.

Managed care companies hire talented people who wish to provide high-quality care and are motivated by many factors, including both economic factors and sincere concern for your welfare. As managed care matures and recognizes that anxiety disorders are very common, often severely crippling, and highly treatable in affordable ways, it is doing an increasingly good job handling these problems. Give your managed care company a chance to help you. Help it help you before you go outside the system. If, in the end, you find your needs are not met, consider writing to the managed care company, or your employer, or both, and encourage them to do a better job in the future of helping people with anxiety disorders. Taking this step may not help you, but it may help other anxious people in the future when they try to use this particular managed care network.

Do not let the financial issues get between you and your recovery. Be realistic about what you need and what you can afford. Be determined to get well. You can often use self-help organizations in your area to help you meet your needs and to find knowledgeable providers of health care services that you can afford.

What Kind of Therapy Do I Need?   There are many forms of the talking cure, or psychotherapy. The traditional form of treatment is psychoanalytical therapy, which focuses on childhood traumas and enduring emotional conflicts. In this view, anxiety is a symptom of deeper conflicts, which can be resolved in the psychotherapeutic relationship, often with frequent visits over a long period of time. The new form of psychotherapy for anxiety disorders is called cognitive-behavioral treatment (CBT). The visits are less frequent and the course of treatment is less prolonged. It focuses on thoughts (cognitions) and behaviors (avoidance), often using journals and structured readings and active practice in the anxiety-generating situation.

There are many other forms of psychotherapy as well; some provide more support and some provide more education. Most real-life therapists today are not doctrinaire practitioners of any particular school of therapy but can best be described as eclectic, meaning that they select components from many sources to fashion the best treatment for each individual patient. No form of psychotherapy works for every anxious patient, and no form of therapy fails to work for any anxious patient. We recommend having an open mind and doing an active search for the best treatment for you at this time in your life, recognizing that your own needs may change over time.

M.D. or not M.D.? Just as there are many approaches to psychotherapy, so are there several categories of caregivers. Psychiatrists are medical doctors who specialize in mental disorders (often including anxiety disorders, the most common of all mental disorders). Psychologists are Ph.D. doctors of psychology who are trained in clinical treatments, including the anxiety disorders. Licensed clinical social workers have master's degrees in social work and are licensed to provide clinical care. All three categories of treatment providers—M.D.s, Ph.D.s, and L.C.S.W.s/M.S.W.s—are licensed by the states to provide psychotherapy. Within managed care networks, it is common to see a social worker or psychologist for talking treatment and an M.D., not necessarily a psychiatrist, for prescribing medicines.

Some people find it helpful to see one doctor for both therapy and medicine (which tilts you toward using a psychiatrist, since only psychiatrists are specialists in mental disorders who are also medical doctors), while other anxious people find it desirable to see a non-M.D. therapist for the talking part of their treatment and to see a psychiatrist or other M.D. for medicines. Often particular M.D.s and non-M.D. therapists are experienced in working together as teams.

We are open to all of these approaches to getting well, and we have seen both good and bad outcomes for all of these many patterns of care. While the professional status of the treating person may be important, we have found that experience and personal characteristics are often more important, and that the therapist who does well with one patient may not necessarily be right for another patient. We recommend that you proceed in therapy as you do with medicines, getting as much information as you can—with an open mind, with a determination to get the best from each provider of care that you see, and with a willingness to try something new if you do not get your needs met in a particular relationship.

How Should I Prepare for an Appointment with My Psychiatrist?

If you have decided to see a psychiatrist to evaluate whether you would benefit from taking medicine, take a few minutes to get organized prior to your appointment. In your journal, review the anxiety history you prepared in Step 1 and any prior history you have of taking psychiatric medicines.

List in your journal all the medicines you have ever used in your efforts to reduce anxiety and insomnia. List the names of the medicines, the maximum dose you used, and the approximate dates you used each of the medicines. Also record the benefits you got from each medicine, the side effects you experienced while on the medicine, and why you stopped using each medicine. This information will be helpful to you and to your prescribing doctors in working out the best care for you in the future.

We have found that many anxious people have tried medicines and then stopped using them without giving the medicines a full chance to work (which for most medicines is two to three months at adequate doses). This happens because anxious people are often frightened of taking medicines and of any possible side effects, so they commonly quit prematurely. We have also found that some anxious patients use medicines alone, without full use of therapy and antianxiety techniques at the same time, concluding that medicines do not work for them or that the medicines do not work well enough. We recommend using medicines long enough, at high enough doses, to get the full potential benefits from them and using them along with therapy and diligent practice in anxiety-provoking situations to achieve the maximum benefits.

Answer the following questions in your journal in preparation for your medicine evaluation:

1. What are my feelings about taking medicines?
2. What do I worry about the most with regard to taking medicine?
3. What do I hope to gain by taking medicine?
4. What do I think my friends and family, and my support person in particular, would think about my taking medicine?
5. What questions do I have about medicine options that I want to ask my doctor?

Four Tips to Help Time Pass

1. Tell yourself you will go one more block before you take a break from practice.
2. Guess how many seconds it will take to go through a tunnel or up an escalator. Count it out, or use your watch, and see if you were close.
3. Look at the seconds tick away on your watch.
4. Knit or crochet.

Tips for Friends and Family

Many people have strong feelings about medicines. Having seen your anxious person working on finding a cure for his or her anxiety, you may feel the need to quickly find a pill that will relieve his or her suffering. On the other hand, you may not like the idea of your anxious person taking medicine of any sort. If you know others who are part of your anxious person's life, you will find that they, too, are likely to have strong feelings about medicine, and they will not always agree with you.

It is important for all of you to step back from this decision so you do not jump to a conclusion that is not the best one for your anxious person. Answer the questions posed earlier in this step about choosing whether to take a medicine or not, and then share your answers with your anxious person or other friends and family.

Do the reading that is suggested for this step, and look in libraries and bookstores for books with current information about psychiatric medicines. You may also want to talk to people in an anxiety support group about their personal experiences with medicine. No two people ever have the same experiences with taking medicine, even if they have taken the same medicine.

It may be helpful for you to find a knowledgeable psychiatrist to help you sort out the risks and benefits of medicine. Even if your anxious person is not ready to take this step, you can certainly have a consultation appointment to review the information that you present. If your anxious person does want to see a psychiatrist, find out if you can go along, or at least submit a list of questions for the psychiatrist to answer. Some psychiatrists will allow a session to be audiotaped, and then you and your anxious person together can listen to the doctor's advice in a quiet, nonstressful environment and talk about the information and your feelings together.

Homework for Step 6

1. Read Step 6.
2. Select and record a goal for this week's practice.
3. Practice in your discomfort zone daily, and record this practice on your Weekly Practice Worksheet.
4. Meet once to practice with your support person and to review your journal.
5. Review your current or potential use of medicine and therapy with your support person.
6. If you have a doctor or therapist, review medicine use with him or her.
7. Fill out your Personal Progress Log.

Readings for Step 6

1. Young, J. E., and J. Klosko. *Reinventing Your Life.*
   Chapter 3: "Understanding Lifetraps"
2. Markway, B. G., C. N. Carmin, C. A. Pollard, and T. Flynn. *Dying of Embarrassment—Help for Social Anxiety & Phobia.*
   Chapter 17: "How Do I Find Professional Help?"

The Benzodiazepines

Pluses: Rapid onset of benefit, few side effects, can be used either as needed or several times a day.

Minuses: Abused by some alcoholics and people addicted to drugs, can be more difficult to stop after months of everyday use, usually taken several times a day if used every day.

Trade Names (Generic)	*Usual Maximum Dose/Day (mg)*
Ativan (lorazepam)	10
Klonopin (clonazepam)	4
Librium (chlordiazepoxide)	100
Serax (oxazepam)	120
Tranxene (clorazepate)	60
Valium (diazepam)	40
Xanax (alprazolam)	4
Xanax XR (alprazolam)	6

All these medicines are commonly used in the daytime for anxiety.

The Antidepressants

Pluses: No abuse potential for addicts and alcoholics, easier to stop, usually taken only once a day.

Minuses: Must be taken consistently for several weeks before beneficial effects are produced. For some people, side effects of sexual dysfunction and weight gain may be a problem.

Trade Names (Generic)	Usual Maximum Dose/Day (mg)
SSRIs	
Celexa (citalopram)	60
Lexapro (escitalopram)	20
Prozac (fluoxetine)	60
Prozac Weekly	90/week
Luvox (fluvoxamine)	300
Paxil (paroxetine)	50
Paxil CR	62.5
Zoloft (sertraline)	200
Tricyclics	
Anafranil (clomipramine)	250
Norpramin (desipramine)	300
Pamelor (nortriptyline)	150
Tofranil (imipramine)	300
MAOIs	
Nardil (phenelzine)	45
Parnate (tranylcypromine)	60
Other	
Effexor XR (venlafaxine)	225
Wellbutrin SR (bupropion)	400
Remeron (mirtazapine)	45
Serzone (nefazodone)	600

CHAPTER 11

Step 7

Structure Your Life without Anxiety

We have found that the lives of many anxious people lack structure. Thinking of your life as having a "structure" may be unfamiliar. Everyone, rich and poor, young and old, on every part of the planet, has exactly the same twenty-four hours each and every day. What distinguishes us is how we use those hours. The uses we make of our time is what we call the "structure" of our lives; it is how we organize our lives. If you make no effort to control your life, your life still has a structure. It may be similar from one day to the next, or it may change every day. Whatever you do, your life has a unique structure, one that you can understand by thinking about how you use your time and recording those uses in your journal.

In this step, the structure of your life refers to the routine, everyday activities of your life, or how you normally spend your time. As we will explain, a chaotic pattern both is caused by anxiety symptoms and contributes to worsening of anxiety. This chicken-and-egg balance of panic and structured living is important to understand, since often people who have become very focused on panicky feelings and who have lost a functional structure in their lives believe it is impossible for them to have structure again. This step will help you think through the role of structure in your life and, with the aid of your support person, rethink areas that have become problems for you.

Structured living is often lost when anxiety hits because your feelings of panic are so overwhelming. They demand attention when they surface, and take precedence over any other plans that had been made. This giving in to feeling-driven scheduling means that it is very hard to stick to any plans. Almost all people who suffer from panicky feelings recognize the dominant role of panic in making daily plans. For some people, this takes an extreme form and leads to avoidance of almost all activities. For others, it means that they are never sure if they will be able to execute a plan when the time comes. Once the anxious feelings become the focus of how you react to life, it is hard to live by any routine without being swayed by how you feel from moment to moment. When this happens the dragon is running your life, not you.

This feeling-based reaction to life is terribly harmful. It leads to instability and to being able to count on nothing—not your feelings, not your actions, not your schedule. Everything in your life is chaotic. All people, but especially people with anxiety problems, need structure to their living. The chaos that is caused by impulsive, feeling-driven planning undermines all structure and exacerbates the feeling of being out of control that characterizes anxiety disorders. We have found that the more choices you are able to exercise over how to spend your time—for example, if you are retired, work in your home, or are a homemaker—the more difficult it is to impose structure on your life. Employment and other obligations that are structured by external forces help keep you from focusing too much attention on your feelings. See Chapter 20 for more thoughts about retirement and anxiety.

Take Charge of Your Actions

By focusing on the areas in your life that are troublesome because they lack structure, you are taking charge of your actions. You are once again affirming that although your feelings are powerful, they are not your master. As you have seen in Part One, and in earlier steps, it is vital to move away from allowing your feelings to govern your actions. You can get a wonderful boost of self-confidence as you live your life according to your personal plans, not your panicked emotions. Try adopting our suggestions to add thoughtfully planned, positive activities to your daily routine. Many anxious people find that these principles make an enormous difference in reducing their symptoms of panic and anxiety, and as the symptoms diminish, so does the role of anxiety in shaping how they spend their time.

When people who have lost huge parts of their lives to chronic anxiety have gained relief, either through medication and/or behavioral approaches, they often are left not knowing how to use their newly created time. In this case as well, try using these suggestions to further enhance your newfound abilities to live a more satisfying life.

Answer the questions on the test below to help focus on the parts of your life that trouble you. Record the answers in your journal, or make a copy of the test before you fill it out and have your support person fill it out for you as well. This is important, because when it comes to these feeling-driven, automatic behaviors, we are all likely to deny important facts to ourselves because we are afraid to change. There are six areas of behavior in which your life may lack structure:

1. Eating
2. Sleeping
3. Exercising
4. Working
5. Relating to other people
6. Having fun

There are several questions to be answered under each of these subheadings. Answer *T* for true and *F* for false for each question, and then evaluate each area as being one of no problem, possible problem, minor problem, or serious problem.

The Structure of Your Life

Area One: Eating

_____ I spend too much time thinking about eating.
_____ I weigh too much or too little by more than fifteen pounds.
_____ I do not have a stable pattern of eating.
_____ I eat in binges and then starve myself.
_____ I almost always eat alone.
_____ I am distressed in some way about my eating. Describe:

_____

_____

_____

My structure of eating is:

_____ No Problem _____ Minor Problem
_____ Possible Problem _____ Serious Problem

Area Two: Sleeping

_____ I do not have a regular bedtime.
_____ I do not have a regular time to awaken.

_____ I do not have a bedtime routine.
_____ I am often sleepy during the day.
_____ I often nap during the day.
_____ I do not get enough sleep.
_____ I am distressed in some way by my sleeping. Describe:

_____

_____

_____

My structure of sleeping is:

_____ No Problem   _____ Minor Problem
_____ Possible Problem   _____ Serious Problem

Area Three: Exercising

_____ I do not exercise for a minimum of twenty minutes at least three times a week.
_____ I often feel out of breath climbing a flight of stairs.
_____ I have frequent aches and pains in my muscles.
_____ I am distressed in some way by my exercising. Describe:

_____

_____

_____

My structure of exercising is:

_____ No Problem   _____ Minor Problem
_____ Possible Problem   _____ Serious Problem

Area Four: Working

_____ I do not like my work.
_____ I am not fulfilled by my work.
_____ My hours are too long or not long enough.
_____ I am not able to learn and grow in my work.
_____ I am not proud of my work.
_____ I am distressed in some way about my work. Describe:

_____

_____

_____

My structure of working is:

_____ No Problem   _____ Minor Problem
_____ Possible Problem   _____ Serious Problem

Area Five: Relating to Other People

_____ I do not have relationships with people who care about me.

_____ I do not have people I enjoy spending time with.

_____ I do not talk with and listen to other people on a regular basis.

_____ I do not have at least three people I can share good and bad news with.

_____ I am distressed in some way by my relationships with other people. Describe:

_____

_____

_____

My structure of relating to others is:

_____ No Problem   _____ Minor Problem

_____ Possible Problem   _____ Serious Problem

Area Six: Having Fun

_____ I do not have a routine for relaxation and having fun.

_____ I do not have activities that give me pleasure.

_____ I do not have fun regularly.

_____ I wish I had more fun.

_____ I am distressed in some way about having fun. Describe:

_____

_____

_____

My structure of having fun is:

_____ No Problem   _____ Minor Problem

_____ Possible Problem   _____ Serious Problem

Make Healthy Changes

Most people—with or without anxiety—have problems with at least some of these areas of their lives. These six areas encompass the most ·fundamental of human behaviors. Now that you have focused on the areas that you could improve, you will use once again the same techniques you have already been using to overcome your anxious thoughts. There are three principles that will enable you to make healthy changes in these behaviors:

1. Plan for change.
2. Implement new behaviors.
3. Make yourself accountable to your support person.

Like the earlier work you have done that has used this progression to overcome your anxiety problems, you can make small changes in behaviors over time, and if you do this work systematically and consistently, you will see a great improvement in your quality of life.

Using the test as a guide, take each area that distresses you and break it into small component parts. Try to find out more information about an area of distress from your physician, self-help groups, or books and other published material. Look at Parts Three and Four of this book for more about some of these topics. Many people who have long-term anxiety problems will need help with this stage of making changes because they have lost all sense of "normal" behavior that is not driven by feelings. If you believe this applies to you, we urge you to seek professional assistance in making plans for change. A therapist can be helpful, but so can your support person, a friend, or an organized program such as Weight Watchers or Overeaters Anonymous for improving eating habits. Tell the person with whom you are working that you need assistance in establishing healthy routines in your life. You need help deciding what is healthy, since you have no idea! As with anxiety problems in general, some therapists and friends will understand this and some will not. Remember, you are the coach of the team of people helping you with your anxiety problem. If you feel a person or a program is not helpful, find another one.

Three Tips to Help Ignore Unwanted Thoughts

1. Sweep your fingers over your forehead to vacuum unwanted thoughts from your mind.
2. Look around at others. Notice that they are not paying any attention to you.
3. Look at yourself in a mirror and see that the panic does not show on your face.

Another helpful way to add structure to your life, particularly if you are retired, a homemaker, or work from home, is to set up a basic schedule for each week. Once you have the basic schedule in place, you will be surprised to find how much less anxious you are once you do not constantly have to decide what to do next every minute of every day. Of course, the basic schedule can be changed if necessary, for example, for vacations or holidays. Having regular routines, a basic structure to your twenty-four-hour day, is calming and helps signal your body that you are in charge of what you do and when, which reduces the need to constantly ask yourself what you *feel* like doing. As you have seen, feeling-driven choices are not always beneficial!

Try filling out daily schedules like the prototypes at the end of this step, and add them to your journal. Fill out one schedule with how you spend your time now. Then make a new schedule to reflect how you would like to spend your time. How different are the two? For the second schedule, don't be limited by your present level of anxiety. For example, if you now take an hour to leave the house in the morning due to OCD rituals, don't put this into your ideal schedule. Seeing how much more time you could have without the limitations of an anxiety disorder is a great motivation to keep working toward your goals. Remember to schedule "down" time—time to take it easy. If you really like to watch daytime TV, assess whether it is realistic to eliminate that completely from your schedule. First, you may try modifying what you do. For example, instead of the average four hours of daytime TV you now watch in your unstructured time, you may choose to watch one or two hours in your new plan. The point of this new schedule is not to overwork yourself but to provide a comfortable routine within which to function, so you can live your life the way you want to live it. Letting anxiety or guilt shape your life is a bad idea.

Be realistic as you begin to move toward implementing your new schedule. For example, if you now get up at 8:30 A.M. and you would like to get up at 6:00 A.M., don't be discouraged if you have some setbacks. Simply try again the next day.

Remember, set small steps. Achieve these steps and then think about taking new small steps. Long journeys are made up of small steps.

The work in this step is exactly like the work that you have already done in earlier steps. This new focus on a healthy lifestyle, rather than on disturbing feelings, takes you a step further in your cure, moving you closer and closer to taking control of the behaviors that make up your life.

Good Pleasures and Bad Pleasures

Healthy pleasures last and lead to increased self-esteem and closer, more positive links with other people. Unhealthy pleasures are brief and lead to lowered self-esteem. They are not suitable for open, honest sharing.

Try this approach with any pleasure, from cookies to cocaine, from walking to TV watching. You do not have to be a rocket scientist to use this approach, you just have to notice what you are doing and think it through for a few hours. Making behavior changes, of course, takes longer, but the first step is clearly identifying the troublesome patterns you have in your life and committing yourself to more healthy living.

Tips for Friends and Family

This step offers another good opportunity, like Step 5, for you to evaluate your own life as your anxious person evaluates his or hers. Then you can help each other make changes. This can be rewarding to do together and can allow you to gain some benefit from the hard work you, too, have been doing as your anxious person recovers. Remember that pleasurable, relaxing activities are important parts of a healthy life. Overscheduling yourself or your anxious person is not an improvement.

It is important, however, to be honest about what is pleasurable. Is that bowl of ice cream before bed a pleasure or a self-destructive habit? Is spending Sunday morning reading the paper a pleasure or an avoidance of finding something more useful or active to do? Only you, with the help of another caring person, can evaluate your particular situation. We urge you to be kind to yourself and your anxious person. If you make a change and then after a month or so miss the old way of doing things, try changing back. The structure of your life is yours to choose each day, and each day you again decide what is truly in your best interest.

Homework for Step 7

1. Read Step 7.
2. Select and record a goal for this week's practice.
3. Practice in your discomfort zone daily and record this practice on your Weekly Practice Worksheet.
4. Meet once to practice with your support person and to review your journal.
5. Complete the test The Structure of Your Life.
6. Complete the How My Time Is Spent forms, one for your current schedule and one for your desired schedule.

Readings for Step 7

1. Bolles, R. N. *What Color Is Your Parachute?—A Practical Manual for Job-Hunters & Career-Changers.*
   Part I: The Parachute Workbook—"The Quick Job-Hunting Map"
2. Burns, D. D. *The Feeling Good Handbook.*
   Chapter 10: "A Prescription for Procrastinators"

How My Time Is Spent—Now

(List Usual Activities)

Time	Monday	Tuesday	Wednesday	Thursday	Friday	Saturday	Sunday
6 A.M.							
7 A.M.							
8 A.M.							
9 A.M.							
10 A.M.							
11 A.M.							
12 noon							
1 P.M.							
2 P.M.							
3 P.M.							
4 P.M.							
5 P.M.							
6 P.M.							
7 P.M.							
8 P.M.							
9 P.M.							
10 P.M.							
11 P.M.							
12 mid.							
1 A.M.							
2 A.M.							
3 A.M.							
4 A.M.							
5 A.M.							

How My Time Is Spent—Goal
(List Ideal Activities)

Time	Monday	Tuesday	Wednesday	Thursday	Friday	Saturday	Sunday
6 A.M.							
7 A.M.							
8 A.M.							
9 A.M.							
10 A.M.							
11 A.M.							
12 noon							
1 P.M.							
2 P.M.							
3 P.M.							
4 P.M.							
5 P.M.							
6 P.M.							
7 P.M.							
8 P.M.							
9 P.M.							
10 P.M.							
11 P.M.							
12 mid.							
1 A.M.							
2 A.M.							
3 A.M.							
4 A.M.							
5 A.M.							

CHAPTER 12

Step 8
Plan for Lifelong Recovery

Expect and allow the panic and the other symptoms of anxiety to reappear. Use Wizard Wisdom to take away the power of the dragon by facing him and practicing acceptance of the distressing feelings and worries that are his weapons. Certainly the panic and anxiety may continue, and certainly they may come back even if they have been gone for a long time. But each time the dragon shows up he is the same, even as he attempts to fool you with ever-new disguises. These disguises may masquerade as mysterious, life-threatening physical illnesses, and it is important to consider this as you work on your anxiety cure.

Setbacks and Springboards

Identifying a setback and turning it into a springboard for coping successfully in the future with an anxiety problem is a crucial part of being cured of anxiety. If you are living your life now with little interference from anxiety, you may be tempted to assume that anxious thoughts and feelings will never bother you again. We urge you not to take this stand. Rather, keep the techniques you have learned for dealing with anxiety accessible to you, and keep up the life changes you have made to prevent the dragon from encroaching on your hard-won freedom.

Panic and anxiety tend to wax and wane over time, with some periods of the sufferer's life being characterized by minor or even nonexistent anxiety problems and other periods being characterized by severe or even crippling symptoms of anxiety. Big upsurges of anxious symptoms often lead to setbacks, times when things that had once seemed easy become terribly difficult. Every one of these distressing experiences of relapse leading to heightened symptoms of anxiety is an opportunity for new growth. That is why we call them springboards, because these setbacks are opportunities for dramatic movement forward. Seeing a difficult experience as a challenge and a chance to grow comes in many forms.

Expect Anxiety to Return

Sue's experience offers a wonderful chance to examine in detail the way a setback in anxiety can turn into a springboard for further learning. Sue is thirty-six years old and has had anxiety problems for most of her life. She has suffered from GAD and has had several bad flare-ups of phobias. She was a diligent follower of the Anxiety Cure method, and after a period of hard work, she had regained control of her life. Then for about a year she had spent only brief periods of time working at reducing her anxiety.

One evening Sue was in the passenger seat as her husband drove to the grocery store. Suddenly Sue banged on the dashboard, yelling, "I am not cured!" She told her husband that her panic and anxiety had returned with a vengeance, and she was angry at the arrogance of any therapist who would tell her that this was a normal way to feel. Sue's husband was understandably concerned at this sudden outburst. He asked her to breathe deeply so he could concentrate on his driving until they reached the grocery store parking lot. They sat in the parking lot and reviewed what had provoked Sue's outburst and her increased anxiety.

Notice how Sue, even when she was completely frustrated by her painful feelings of anxiety, was able to reach out to her husband for help. Notice also the sign of a loving, trained support person in the way her husband refocused the experience on the here and now and the short term, asking her to be quiet for safety's sake and to work on breathing only until the parking lot was reached, a few minutes away. In this brief interaction, you can see the calming effect of the outreach and response even before their more formal reevaluation occurred.

In the Anxiety Cure we ask you to rate your anxiety level from 0 (no anxiety) to 10 (the worst anxiety you ever had). This interlude allowed Sue to reduce her anxiety from a level 8 to a level 5 prior to reaching the parking lot.

Once Sue and her husband began to review the problem, they quickly assessed Sue's anxiety level and agreed that, at a level 5, they could continue to talk without stopping to calm the anxiety before they began to figure out the problem and the solution. Sue's husband noted that there were a number of different reasons for her anxiety to be more active and intense at this time. This seemed to be a reasonable time for the panic dragon to be more aggressive, given how much was going on in Sue's life. Sue's husband listed the following reasons for her increased anxiety:

1. Sue had arrived home from work late and had not yet eaten dinner, which they knew from past experience always made it harder for her to deal with anxiety.

2. It was the night before her final day of work prior to a promotion into a new department. Even good changes were always hard for Sue, as her worry machine pumped out every possible problem she might encounter in the new, unfamiliar situation.

3. In her present department, it was traditional for each employee who was departing because of a promotion to bake and bring in a fancy cake on the final day of work as a farewell gesture. People in the department competed about bringing in fancy "farewell" cakes. Sue had talked all week about her worry that her offering would not measure up to the lavish work of others.

4. Sue and her husband usually enjoyed biking together three or four times a week for exercise, but they had not managed to find time for biking during the last week. Not having a physical outlet for her tension had made it hard for Sue to sleep at night and added to her anxiety.

5. Sue had not slept well for two nights, complaining when she woke in the morning that she did not feel refreshed. She also had nightmares. Not sleeping well made her feel tired and slower at work, and that meant she had worked longer hours to compensate for feeling groggy during the day.

You can see from her husband's summary of this setback how, in hindsight, it was almost inevitable. Each contributing factor laid the groundwork for another part of the anxiety problem. Sue's carefully worked out anxiety reducers had been put aside the previous week without thought of the likely consequences.

Sue agreed with her husband's assessment. However, she was unable to sort out all those factors herself when she was in the middle of a setback. This was normal, even for someone who has been "cured" of his or her anxiety. Remember, when your anxiety is over about a level 6, it is hard to get any perspective on yourself. What is needed is exactly what

Sue did—reach out to your support person, family member, friend, or therapist. The two of you together can more quickly reactivate the techniques you have learned from all of your hard work.

Remember at a time like this that your hard work has not been useless. Notice how, within minutes of her peak anxiety, Sue was once again in control because she knew the cause of her anxiety and the solutions to the problem. This was enormous progress for Sue and her husband.

For most people who suffer from anxiety without the Anxiety Cure method, this outburst of Sue's would have resulted in increased anxiety for her, and her husband would have been frightened and unsure of what to do. They would not have come up with good solutions to a problem they did not understand. In fact, they could easily have reached several erroneous conclusions that would have made all of the five problems listed above even worse. For example, they could have gone right home without getting any food at the grocery store, and instead of eating, they could have sat up far into the night worrying together about why Sue was so upset. Sue's husband could have become angry at her as well as scared, and that would have further upset them both and driven them further apart, worsening both of their problems.

Specific Solutions to a Specific Anxiety Problem

Here were the good solutions to these problems that Sue and her husband came up with together:

Solution 1. Instead of buying food that needed to be prepared, Sue and her husband got take-out sandwiches and sodas from the deli counter. They also got a quick-to-fix dinner for the following night so they would not again arrive home to find nothing to eat.

Solution 2. Sue spent a few minutes over dinner focusing on the sadness she felt about leaving her old job and her former coworkers and the fear she felt at facing a new, more challenging job. She had been afraid to share these feelings before, but she knew that talking about something frightening helped her not to have nightmares.

Solution 3. Sue bought a prepared cake at the store, and she did not stay up late baking, as she had planned to do. She had been worried about how her store-bought cake would be viewed by her coworkers, but the type of cake actually received less attention than she had recalled from previous parties, and it was eaten quickly. No one commented on the fact that she had not spent time baking it.

Solution 4. Sue and her husband, with their purchased sandwiches and sodas, went on a short bike ride to a local park and had a picnic. They promised each other that they would take a longer ride on the weekend and set a day and time so they would not forget.

Solution 5. Lack of sleep had been an ongoing problem that Sue felt she had not fully resolved prior to this flare-up in her anxiety. She had recently bought a yoga videotape and resolved to try yoga prior to going to bed on nights she felt anxious to see if that would help her get a more restful night's sleep. She planned to leave on time from work the following day instead of staying late to do final wrap-ups on work-related projects, which she knew she probably would have done without this setback.

By reaching out for help when anxiety reappeared and by sticking with the lessons she had learned from her work with the Anxiety Cure, Sue was able to turn an anxious moment into a pleasant evening. She was not anxiety free, but anxiety at level 3 or 4 seemed reasonable and manageable to her, given that she was going through an understandably stressful time. Handling this stress well, and even adding the future plan of yoga to her regular routine, turned this setback into a springboard of increased self-confidence for more future success for Sue and into an improved relationship with her husband.

Most people with anxiety, and the family and friends who care about an anxious person, will see that this example of a setback is common in terms of how it grew from a positive event—Sue's promotion. Many anxious people do almost anything to avoid change, even to the point of turning down promotions or awards for excellence. Anxiety is too often the driving force in an anxious person's life. The Anxiety Cure turns this around by looking not at the feelings of anxiety, but at the contributing factors and at the practical and positive solutions to lowering anxiety. In Sue's case, it is clear how this normalization of her feelings, combined with some creative problem solving, moved her quickly from anxious to able to enjoy her life.

Sue's husband felt good after this setback. He had learned what to do to help Sue. He did it, and it worked for Sue and for him. Both Sue and her husband remembered the Anxiety Cure's definition of "cure"— knowing what is wrong and what to do about it. They concluded, with pride in their hard work and their achievements, that in just that sense not only was Sue cured, but so was her husband.

Setbacks are sometimes triggered by unexpected changes, and sometimes setbacks are triggered by not having been exposed to an event or an activity for a period of time, such as occasionally occurs with fear of flying. It is often hard to separate lack of opportunity to fly in a plane from avoidance of flying, and if you do not seek out opportunities to practice in areas that once caused anxiety or panic, the dragon can easily take back parts of your life. Sometimes setbacks occur in a different form from the expected, so that someone who was phobic of driving now has a fear of walking across a footbridge. Phobias do not commonly transfer themselves, but it does happen. Often there is no explanation for why a setback occurs. It is as likely to come after good news as bad news, and it is as likely to come for no reason as for an apparently good reason.

However a setback occurs, it is never as bad as the first episodes of anxiety because, after you have done your work in the Anxiety Cure, you know that fear of the fear is an anxiety disorder, and you know you can get over this fear of the fear. You know what you need to do to get better. This knowledge takes much of the fear out of having an anxiety problem, but even so, when you are in the middle of a setback, it is sometimes hard to gain enough perspective to know what to do first. If possible, plan ahead, and during a time when you are doing well, answer the following questions in your journal so you will have the answers on hand when a setback occurs.

Questions to Help Me Plan
for When I Have a Setback

1. What support people will I talk to?
2. What chapters in *The Anxiety Cure* or other books will I reread?
3. What new life habits have I found to be helpful?
4. What external sources of anxiety will I watch for?
5. What techniques have I found helpful in the past in dealing with anxiety?
6. What medicines will I use?

Answering these questions now in writing in your journal will also help you keep the surprise of a setback from overwhelming you, since you acknowledge to yourself that it is possible that your anxiety will increase sometime in the future. You may want to put a paper clip on the page of your journal that lists your plan in the event of a setback, because you may want help fast in the future.

If you are reading this amid a setback, it may not be possible for you to make a plan ahead of time. Rather, answer the following questions to help you get back on track with your anxiety cure. Be sure to date this entry because you want to keep close track of setbacks as you evaluate your progress into the future.

Evaluating a Setback—Gaining Perspective
1. On a 0–10 scale, what is my anxiety level right now?
2. Who can help me evaluate this setback?
3. Is this setback a surprise?
4. When did I first notice increased anxiety?
5. What have I tried so far to help with this setback?
6. What dose and type of antianxiety medicine am I using, and when did I last evaluate my use of the medicine?
7. How have I been sleeping recently?
8. Have I been exercising/stretching regularly?
9. What might have contributed to this setback? Am I using any over-the-counter or prescription medicines or street drugs? Am I drinking alcohol or beverages with caffeine?
10. When did I last eat/how have I been eating recently?
11. Have I been avoiding situations because of anxiety (or, for OCD, Have I resumed compulsive behaviors) that I had stopped while I was doing well?
12. Is there any unusual stress in my life right now?

The next step is to figure out what to do about the setback and how to move forward with your anxiety cure. Answering the above questions has put you on track already, as it will help you sort out the individual pieces that may have contributed to this setback. Now you can put your past experience with the Anxiety Cure to work for you as you answer the following questions in your journal.

Treating a Setback—Turning It into a Springboard

1. When I was using the Anxiety Cure in the past, what techniques helped me to keep myself in the here and now?
2. When can I get in touch with my support person?
3. Do I need to take medicine for this attack now?
4. Do I need to call my doctor today/tomorrow to review my use of medicine?
5. How could I improve the quality/quantity of my sleep tonight?
6. Could I find time to exercise/stretch today or tomorrow?

7. Do I need to evaluate any medicines I am taking for possible anxiety side effects? Should I call the pharmacist? My doctor?

8. Do I need to cut back/cut out use of alcohol, caffeine, or street drugs?

9. Do I need to eat? What is my plan for eating during the next twenty-four hours?

10. Do I need to begin practicing my automatic anxiety techniques systematically?

11. What can I do about the stressful things in my life? Do I need to talk this over with my support person? An anxiety group? My doctor? A therapist?

12. What can I learn from this attack to help lessen anxiety in the future?

It is important during an upsurge of anxiety to stay in the present when working to make your life better. There is a tendency to generalize this painful but predictable experience into a catastrophe that proves you will never be well. Answering these questions can help avoid that trap, a trap that may lead to your feeling out of control and result in a worsening of your anxiety.

Remember that the only food the dragon can eat is your fear of him. Try to step back from this setback and counsel yourself as you would want a good friend to counsel you if you could talk to someone immediately. Say calm things to yourself: "It is going to be okay." "This will pass." "I have been here before, and I know I can handle it."

During a setback and in the days that follow, you will be glad that you kept your hard-learned lessons documented in the pages of your journal. You are your own best teacher because the anxiety is your own and no one else's.

Work in Progress

Every setback is a springboard for you to make further progress, to increase your understanding of your anxiety disorder, and to increase your self-esteem by rolling up your sleeves and getting on with the work needed to solve your anxiety problem. You need to have your support systems in place for a lifetime. That means keeping track of your books and information about anxiety so you can understand the problem, even when the dragon comes at you in an entirely new disguise. It means keeping your support person educated and informed. *If you lose one support person, recruit and train another one.* It means finding therapists and doctors who understand anxiety disorders and who can help you, whatever the problems are that you are facing at any point in your life.

Evaluate Medical Problems

Medical problems can confound even people who have been free of anxiety for many years. Facing a new medical problem that may or may not be related to the anxiety disorder is confusing and frightening. We hesitate to list the medical problems or symptoms that may be rooted in anxiety for two reasons. One reason is a fear of giving anxious people more bodily symptoms to watch for anxiously. The other reason is that sometimes a symptom is not caused by anxiety and needs medical intervention.

Gut Dilemma

Cheryl, a twenty-four-year-old woman, offers us an example of the complexity of a person with anxiety having even a relatively simple medical problem. For two years Cheryl had been living her life fully, without constraint from the GAD and depression that had brought her to seek help.

Without warning, she developed diarrhea, and after three weeks of being afraid to eat away from home because the food went through her too quickly for her to get to a public bathroom, she sought help from a family doctor. The doctor wisely suggested over-the-counter remedies and a bland diet for a week and told Cheryl to call him at the end of the week to report how she was doing.

Cheryl had been horribly frightened that the doctor was going to tell her there was something seriously wrong with her, and when the doctor was so calm about a problem that had been terribly worrisome to her, she thought to get out Evaluating a Setback—Gaining Perspective, the checklist from this chapter of *The Anxiety Cure*.

In her evaluation of her anxiety, she realized that the anxiety increase had predated the onset of the diarrhea and that her sleeping had been disrupted because of the increased anxiety and diarrhea. She had stopped her daily walks when she began to feel sick. Her stress, she now noticed, was also quite high from an external cause. She was planning to move into her boyfriend's apartment in a month and was having second thoughts about the relationship.

Once Cheryl recognized that the diarrhea was in all likelihood a new anxiety symptom, she was quick to use Treating a Setback—Turning It into a Springboard from this chapter and to call her therapist to talk over her ambivalence about her relationship with her boyfriend. After a week Cheryl felt so much better that she forgot to call her family doctor to report her progress. She was surprised when her doctor called to check on her. She was happy to report that the diarrhea was gone.

With any medical problem that may or may not be anxiety, it is important to seek reasonable medical advice, but it is also important to try to gauge the impact that anxiety may be having in either causing or continuing the medical problem. Not all doctors are as sensitive to the role of anxiety as was Cheryl's.

A Cautionary Tale

Tony, a sixty-five-year-old retiree, only learned of the likely impact of anxiety on his backaches after he had had a surgical procedure to help with back pain. But the surgery caused such severe chronic pain that he was bedridden for six months. Only when his physical therapist told him that his anxiety was too high for physical therapy to make any improvement in his pain did Tony seek help for his anxiety. By that point, he had so many physical complications from the surgery and the subsequent bed rest that the treatment of his anxiety was both complicated and prolonged.

We urge you to draft a letter to your doctors, alerting them to your anxiety and any medicines you take to help deal with the problem. The letter can help if you are in need of emergency dental work, for example. Novocaine is usually formulated with epinephrine. Epinephrine, however, can cause paniclike symptoms in susceptible people. If a dentist or doctor is aware of your susceptibility to anxiety, it is easy to avoid the epinephrine formulation, and a great deal of unnecessary distress can be avoided.

This letter can also be a help if you need surgery and in the hospital will be in contact with a number of nurses and doctors who may not be aware of your anxiety disorder. Such a letter documenting your specific worries can help you deal with recovery rooms with no windows or support your request to follow closely your medicine schedule. Use your anxiety history from Step 1 to write this general Dear Doctor letter. Be sure your family is aware of this letter so they can help to get this information to the medical personnel who need it in the event of an emergency.

We are indebted to a longtime patient of ours for sharing a copy of the letter she wrote when she was expecting her second child. She found this letter helpful in dealing with her obstetrician, pediatrician, and the nurses and doctors in the hospital when her healthy daughter was born. Because she is a nurse herself, she had a clear idea of how to draft this letter. You may wish to have your letter follow her format. If you are on medicine for an anxiety disorder, it is a good idea to include your prescribing doctor's name and telephone number should any questions arise.

Example of Dear Doctor Letter

Dear Doctor:

Our family is expecting a baby in the spring. We are very excited about the new arrival. We have a few questions for you and a few things to tell you about this pregnancy. I have an appointment to see you next week to discuss these questions.

The pregnancy has been going well—both mother and baby appear to be in good health. However, I have a familial anxiety disorder for which I take diazepam daily in small dosages. The diazepam eliminates the physical symptoms associated with the anxiety disorder and greatly reduces the anxious thoughts and ideas. Understanding the risks and benefits, I have continued to take the diazepam during the pregnancy.

My obstetrician is not comfortable with my taking the diazepam until the due date arrives. She is concerned that the baby may go through withdrawal.

I have received genetic counseling and discussed the possible dangers of taking medicine during pregnancy with my psychiatrist at length. My psychiatrist is comfortable with my taking the diazepam throughout the entire pregnancy. He has followed other pregnant women in similar situations; from his experience, he does not expect any withdrawal symptoms to occur at such a low dosage. However, he recommended that I share the obstetrician's concerns with you.

At our appointment next week, I would like to get your thoughts on the following:

1. A plan of action should the baby experience withdrawal symptoms such as irritability.
2. A recommendation about formula for the baby. (Nursing and diazepam consumption appear to be contraindicated.)

I appreciate your taking the time to answer my questions. Thank you for helping me to continue to do what is best for both me and my baby.

Sincerely,

[Your Name]

Anxiety and Cancer

Confronting an anxiety disorder and regaining control of your life can be terribly hard, but it also can be a terrifically valuable lesson in life. We have a friend whom we admire greatly who became an expert at using these antianxiety techniques. She was diagnosed with malignant melanoma, a form of cancer for which there was no effective treatment. Her primary cancer was removed from her back, but six months later she had a recurrence of the cancer in a lymph node under her arm and the diagnosis of metastatic malignant cancer. This woman asked her oncologist what the treatment was for the recurrence. Her doctor said that radiation and chemotherapy could not help. The diseased lymph node could be removed, but that was all that could be done. The potentially fatal cancer might or might not have spread beyond that node.

Imagine her terror. She said later that she used her antianxiety techniques of staying in the present: "I just reminded myself that once that malignant lymph node was gone, I didn't have a recurrence of the cancer until the doctor told me I did. My anxious mind kept running ahead to the horrible 'what if,' but I kept pulling my thinking back to the 'what is' of the situation. I used my anxiety disorder techniques every day. The oncologist told me that the five-year survival rate for melanoma with the factors I had was only 20 percent. That meant that one person in five who had what I did lived for five years and that 80 percent were dead before five years. Those were not good odds, but they were my odds. I reminded myself often that until I got a diagnosis of the spread of cancer beyond that lymph node, I was still in the 20 percent who were making it one day at a time."

Twenty years have passed since that event, and this brave woman has had no recurrence of that cancer. We do not claim that her use of these antianxiety techniques, which she had learned when facing her own phobia, has kept her from having a recurrence of cancer. Her use of these antipanic techniques helped her to live a far more normal and happy life during that time than she would have if those "what ifs" had gripped her, as they threatened to when she had her second operation.

Three Tips to Occupy Your Mind

1. Count backward from a hundred by threes or by sevens.
2. Say the alphabet backward.
3. Do crossword puzzles.

Find a Support Group

Another strategy for getting and staying well from an anxiety disorder means getting in touch with local support groups that can help you. See the Resources in the back of this book.

The founder of a local anxiety support group noticed that although she had made efforts to build a core group of participants, most group meetings were made up of newcomers, people who had been diagnosed with anxiety relatively recently. This may happen because, as people get better, they no longer need to go to support group meetings. Friends and family may also find these groups helpful in seeing how common the experiences are that their anxious person is reporting. Some self-help support groups are specifically targeted to OCD, social phobia, or panic, while others are for people with mental health problems in general. There are many types of groups throughout the country. Support groups can help you feel less alone and help you connect with local doctors and therapists who have been successful in treating others with anxiety. Every support group is different. If you find a group that does not address your needs, simply try another group. Often, if you talk informally to people after the meeting, you can learn of similar groups that may fit your needs more closely.

Think about your answers to the following questions prior to going to a group. Bring your journal to the group so you can write down ideas and phone numbers you learn at the meeting.

Seeking an Anxiety Support Group
1. What do I hope to find at an anxiety support group meeting?
2. What questions do I want to ask at or after the meeting?
3. What referrals to support groups do I have so far? (See the Resources for a place to start).
4. What information did I gather at the group meeting?
5. Are there other resources I want to explore?

Connect with a Higher Power

There is a final dimension to finding a cure for anxiety disorders that we write about with more hesitancy, since it is more personal and more subject to misinterpretation: finding help in a spiritual connection with a Higher Power. This means turning over personal problems to a Higher Power or, as one patient phrased it, "let go and trust your body." For most people, the most reliable beacon to lasting serenity is to be found in our relationship with God as we know him. From this perspective, the prescription is "let go and let God."

This is not an argument for any specific religion, although most of us find God in highly individual, often religious ways. *It is a simple fact that one of the best ways to gain control of your life and to find serenity is to find a spiritual base for your new growth.* All of the great religious traditions share the sense that you can find the strength to live by submerging your personal will into the will of God. All religions deal with fear directly and often. This means thinking about what is good in a larger sense than can be found in one individual and instead turning to a force of good or a world good.

Not every reader will find this advice useful or even acceptable. But before rejecting this idea, talk it over with your support person. Remember that to relate to your Higher Power, it is not necessary to become involved with a formal, religious organization. This spiritual dimension to your continued self-growth may take many forms. Some people find their Higher Power in nature and regularly seek to spend quiet time in a beautiful spot as a way to make a connection to a larger meaning of life. Others find that being involved with art leads them to their Higher Power. For some people, an organized religion can be both a wonderful way to benefit from structured time focusing on their Higher Power as well as a powerful source of community.

Tips for Friends and Family

Accept the unknown. It is important to learn to live with the uncertainty of anxiety. Know that your anxious person has an anxiety disorder and allow the dragon to do what he wants to do. Keep track of what has and has not worked for you in relating to your anxious person so that you will not need to start from scratch in the future. If the dragon comes, he comes. If he does not come now, he may come in the future. Either way, you have learned how to live your life and let your anxious person live his or her life not only with the anxiety disorder but also with whatever other challenges you each find on your paths. Each problem in your life is a growth opportunity waiting to be utilized, including having a family member or friend with an anxiety disorder.

Homework for Step 8

1. Read Step 8.
2. Select and record a goal for this week's practice.
3. Practice in your discomfort zone daily and record this practice on your Weekly Practice Worksheet.
4. Meet once to practice with your support person and to review your journal.
5. Fill in your Personal Progress Log.
6. Review your need for an ongoing support group or religious organization.

Readings for Step 8

1. Ross, J. *Triumph over Fear—A Book of Help and Hope for People with Anxiety, Panic Attacks, and Phobias.*
   Chapter 23: "Becoming Acquainted with the New You"
2. Kübler-Ross, E., and D. Kessler. *Life Lessons.*

PART THREE

Dimensions of Anxiety

CHAPTER 13

Anxiety and Terrorism

September 11, 2001, marked a turning point in the understanding of fear and anxiety. On that day nineteen terrorists hijacked four commercial airplanes with devastating results. The crashes in Pennsylvania and at the Pentagon were within the range of earlier terrorist attacks. The two planes that crashed into the World Trade Center in New York City were utterly outside of any previous experience.

Within weeks of the September 11 attacks, another menacing terrorist threat emerged in which anthrax spores were spread through the mail. The anthrax scare extended the threat of terrorism into bioterrorism. It was not contained by time and place or restricted to airplanes and monumental buildings. No one claimed responsibility, so it was not possible to identify the enemy who was killing Americans or to know the motivation of the killer. Suddenly the threat of death from terrorism was as ubiquitous as the daily mail and as mysterious as the worst horror movie.

Beginning on October 2, 2002, two snipers terrorized the nation's capital area for three weeks. They killed ten people and grievously wounded three more in acts of terrorism that dramatically changed life in the region. Day after day those attacks produced headlines around the world. No one over a wide area was safe from the unknown and deadly assailants. Children were kept inside schools. Shopping and nonessential travel came to a near standstill. People pumped gas into their cars from a crouching position. Streets were progressively more deserted as fear escalated.

Those three experiences of modern terrorism, each relatively localized geographically, led to anxiety and posttraumatic stress symptoms on a global scale. The political and economic changes that followed, as well as the emergence of a new kind of war, were the result of these painful but understandable experiences. Coping with the fear of terrorism is a new imperative of modern life if millions of people are not to become as housebound as suffering agoraphobics.

In this chapter we look at what happened in the recent past, making use of new knowledge about the brain biology of fear and more than two decades of our own experience helping people with anxiety problems. With these twin perspectives we explore how best to handle the anxiety caused by modern terrorism.

The use of fear in war is not new. In the late thirteenth century, Genghis Khan created the largest empire the world ever saw using mass terror. The fear of the Golden Horde from the Asian steppes was the result of the suddenness and brutality of his assaults. In cities and nations that resisted Genghis Khan's invading forces, women were raped and then, in great numbers, men, women, and children were killed. Few areas of the world resisted the warriors from the Gobi Desert once word spread of their vicious onslaughts. Terror was the greatest weapon of the invading Mongols. Whole empires collapsed in fear without defending themselves. Similarly, when Hitler attacked with his blitzkrieg, or "lightning war," early in World War II fear was his most devastating weapon.

Modern Terrorism

Although modern terrorism uses fear to achieve its goals, it does not rely on the tactics used by Genghis Khan and Adolf Hitler. Today's terrorists are not countries with powerful armies. Some modern terrorists are individuals, quite often native-born Americans, like Ted Kaczynski, the Unabomber, Timothy McVeigh, the bomber of Oklahoma City on April 19, 1995, and John Allen Muhammad, one of the accused Washington, D.C., snipers in 2002. These terrorists, and more like them, have passionate, if eccentric, political agendas. Other modern terrorists have come together in highly organized groups, such as the Irish Republican Army (IRA), the Tamil Tigers in Sri Lanka, the Palestinian terrorist groups, and Osama bin Laden's al-Qaeda network. These terrorist groups are well funded and highly disciplined. Over long periods of time they carry out well-planned attacks. Modern terrorist organizations are determined, effective, resilient, clandestine guerrilla organizations.

Modern terrorists lack the resources to conquer their enemies, as did Genghis Khan and Adolf Hitler. To achieve their political goals modern terrorists rely on intense and prolonged fear to overwhelm and ultimately to demoralize their enemies. Their aim is to force their political opponents to give up out of fear of future attacks. Terrorists do this by injuring and killing relatively few people. They cannot cripple their enemies by killing people or even by destroying the material support of nations, such as airplanes, bridges, or buildings. Modern terrorists kill people and destroy property to create fear of the next surprise attack. They seek to cripple their enemies by spreading the fear that terrorists, invisible in their target's population, could strike anyone, anywhere, at anytime. Modern terrorists want their enemies to feel that they can never be safe from lethal attacks. Terrorists continue their efforts over long periods of time to reinforce this fear and to exhaust their enemy's will to resist.

While terrorism itself is not new, the current forms of terrorism are distinctly new, having first appeared during the past few decades. These new strategies of terrorism have been used in many parts of the world and have become more effective over time. Why are modern nations, many of which possess overwhelmingly powerful armies to defend themselves, so much more vulnerable to terrorism than were our ancestors who lacked such potent armies and such powerful weapons? The elevated risk of terrorism is not because the terrorists have new and more potent weapons, although there is a fear that some terrorists may obtain such weapons in the future. Up to this point, however, the weapons used by terrorists are old-fashioned. In the attacks on September 11, 2001, the weapons used by the terrorists were box cutters and airplanes. The anthrax killer used as a modern weapon one of the oldest lethal bacteria in the world. Anthrax remains common in many parts of the world, including the American West, where farmers are so familiar with anthrax and its treatment that they do not fear it. In contrast, for most Americans today anthrax is as unfamiliar and as fear-causing as the bubonic plague. John Muhammad and Lee Malvo are believed to have used an easily available rifle and an old car to cripple the capital of the world's most powerful nation for three weeks.

Not only is the new power of terrorist attacks not due to new weapons, it is not due to a change in human brain biology. The biology of human fear has been what is for the 100,000 years *Homo sapiens* have existed. What is new in the world is not the weapons of the terrorists nor is it the human vulnerability to fear. What is new that makes terrorism so powerful is the role of the global mass media, the unwitting vector for the fear that is the primary weapon of modern terrorism.

What Anxiety Problems Can Teach Us about the Fear of Terrorism

Let's take another look at the events of recent years from the perspective of anxiety problems. Before we look in detail at those painful events, however, let's think about a modern fear with which we are more familiar, the fear of flying. About 15 percent of Americans are so afraid of flying that they either do not fly at all or they severely curtail their flying. When fearful flyers even think of flying they suffer from painful anxiety.

Some numbers help our perspective. In commercial aviation, including commuter fights, there are about 2,000,000 people flying each day in the United States in approximately 20,000 separate takeoffs and landings. In bad years over the past two decades there have been as many as 600 deaths per year in all commercial aviation in the United States. In many years during that time, there were no deaths in commercial aviation at all. The average over this time has been about 300 deaths a year in U.S. commercial aviation.

Based on these numbers, let's look at the odds of dying in an airplane crash. That comes to about one chance of death in 2 million flights. Those odds are similar to the odds of winning for a person who buys a single lottery ticket. Is it any wonder that commercial pilots and flight attendants who are in the air for thirty hours a week for careers of forty years or more do not pay any additional premium for life insurance compared to people in other occupations? Nevertheless, fear of flying is widespread, and, for those who suffer from it, fear of flying is extremely painful. Fear of flying is also persistent and not easily overcome.

Now think about driving automobiles. About 40,000 Americans each year die in automobile crashes. That means that about one in every 7,000 Americans dies in a car crash each year. Those odds explain why so many Americans have family and friends who have died in automobile accidents and why so few have family or friends who have died in airplane crashes. What's going on here? Why do so many people fear flying (when the risk of dying in a plane crash is so unbelievably small) while so few people fear driving in automobiles (when the risk of dying in a car crash is not tiny)?

Let's start with some possible reasons for this disparity between risk and fear. Here are some factors that do not explain the disparity. The millions of fearful flyers are not ignorant of the facts about aviation safety. They have heard those numbers a thousand times. When confronted by reassuring risk numbers one fearful flyer said in therapy, "Doctor, don't waste your time with statistics. The only risk-related statistic that matters to me about airplane crashes is fifty-fifty. When I get in a plane the odds of my crashing are fifty-fifty. Those odds are terrible." When asked to explain where he got that alarming number, he said simply, "I figured it out myself. Each time I fly I either crash or I do not. That is fifty-fifty!" So much for the role of logic and information in explaining crippling anxiety.

Another factor that does not explain this disparity between fear and risk is intelligence. People who have a serious fear of flying are not less intelligent than people who are not afraid to fly. Men and women both are fearful flyers, young and old, rich and poor. Those variables do not explain fear of flying or the more general disparity between what is widely feared and where the major risks of death in the United States are to be found.

One variable that explains some cases is the presence of anxiety problems. Many, but not all, fearful flyers have other anxiety problems as well as the fear of flying. Their nervous systems are on hair-trigger for anxiety. Many of the people at high risk of the fear of flying have brains that are primed, genetically and by experience, to send out false alarms of danger. The tendency to experience false alarms of danger, as you have learned in this book, is the hallmark of anxiety problems.

It is important to recognize that in any population exposed to a terrifying event, both the risk of acute fear and the risk of persistent problems of anxiety following the initial exposure to danger are varied. Some people who survive an airplane crash or an automobile crash recover from their acute fears quickly and resume these activities with little or no persistent anxiety. Other people, suffering exactly the same frightening experience, endure problems of anxiety that lead to long-term avoidance and substantial pain and disability.

The point is that risk of fearful reactions to dangerous or frightening situations is highly varied in human populations. Part of that difference is genetic. Some people are naturally fearful and others are naturally fearless. Part of the difference relates to the range of experiences different people have had over their lifetimes. Some people have experienced fear-generating situations in the past and developed successful strategies for coping with them. Others have had fear-generating experiences and have been overwhelmed by these experiences. The experience of severe anxiety in the past sets the stage for sensitization to future anxiety-generating experiences. Anxiety itself leads to preoccupation with the possibility of future fear. Anxiety also leads anxious people to avoid some particular ordinary experiences, since these experiences might be associated with danger and could, in any event, cause the painful fear reaction to reoccur.

During the three weeks of terror in the Washington area in October of 2002, we were busy practicing as mental health professionals. We were often asked if we had a huge influx of new anxious patients spurred into therapy by the snipers. The answer may surprise you: Not a single patient sought our help during those three weeks because of the terror that so clearly gripped our region. Here is another observation from our practice that may be almost as surprising: Our most anxious patients were not particularly disturbed by the snipers' bullets during that reign of terror. Many of our anxious patients were even relieved during that time in what at first appears to be an odd way. They felt more normal in their fears when everyone around them was so clearly disturbed by fear.

One patient said, "I feel sorry for these 'normal' people who have not had fear like this before. They don't know what is happening to them. They have no idea what to do about it. For me the sniper is just one more fear to add to the long list of dreadful fears that I have endured for decades. Every day my son goes to school I fear that he will be kidnapped or killed in an automobile accident. Every day of my life when I have a pain in my stomach or my head I am sure that it's a fatal cancer. The sniper is bad and I or someone in my family may be his next target, but this fear is easier to deal with than most fears of mine because with this fear I have so much company. When I fear that my boy will be kidnapped on his way to school or when I think that my headache must be a brain tumor everyone looks at me like I am a nutcase. When I say I'm afraid of the sniper I feel normal. Other people treat me as if I was normal. What I know but do not say, is that the sniper is no big deal when it comes to fear. That is how I really feel. I don't say that because if I did say it normal people who are suddenly terrified of the sniper would be sure I was a mental case!"

While no surveys have been done to test the hypothesis that most people suffering from the fear of terrorism are not also suffering from a pre-existing anxiety disorder, we are convinced by our clinical experience that most people who were severely affected by fear of the snipers in the Washington area in October of 2002 did not suffer from anxiety disorders. What they did suffer from was pathological anxiety that was painful and sometimes crippling. That pathological anxiety was caused by the threat of terrorist attacks. This observation makes the point that the powerful and potentially disorganizing fear mechanisms in the human brain are in everyone's brains, not just in the brains of those who suffer from anxiety disorders. By studying people with anxiety problems we have learned about these brain mechanisms and how to help people when their fear mechanisms go awry.

The Five Environmental Factors That Promote Fear

Much of the risk of anxiety is found in the social environment outside the individual who has a disabling anxiety. These environmental factors interact powerfully with the biologically determined risk factors for anxiety problems. Work with thousands of anxious people has shown us that there are five environmental factors in anxieties that are out of proportion to actual risk, such as the fear of flying and fear of terrorism. They are: familiarity of the experience, personal control over exposure to the possible danger, potential for catastrophic events, apparent predictability of danger, and, finally, whether the risks are thought of as natural or as having human causes.

Let's start by looking separately at each of these five factors when it comes to the fear of flying, a fear that is easy for most people to think clearly about. Then we will use these same five factors to understand the fear of modern terrorism.

1. *Familiarity*. Recall that the locus ceruleus in the midbrain is the biological source of the experience of panic. The locus ceruleus is the brain's red button of danger. This center of neurons using the neurotransmitter norepinephrine is the brain's novelty detector. It fires a warning of possible danger in novel situations because novelty is associated with possible danger. In clear contrast, familiarity is associated with a sense of safety.

This simple biological truth explains how all effective therapies work for anxiety. The goal of therapy for anxiety problems is to encourage the sufferer to voluntarily experience the feared activity over and over again until the once-feared experience is so familiar that the activity is no longer feared. When that happens the locus ceruleus no longer fires in this particular experience. The treatment of anxiety problems is so difficult and so uncertain because it is so hard to get an anxious person to go into feared situations even when outside observers are confident that there is little or no actual danger in the feared situation. Convincing a flying phobic to get on an airplane is a major therapeutic challenge.

Driving cars is familiar to everyone in America today, unlike flying, which is personally unfamiliar to many Americans. For this reason there is little fear of driving. When cars were introduced early in the twentieth century, there was widespread fear of riding in them. With increasing familiarity that fear all but disappeared. Fearful flyers either don't fly (the most typical pattern) or they fly infrequently and with great distress.

2. *Personal Control.* Car drivers believe that they can avoid possible accidents because they have the feeling of being personally in control of the car. Often this is an illusion. An accident means that what happened was out of the driver's control. Nevertheless, in terms of the psychology of fear, the driver of an automobile usually has the sense of being in control of the risk of a car crash. This sense of personal control, no matter what the reality may be, greatly reduces the likelihood of anxiety as a result of driving in a car. Even the passenger in an automobile has a sense of personal control since the passenger can alert the driver to impending danger.

In an airplane the passenger has no control as well as no illusion of control. The control of the airplane is with the pilot, the aircraft maintenance workers, the air traffic controllers, and many others over whom the passenger has no control. The airplane passenger even lacks knowledge about who these people are. We have worked with some pilots who can fly a plane with no anxiety but who experience panic when someone else is flying the plane. As one of these fearful pilots said in therapy, "When I am the pilot I know that I can land anytime I choose but when someone else is flying and I am just a passenger I have no control over when and where we land. Being out of control in an airplane scares me!"

An instructional exception to the statement that Americans today do not fear driving automobiles relates to the anxiety disorder agoraphobia, a fear of being separated from safe places and safe people. Agoraphobics, who suffer from unexpected panic attacks, are afraid to drive automobiles themselves although they can usually ride comfortably in cars as passengers. How does this fit with the general picture of fear being developed here? Agoraphobics fear that they will lose control of themselves because of their terrifying panic attacks. Being the driver of a car scares them because they fear their own loss of control. So for the agoraphobic, subject to unpredictable panic attacks, it is being the driver of an automobile that causes the threat of being out of control.

Another interesting aspect of the fear of driving is that many agoraphobic people can drive on local roads but they cannot drive on limited access highways, such as interstate highways. Why is this, when the statistics are clear that drivers are safer on modern limited access roads than they are on older local roads where the traffic is less controlled and where there is little highway engineering to prevent harm in the event of an accident? The answer is that on local roads the agoraphobics have the sense that they can stop anywhere they choose, while on limited access highways they are trapped until they reach the next exit, which can be many miles away. These examples show the importance of a sense of being in control when it comes to the fear of situations of possible danger.

3. *Potential for Catastrophic Events.* Car crashes are not news, even fatal car crashes, unless many people are killed in a single accident, and even then fatal automobile accidents are minor, local news. Every airplane crash is headline news all around the world, sometimes for weeks or months. When a risk is associated with a catastrophe there is a heightened sense of risk because catastrophes are, by definition, unfamiliar and overwhelming. A catastrophe is out of the range of normal experience; that is why even that word, "catastrophe," is scary. When our brains are confronted by catastrophes we have heightened fears. Those fears are often prolonged and intense even if the risks themselves are small.

4. *Predictability of Risk.* The person who flies or drives has an ability to predict the risk because the risk is connected to getting on an airplane or into a car. People at risk of modern terrorism have little ability to predict their risks and no way of knowing whether or not they are at risk at any particular moment. When danger can come at any time, it is feared much more than when its appearance is predictable. This is one of the reasons so few people fear smoking cigarettes despite the risk of horrible illness and death that result directly from cigarette smoking. For individuals who have fears of cigarette smoking, they can avoid it. In contrast, secondhand smoke, although far less dangerous, is widely feared because it is not a risk that is chosen and it is not a risk that easily can be avoided.

When people voluntarily and knowingly take a risk, like riding on a motorcycle without a helmet, they are too seldom afraid. This is the flip side of too much anxiety—too little anxiety for some people when they choose their risks. That is why many states have enacted laws to protect motorcycle drivers from their own dangerous fearlessness. Not many people with anxiety problems ride motorcycles with or without helmets, but many people with anxiety problems do smoke cigarettes.

5. *Natural versus Human Causes of Danger*. When life is lost in what is thought of as a natural disaster there is less likely to be intense fear, in part because this danger is thought by some to be an act of God. Because a natural disaster, such as a hurricane, is not caused by anyone in particular it provokes relatively less fear. There is no one to blame for natural disasters. Natural disasters are more familiar over the course of human history. These distinctions between natural and human-caused disasters are not always as clear as they may at first seem. Floods, fires, and earthquakes take lives from natural causes but there is often someone to blame for not better protecting people from these natural risks.

The Two Social Multipliers of Fear

The five factors that control the psychology of risk are found in the social environment outside of the anxious individual. They are strongly influenced by two additional factors from the larger society, each of which not only adds to fear but multiplies it. The first big multiplier is the modern mass media. The global media has great power over what each of us thinks and feels. The bigger the news, the more potent is its effect on our thoughts and feelings. When it comes to airplane crashes, and even more when it comes to terrorism, the media intensifies, extends, and prolongs fear-inducing exposures.

The media is not to blame for the role it plays in promoting fear. The media not only seeks our attention, but absolutely requires our attention for its survival. TV news depends on ratings—the more people who watch the TV news the more money a program earns. Even public broadcasting, with less commercial sponsorship, seeks the largest audience possible to add to its funding base and to justify its claim for public support. This dependence of the media on audience size is equally true for the Internet and for print media. It is our own psychology that forces the modern media to deliver fear to us precisely because fear rivets our attention like nothing else.

There is more to the role of the media in modern fears than economics. Even if the media were immune to economic factors we would insist that they provide us with instant and in-depth information about imminent dangers in our lives. When a tornado is in our area we turn on the radio, the TV, or the Internet. When there is a terrorist attack, or the threat of one, we tune into the media regularly if not continuously. Our fears rule us. We demand that the media provide us with information—the more information the better—about what we fear. The media are as much creatures of the human brain biology of fear as we are as individuals.

In addition to the media, the second social multiplier of fear is whether there is an incentive for individuals and groups to emphasize particular fears. People who seek to curb tobacco smoking and illegal drug use, for example, are interested in encouraging fears of secondhand cigarette smoke and fears of illegal drugs as ways of discouraging the use of these unhealthy products. Fear of nuclear power has been encouraged by people who oppose nuclear power in a similar way. There is no advocacy or political agenda behind the fear of flying, but there is a political dimension to the fear of terrorism. Recall that the goal of terrorism is to spread fear for political purposes. There are forces in society, many of them prosocial, that are eager to spread the fear of terrorism just as there are forces that seek to spread the fears of secondhand cigarette smoke and nuclear power, even when the risks themselves are relatively small.

It is this political dimension that makes even the discussion of "irrational" fear controversial. By definition, any political position has many people who support it and many who oppose it. All sides in political battles seek to use whatever means they can to win. Quite often advocates of various points of view use fear just as they use other psychological forces to achieve their goals, goals that we as individuals may or may not consider to be worthy. Like the role of the media in magnifying social fears, the role of advocacy is contentious but nevertheless so important that it cannot be ignored if we hope to understand what is going on when it comes to widespread fears, especially the fear of terrorism.

The Anthrax Episode

Let's look at the anthrax attacks from the fall of 2001. A total of about twenty people in a nation of more than 270 million were infected with the deadly anthrax bacteria that fall. Five died. The terrorist who spread that scourge was no fool; he or she sent those infectious spores to prominent people to maximize the public fear. The murderous letters went to TV celebrities and prominent politicians. A few anthrax-laced letters were mailed over an extended period of time to insure a buildup of fear. How many Americans changed their behaviors during those months of terror? How much money was spent as a result of our fears of anthrax "contamination"? How much that was important to our nation did not get done because of the widespread fear of anthrax? When the anthrax threat was over, as it now appears to be, how much damage was done by the bacteria and how much damage was done by the fear of anthrax?

On American highways an average of five people die each hour of the day every day of the year. A death is a death. People killed in car crashes are as dead and mostly as innocent as those who died of anthrax in late 2001. Why do some deaths appear to count for so much and others appear to count for so little in terms of human psychology? Seldom have five deaths been such big news for so long as happened in the fall of 2001 when the nation was mesmerized by its fear of anthrax.

Here's another perspective on the fears generated in the fall of 2001. How much energy has been spent in public consideration of possible terrorist threats in the future? Our scientists and media experts have been conducting the most remarkable public exercise in analyzing possible future terrorist targets and weapons. Each potential target and each potential weapon is discussed in exquisite detail with the pluses and minuses carefully weighed, focusing most intently on the mass fear that each would provoke.

Look at the threat of smallpox. Anthrax, we have learned, is not contagious. Anthrax is not spread from one person to another. Smallpox is contagious. One person infected with smallpox becomes a vector spreading the virus to those who come within a few feet of that person. Out of fear of smallpox in the hands of a terrorist in the future, the nation is considering vaccinating the entire population against a threat that is, at this time, entirely in our own fearful imaginations. We will need to weigh not only the dollar costs of such an endeavor but also its opportunity costs. What other things could have been done with that time and money that would have had beneficial effects in our society? Additionally we will need to calculate the predicable costs of illnesses and deaths caused by such a massive smallpox vaccination program and weigh them against potential risks of the alternative, which is to vaccinate against this disease only after the first cases of smallpox have been identified.

A panel of experts called the Advisory Committee on Immunization Practices advised President Bush about the dangers of smallpox as a terrorist weapon and the options for vaccination to protect Americans. The experts recommended an initial vaccination of about 500,000 "first responders," health care workers who would be most likely to contact any victims of smallpox. Later up to 10 million health workers would be vaccinated, presumably including the three of us, but probably not until the vaccine was licensed in 2004. The panel estimated that about fifteen people per million people vaccinated would experience "life-threatening complications" from the vaccine itself, including one or two per million people vaccinated who would die of these complications while others would suffer blindness and similar grave illnesses. Because of these predictable risks the panel did not recommend immediate vaccination of the entire American population because the vaccine's benefits do not outweigh its risks for the general public.

The 30 to 50 million Americans who have compromised immune systems would not be candidates for vaccination because they are at higher risk of complications. That leaves about 220 million Americans to consider for smallpox vaccination. If fifteen per million were to suffer "life-threatening complications" that comes to 3,300, or just a few more than the number who perished on September 11, 2001. In a clear bow to the psychology of fear, the panel recommended that in the future members of the public be given the opportunity to decide for themselves whether to choose to be vaccinated against smallpox or not. Recall that one of the key factors in reducing fear is the sense of control over the risk. This particular example of balancing the risks and benefits of an action in the distorting crucible of the fear of terrorism now is being played out publicly.

Fear is not the only legacy of the terrorist attacks during the past two years. These attacks produced some benefits. They led to an international bonding fired by the terrorist attacks. There was a gratifying sense of national identity and a patriotism not seen since the Second World War. The differences between Americans that were so glaring before September 11 seemed less important as many people developed a sense of national solidarity that flowed from those terrible deeds. Many Americans responded to the fear of terrorism by turning to their religious faiths. Other Americans had a heightened sense of the joys and wonders of their everyday lives in the midst of this new and unpredictable threat to their existence. Some Americans reached out to their neighbors and even to complete strangers with a new sense of caring and generosity.

Another remarkable change after the terrorist attacks has been the dramatic rise in the public appreciation for the military, police, fire, and rescue workers. These are all jobs that have been disparaged in the media and by politicians in recent decades. When we feel threatened we turn to these hardworking, relatively low-paid, and usually unsung heroes as our best hopes for survival—as individuals and as a nation. This change of public perception has been dramatic over the past two years. It has been beneficial for all Americans. Not to ignore those important positive dimensions to the response to terrorism, this chapter focuses on public fear because the fear of terrorism is the most powerful weapon of modern terrorists.

The Five Fear Factors and the Events of September 11

To help us sort out the surprising twists and turns to risk and fear, let's go back to the five factors that shape our fears and look at them specifically in terms of terrorism. We can start by focusing on the mother of all terrorist attacks, the events of September 11, 2001. When we do that we can see more clearly precisely why terrorism is so terrifying. We can begin to see what needs to be done to protect ourselves, our families, our nation, and our world from the fear of terrorism. When we take the inventory of the fear of terrorism we see that it is our fears that keep terrorism alive. Worse yet, our fears feed and encourage the growth of terrorism in the future. We begin to grasp the most important fact of all: When we no longer fear terrorism, then terrorism will end, because it will no longer work as a strategy of modern war.

The first factor in the equation of fear is *familiarity*. Despite how widespread terrorism has become around the world in recent decades, it remains unfamiliar, especially to Americans. Europeans, like most other people in all parts of the world, were overwhelmingly sympathetic to Americans as a result of the devastating losses we suffered on September 11, 2001. Nevertheless, one of the common European reactions to those tragic events was a certain satisfaction that now, at long last, Americans would understand firsthand the effects of terrorism that most Europeans had endured for nearly a generation. Because terrorism is unfamiliar in the United States, the fear of terrorism was especially magnified and prolonged in this country after September 11.

The second factor promoting fear is *personal control*. The risks of modern terrorism are unchosen, in contrast to how the risks of cigarette smoking or even the risks of airplane travel are chosen. Americans know that when it comes to terrorism they have little or no control over their risks. Americans can choose not to smoke and not to fly. Some Americans choose not to go into tall or historic buildings. Can Americans avoid handling the mail or going to public places such as shopping centers, sporting events, and schools?

The third factor in determining public fear of a particular risk is the *possibility of a catastrophic event*. Surely terrorism is the modern definition of catastrophe. Especially disturbing is the linkage of terrorism to weapons of mass destruction, including chemical, biological, and nuclear weapons, as is expressed in the recent mantra of danger in the new sort of war that will be waged by tomorrow's terrorists.

The fourth factor governing fear is the *predictability of risk*. The terrorist threat is the embodiment of unpredictability. The special power of terrorism is that it is unpredictable. Even long periods during which there are no terrorist attacks do not reassure the American public because they assume the time is being used to plan even bigger and even more fiendish attacks.

Finally, terrorism is not a *natural risk*. Terrorism is, without a doubt, a human-caused risk based on hatred. This is as true for homegrown solitary terrorists as it is for hostile foreign terrorist networks. In all five areas governing the intensity of fear induced by a particular risk, terrorist threats are at the top of the list of modern fears. In each of the five factors, terrorism heads the list of the most dreaded fears. Terrorists may be vicious, they even may be insane, but they are not stupid. They have learned the lessons of the past three decades and fashioned a thoroughly modern weapon that does not require the support of a state. Terrorism is a weapon that can be wielded on the cheap. The attacks of September 11 appear to have cost less than $1 million, what the U.S. military spends for a single missile. The secret weapon of terrorism is our own fear. The terrorists have learned important lessons about what drives human fears.

Add to these five fear factors from outside the individual the two social multipliers of fear: the mass media and the advocacy dimension of the risk of terrorism. Here again terrorism is at the top of the hierarchy of danger. Is it possible to imagine a threat that is more irresistible for the media than the threat of modern terrorism? When it comes to advocacy motivations for intensifying fears, it is clear that political motivations are the driving force behind everything terrorists do. It is also true that many of the opponents of terrorism have political motivations, even if those motivations are as innocent as trying to protect the population.

This analysis of the fear of terrorism gets more complex when you realize that the United States went to war after September 11, 2001. The leaders of the country, from both parties, need to get public attention to support the sacrifices that war requires. Fear is a major motivator for just those behaviors that are needed to go to war and to successfully wage war over a prolonged period. We have learned from our practices over many years that the more you fear your fears, the bigger they grow. The less you fear your fears, the more they wither away and die of neglect.

Understanding Anxiety Problems Helps Cope with the Fear of Modern Terrorism

Understanding the brain biology of fear and the lessons from helping people overcome anxiety problems can reduce the fear of terrorism. The central purpose of terrorism is to foment widespread, intense, and prolonged fear. The more we fear terrorism the more the terrorists succeed and the more incentive other terrorists have to wage this new kind of war in the future. In this regard, the problem faced by the society at large is similar to the problem faced by the person suffering from a serious anxiety problem. The only way out of the problem is to go toward the fear and not away from it. In fact the more the fear is nurtured by avoidance the stronger and more dominating that fear becomes.

One of the most curious aspects of the fear of terrorism is that America is so vulnerable to this fear now. One reason for this heightened risk of fear of terrorism is the great and still-growing power of the global media in our lives. No other people in history has ever been so connected to the news as Americans are today. Although the media is everywhere it is not monolithic. We have access to hundreds of news outlets every moment in our lives. As the media has become more diverse it has become more ubiquitous and more important in our daily lives.

The factor most overlooked in the recent upsurge in vulnerability to the fear of terrorism, like many other factors we previously have described, is paradoxical. At no time in human history have any people ever been so safe and faced so few threats of death as Americans now face. This is especially true for American children, who now have a better chance of living to old age than any children have ever before had, anywhere in the world. This is true even when we add in the risks of terrorism, risks that are, as we have see, statistically small. So here is the paradox: If we are so safe why do we experience so much fear and insecurity? The new ingredient is that as death prior to old age has become more uncommon it has become more frightening.

We fear excessively what is unfamiliar. That is why American parents today are so afraid for the safety of their children: They have become unfamiliar with what in all prior human generations was common, and that is the death of young children. Within the past generation in much of the world half of all children did not reach adulthood. In earlier times this sort of infant and childhood mortality was universal. When it was, people took it for granted. They were sad when their children died but they did not fear for their children's safety the way we do today.

Fears cannot be overcome by facts, no matter how powerful those facts are. Nevertheless, facts are needed to establish the basis for confronting fears. When it comes to getting on airplanes, it is not possible to reassure fearful flyers that the particular planes they are getting on will not crash on their particular flights. In fact each particular fearful flyer's plane may crash. Even if a person flies a thousand times safely, the thousand and first flight may be fatal. We know, even if we seldom think of it, that this same reality confronts us whenever we get into an automobile or just go about our everyday lives.

To overcome fears we need to be able to identify activities that are generally desirable and that have acceptable risks even if we have severe fears. Examples include flying and driving in a car. In contrast, smoking cigarettes and riding on a motorcycle without a helmet are risky behaviors where the risks are not justified by the benefits to the individual, whether the individual has or does not have fear. Making those distinctions is important even though those distinctions will not, themselves, solve the paradox of fear and risk.

We have thought a lot about helping people overcome their fear of flying, an activity in which we are often engaged. Fearful flyers don't fly. Therefore they cannot die in a plane crash. Someday one of the great numbers of people we have helped overcome their fears of flying will die in an airplane crash. How will we feel then? It helps in answering that question to know that we fly regularly. Our planes are no more and no less likely to crash than anyone else's plane. The answer is that we will feel good about our work with that person who overcame his or her fear of flying because that person assumed the normal and healthy risks associated with flying on commercial airplanes. We do not help people overcome fears of cigarette smoking, illegal drug use, or motorcycle riding! In any event, over the past twenty years we have not seen the first person come into our mental health practices seeking our help in overcoming these socially appropriate fears.

To better cope with the fear of terrorism, we need to see that the risks of terrorism are exceedingly small based on all past experience. Yes, like the fear of nuclear power, there is a case being made that the past may not be a good guide for future risks. Nevertheless the past is a good place to start in considering all risks, including those posed by terrorism, just as the past is a good place to start when it comes to the risks of nuclear power. When we look at the risk in that way we begin to feel less alone as well as less afraid. We see that the terrorism we now face is not so different from the terrorism that has been and is being visited upon many other nations. We can learn from Germany, France, Italy, and Britain as well as from India, Sri Lanka, Indonesia, and Israel. There are better and worse ways to cope with the fear of terrorism. The worst way is to succumb to it by diverting national attention from important activities such as keeping our lives running and focused on productive activities. We cannot win this new war by hiding our heads in the sand.

Steps Individuals Can Take

When we divert our attention from the activities that make us strong, the terrorists win and we lose. To the extent that we can put the risk of terrorism into the context of the other serious risks we face—risks that are far more familiar and about which we can think more clearly—we will deal with modern terrorist attacks with the one-word antidote for all fears: acceptance. This will not be easy when the next terrorist attack occurs, because, unlike the fear of flying or the fear of getting stuck on an elevator, there are many voices in the society, some of them magnified in the media and by strong advocates, which tell us that the risks of terrorism are not similar to the other serious risks we have experienced in the past. These voices emphasize that the next terrorist attack may be truly catastrophic and entirely outside of our prior experiences.

When we hear that we need to say "Yes, that may be true, but the risks of giving in to our fears are even greater." The best answer to modern terrorism for most of us is to continue to live our lives without becoming preoccupied with the terrorists' despicable acts or our own understandable fears.

There is one more thing we need to do to cope successfully with our fears of modern terrorism. Ted Kaczynski is a paranoid schizophrenic loner. Tim McVeigh was a political extremist. John Muhammad is African American. Osama bin Laden and the perpetrators of September 11 atrocities were Arabs. One of the worst, most unfair, and ultimately most self-defeating ways to handle our fears of terrorism is to stigmatize whole groups of people, including paranoid schizophrenics, political mavericks, Muslims, Arabs, blacks, and recent immigrants to this country. Only a tiny percentage of these groups is a terrorist threat. Our country is made strong by inclusion and by respecting each other in our rich diversity.

Here is a good way to deal with the threat of modern terrorism at a personal level. If you are not in one of the groups of Americans associated with the recent terrorist attacks, seek out recent immigrants—Arabs, Muslims, and others in these groups—and welcome them to our country. Let them know that you respect them and appreciate their contributions to our country. Find a Muslim in your neighborhood or at your job and let that person know you respect the religion of Islam. Reach out to political mavericks and even to the hardest group to reach, the severely mentally ill, including paranoid schizophrenics. Let them know that you care about them. Let the people in all of these groups know that the latest terrorist attack has not made them your enemies.

If you are a member of one of these groups, do not hide this fact. Be proud of it. Take the time to reach out to your fellow Americans to tell them about yourself, your community, and your views of modern terrorism. This step is especially important if the United States is to reduce the risk of future terrorism, and even more if the nation is not to let the terrorists win this new kind of war by causing our fears to tear us apart along the many fault lines of American culture.

Modern terrorists seek to demoralize America by provoking mass terror with relatively small attacks that produce relatively small loss of life. They seek to cripple the nation by exhausting us with fear. They want to get us to give up, to retreat from the larger world, and to become the modern equivalents of house-bound agoraphobics, huddled in our homes afraid to go out. Many American parents and grandparents today lament the harsh and dangerous realities of modern life, saying they now regret bringing children into this troubled world. Fear of terrorism is behind many of these disturbing sentiments. This sort of capitulation to fear is familiar to us from our work with many people suffering from anxiety disorders. It is understandable, but it is also irrational. Perspective helps to overcome fear. Knowledge and information help, too. In the end, the only way out of the prison of fear is by confronting one's deepest and most painful fears. This can seldom be done alone but it can definitely be done with others by working together over a long period of time.

Our clinical experience has shown us that when people confront their fears, not only do they reclaim their lives as they break the bonds of fear, but their self-esteem takes a huge leap up. Many anxious people who have overcome their fears are eager to help others who are still trapped in fear. It is our hope that modern terrorism will catalyze this recovery process on a community level. If that happens, then terrorism will prove not to be a crippling threat but a call to psychological arms that will generate enduring benefits. Perhaps Americans, as a people, can develop an immunity to the fear of terrorism. If our country does that we will have struck a fatal blow against modern terrorism. When we no longer fear it, modern terrorism will disappear as a political weapon.

Let's review the eight steps we are recommending for individuals to reduce the fear of terrorism:

1. Understand that the central goal of terrorists is to provoke terror. Fear terrorism and it grows. Stop fearing terrorism and it withers away and will, eventually, disappear because terrorism will no longer work as a political weapon.
2. Put the risks of terrorist attacks into the perspective of other serious, but more familiar, risks to both adults and children.
3. Support the efforts of the authorities to curb terrorism and to punish terrorist perpetrators.
4. Encourage leaders who help people put the risks of terrorism into perspective and who balance their efforts to combat terrorism with other important priorities.
5. Limit the time you and your families spend with the media during terrorist threats to no more than fifteen minutes a day.
6. Help children to face the treats of terrorism realistically and to feel confident that they are protected by caring adults, including their teachers and parents as well as the police.
7. Reach out in friendship to people in all groups in American society. Avoid stigmatizing whole groups of Americans, including Muslims, Arabs, political radicals, and blacks. If you are a member of one of these groups, reach out to other Americans and let them know what you think about modern terrorism.
8. Go about your daily activities being productive and active despite terrorist threats.

Americans need to take these difficult steps with a sense of community—a large community that includes all the people of the world—since it is in that shared sense of community that we Americans can find our greatest strength. The threat of modern terrorism is not America's alone. This threat is part of life in the modern world. Coping with painful fears of terrorism needs to be as much a part of our modern armamentarium to defend ourselves against terrorism as smallpox vaccination, antibiotic treatments for anthrax, and searches at airports.

CHAPTER 14

Anxiety and Depression

Depression is part of the general class of mood disorders, which, like the anxiety disorders, is a group of related brain disorders. Moods are feeling states. People with mood disorders feel extremely down or, more rarely, extremely up; they feel abnormally depressed or abnormally elated. To be diagnosed as a mood disorder, these mood extremes are not just minor and not just for a brief period of time but to an extent and for a time that seriously erodes the sufferer's quality of life, causing major deficits in important areas of life functioning, such as family life and work. Mood disorders cause significant distress and mental pain.

Depression is worry about the past and about your failures and inadequacies. Depression—a sense of hopelessness that the future will be no better than the past—is linked to a feeling of helplessness about being able to make the future any better than the past. As with anxiety disorders, there is a characteristic distortion of thinking with depression. When you are depressed, you feel so hopeless and helpless that no amount of talking and no amount of realistic assessment of the past, present, and future can shake the conviction, born of your depression, that misery is your deserved lot in life. Also like anxiety disorders, depression comes in grades, from relatively minor to hugely disruptive. Again, like anxiety disorders, depression tends to wax and wane over time. Unlike anxiety disorders, however, it is common for depressed people to have periods, which can often last for many years, when they have no depressive symptoms at all and then to have another depression, called a "depressive episode."

Elation, or mania, is the reverse of depression. A manic person believes he or she can do anything and that the outcome of every event will be positive. The manic person buys a lottery ticket knowing it will be the winning number. The manic person thinks his or her words and ideas are the cleverest in the world. Depression is associated with lowered energy, while mania is associated with excessive energy. The manic person needs little or no sleep and seldom feels tired. Mania is an unrealistic optimism that is usually short-lived. But then the person heads for an inevitable crash in mood and the crushing burden of the bad judgments made in the manic state (for example, reckless spending and promiscuous sexual behavior).

When depression is part of a disorder of mood swings, over days or more often months and years, with extremes of both depression and mania, it is called bipolar disorder or what used to be called manic-depressive disorder. When the person suffers from depression without manic episodes, the depression is called unipolar, meaning there are episodes of depression without mania. Depressions can be single episodes in a person's life or they can be recurrent. They can also be more or less continuous, or they can be episodes separated by longer or shorter periods of normal moods, called euthymia (a normal mood state in which the swings between high and low are not extreme and are usually related to changes in your life circumstances). When not depressed and not elated, a normal person feels a bit down when something unpleasant happens and a bit elated when something good happens, but all these mood changes are in a normal range of moods.

When you have relatively mild but more or less continuous depression without depressive or manic episodes, it is called dysthymic disorder, meaning you feel mildly but chronically depressed. The mood disorders include major depressive disorder (either single episode or recurrent episodes) and dysthymic disorder. Bipolar disorder is more complex, including a single episode, which can be primarily depressed or manic, or a relatively mild manic episode called hypomania. Bipolar II is a less common form of bipolar disorder and is characterized by serious depressive episodes mixed with relatively mild manic episodes. Cyclothymia is a relatively minor form of bipolar disorder, with both minor mania and minor depression alternating. Cyclothymia is similar to dysthymia.

Anxiety Contrasted with Depression

In Part One of this book, you became familiar with the various anxiety disorders; for example, you know that agoraphobia is different from obsessive-compulsive disorder even though both are anxiety disorders. The anxiety disorders share a common core: excessive worry, tension, and irritability. In contrast to mood disorders, the anxiety disorders typically are disorders of future thinking, of what will happen. They are malignant diseases of the "what if's." Recall that for a person to be identified as having a diagnosable anxiety disorder, the problems must be serious and prolonged.

About one-third of people with depression are comorbid for anxiety—that is, they have both disorders—and about one-third of people with anxiety have depressions at the same time. These numbers also make clear that many people have one disorder and not the other. Although there are differences in the thought patterns of depressed and anxious people, many of the symptoms of depression are similar to the symptoms of anxiety disorders, including sleep disturbance, excessive worry, and low self-esteem.

There are four ways that depression and anxiety are linked:

1. The two disorders are often confused, so some people who are depressed mislabel themselves, or they are mislabeled by their therapists or physicians, as suffering from anxiety disorders.
2. Both anxiety and depression are commonly seen in the same people because the groups of disorders share similar brain mechanisms and similar genetic backgrounds. It is common to find histories of depression in families of people with anxiety disorders, as it is common to find histories of anxiety disorders in families of people with depression.
3. One disorder can lead to the other in the sense that you can have an anxiety disorder and get so demoralized that you have a secondary depression, or you can be so anxious in a serious depression that you develop a secondary anxiety disorder.
4. You can have both disorders, and even though they are not related, they can be coexistent. This can happen just the way you can have an anxiety disorder and diabetes mellitus at the same time even though they are unrelated disorders.

Depression or Anxiety?

Depression is secondary to an anxiety disorder when the anxiety disorder came first in time and when the anxiety disorder dominates your problems. On the other hand, the depression is primary when it came first and when it dominates your life (and your symptoms of anxiety). Usually it is possible to discern which came first and which is dominant, anxiety or depression, but sometimes they are both primary disorders in the sense that they either occurred at the same time or they are about equally disabling. If both are primary disorders, then your anxiety did not make you depressed and your depression did not make you anxious.

Though not ideal, the reality is that some therapists are expert in dealing with anxiety but not so expert in dealing with depression, and vice versa. Health care professionals who have an orientation that is clearly toward one or the other of these two classes of disorders tend to see in their patients the problems with which they are most familiar. It may be useful to talk over with your therapists and your doctors what they think about this distinction between anxiety and depression as it relates to your symptoms and to your treatment.

Treatment for Depression and Anxiety

Some of the medicines used to treat anxiety disorders also treat depression. These medicines are the antidepressants, including the selective serotonin reuptake inhibitors (SSRIs), such as Prozac, Zoloft, Paxil, and Luvox, as well as the older tricyclic antidepressants (TCAs), such as Tofranil, Norpramin, Pamelor, Sinequan, and Elavil. There is a group of new antidepressants that are not SSRIs. This group includes Wellbutrin, Serzone, Effexor, and Remeron. Because of the success of these medicines in the marketplace (which reflects their good results with many patients), new antidepressants are being introduced every year. By the time this book is published, several new antidepressants are likely to have been marketed. All of these antidepressant medicines take several weeks to produce their full effects (for both depression and anxiety), and they all are effective against both depression and anxiety.

Another class of antianxiety medicines, the benzodiazepines, are powerful antipanic and antianxiety medicines, but they are not effective antidepressants. If you are using a benzodiazepine for anxiety and you also have depression, you will want to discuss this with your prescribing doctor, since you may need a medicine that has antidepressant properties. Because many people with anxiety disorders have secondary depression, when their anxious symptoms are reduced by using a benzodiazepine, their hope returns and their depression lifts. If the depression is primary, and if it persists despite resolution of the anxiety symptoms, then using an antidepressant is an option you need to discuss with your physician.

Just as many of the medicines that are used to treat anxiety are also effective against depression and vice versa, so it is with nonpharmacological treatments. Therapy for depression also reduces anxiety, while therapy for anxiety often reduces depression. Books written about the mood disorders often have major sections discussing the anxiety disorders, since they are closely related problems. When a person has both depression and anxiety, it usually means the disability is greater and the challenge of treatment is also greater than if the person has only one disorder. Comorbidity does not mean the prognosis is any better or any worse for people with one disorder or the other, as opposed to people who have both disorders. Both depression and anxiety are biopsychosocial disorders, meaning that they have biological, psychological, and social dimensions to their causes and their treatments.

Mood disorders and the anxiety disorders are usually long-term, if not lifelong, problems that require substantial efforts over prolonged periods of time to overcome. We want you to understand your problems. We do not want you to be discouraged or overwhelmed by them. A step-by-step approach will help you with mood disorders, as it does with anxiety disorders. We encourage you to learn more about mood disorders, to join with others who have them, to read about them, and to talk openly about them with people who can help you overcome whatever disability and distress they are causing you.

Depression is a serious, biologically based, real, and treatable disorder. But like the anxiety disorders, it can be treated with medicines or with nonmedicine therapies. We urge you to identify depression when it exists and be sure that you get good care, whether it exists alone or along with an anxiety disorder. Most of the treatments for depression are also effective against anxiety, and most of the treatments for anxiety are effective for depression. But in some cases, highly specific treatments are needed. Your therapist or doctor can help you sort out your personal needs.

CHAPTER 15

Anxiety and Insomnia

Insomnia is having difficulty sleeping that causes distress or disability. Insomnia, like pain, is a symptom, rather than a disease, that can be caused by many illnesses, from arthritis to depression. It also can be caused by serious sleep-related illnesses, such as sleep apnea and narcolepsy. If you have had anxiety for a long time and only recently have developed insomnia, that suggests your insomnia may not be part of your anxiety disorder. If insomnia is a major problem for you, we suggest that you talk it over with your doctor to see if you need a specialized sleep study to identify the cause of your insomnia. Many times when the underlying disorder is treated, insomnia is reduced or disappears. For example, when arthritis pain is reduced, the patient's sleep is more normal. When depression is well treated, insomnia usually disappears.

Having said that, however, it is also true that many clinically anxious people suffer from sleep disorders that have no other cause. These people have insomnia as part of their anxiety disorder, which means it has waxed and waned with other anxiety symptoms from the onset of the anxiety disorder itself.

Sleeping Like a Cat

To understand how anxiety and insomnia are related, think about a pet—a dog or a cat. Now think of the pet having insomnia. You will quickly conclude that even though the animal may have many maladies, it does not have insomnia, as do many anxious people. The dog may sleep soundly through the night (uncommon for a dog), or it may wake several times (more likely). It may sleep in the day. It may sleep a lot or a little. But one thing you can be sure about is that no matter how solicitous the dog's owner, the dog will never be taken to the veterinarian for "insomnia," because the owner will never identify that as a problem for the animal.

The reason pets do not have insomnia is that most insomnia is sleep worry. Without the worry, there is no insomnia. Animals (including unworried humans) may sleep a lot or a little, but they do not have sleep worry, or insomnia. Studies of human insomniacs show that they sleep an average of twenty minutes less each night than do age- and sex-matched control noninsomniac subjects. That twenty minutes is not much difference in total sleep. In both the insomniac and the normal-sleep groups, there is a huge variation in sleep, from less than six hours to more than nine hours. Babies sleep about twelve to fifteen hours, while elder adults sleep about six or seven hours. In other words, the need for sleep normally decreases as we age. The sleep of older people often gets lighter than the sleep of younger people. That is normal, and it is not something to be worried or upset about. Sleep is similar to sexual responsiveness in that it cannot be willed. The harder you try to make yourself sleep, the harder it is to sleep. You have to "let" yourself fall asleep, you cannot "make" yourself fall asleep. Worry, tension, and irritability keep the anxious insomniac awake. The content of these typical nighttime worries is varied. The worry may relate to the activities of the day. The worries may be focused on chronic problems that the particular person has both day and night without respect to the events of the particular day. Most insomniacs worry about insomnia. They worry that sleep will not come. "Oh, no, another night when I cannot fall asleep, which will surely lead to another day when I am tired." This fear of insomnia is heightened by the fact that when sleep is poor, the anxiety dragon has an easier target—lack of sleep usually adds to daytime anxiety and panic. You can easily see the vicious cycle: the more worry, the less sleep; the less sleep, the more worry. Fear of insomnia is the nighttime equivalent of daytime fear of fear.

Nonmedication Treatment of Insomnia

Nonpharmacological approaches to insomnia work just the way nonpharmacological approaches to daytime worry work. To get well you need to learn to let go of your worry. You need to accept your worry and not to add to it with your "what-if" anxious thoughts. Acceptance is the one-word antidote for anxiety, whether it occurs in the day or in the night. Stop fighting your anxiety, and it will fade away from neglect.

When it comes to insomnia, use your antianxiety techniques, which means accepting that you (like your cat or dog) may sleep a lot or a little on any particular night, but that your body will get the sleep it needs, if not tonight, then tomorrow night or the night after. *Let go and give up the fight for sleep. Let sleep find you.*

Get a Sleep Window

You need to set up a sleep window of not more than seven to eight hours. If you try to sleep longer, you are sure to spend time awake in bed, since it is unlikely your body can sleep more than seven or eight hours. Many insomniacs have wide-open sleep windows, going to bed early because they are tired from sleeping poorly the night before and staying in bed late because they sleep so poorly each night. Going to bed at 9 or 10 P.M. is common for insomniacs, and getting up at 9 or 10 A.M. is also common. If you understand that your body cannot sleep more than about seven hours, you realize that this big sleep window ensures that the worried person will have four hours or more of awake time each night. The simple next step to get well is to close that window to a maximum of six or seven hours.

Pick times to go to bed and to get up that work for you, for example, 11 P.M. to 6 A.M. Use that as your sleep window. Make sure that your sleep window is not more than seven hours. Once you set the time, do not go to bed before 11 P.M., no matter how tired you are. Do not stay in bed past 6 A.M., no matter how poorly you sleep. You need to train your brain to sleep the way you would train an animal, with consistency. You should be out of bed except for the seven-hour period of your sleep window.

If you are not sleepy during your sleep window, you can get out of bed and read or do anything else that you like to do until you are tired and ready to go sleep. Do not get back in bed until you are sleepy. *If you wake up but are in a mental twilight or half asleep, stay in bed and figure that your body is resting.* You are probably sleeping more than you think at these times. Count this twilight time as sleep in your mental accounting of your sleep. Only get out of bed during your sleep window if you are wide awake.

Bed is for sleep and sex, period. No food, no reading (except for a few minutes to fall asleep). No conversations or TV. Just use your bed for sleep as you train your body that when you get in bed, you sleep.

Use a Sleep Routine

A routine before bed will help signal to your brain that it is time to quiet down for the night. A routine is anything that promotes a smooth transition from being awake to being asleep. For most people this routine will include using the bathroom, brushing teeth, changing into nightclothes, and getting into bed. If you currently have a routine, be sure it is simple, brief, and comfortable, and then work to perform your routine consistently at the time you have chosen to begin your sleep window. For example, if your sleep routine takes you ten minutes and you have decided that your sleep window starts at 11 P.M., then you will start your sleep ritual at about 10:50 P.M. every night. This will help you with your transition to sleep in another way, in that it will alert you that this is not the time for phone calls, TV, or any other distraction that can stimulate you and keep you from feeling tired just before bed.

If you do not already have a routine before bed, consider what to include. While some people enjoy reading or watching TV right before sleep, remember that it is not a good idea to do these things in bed if you are having trouble with insomnia. Your sleep routine may include your pets, children, spouse, or others who live with you. For example, Kim, a twenty-five-year-old with agoraphobia who developed a terrible fear of falling asleep, found it soothing to get ready for bed and then sit in a chair by her bed while she held her dog on her lap. She stroked the dog and reminded herself about all of the good things that had happened during the day, and then in her mind she rehearsed getting into bed and turning off the light. Initially this increased her panic, but as she let time pass while stroking her dog, Kim found that she could calm down enough to finally put the dog in his bed and go to sleep herself.

In Step 5 you learned several techniques that may be useful as you deal with insomnia. Relaxation, yoga, tai chi, and exercise are all areas to explore as you try to improve your sleep. Relaxation exercises like those in Step 5 may be useful to quiet your mind from the anxiety of the day. Remember to do these exercises before you get into bed. Then when you do get into bed, try to re-create the feeling of peace and relaxation that you found while listening to your tape.

Though these quiet exercises may be helpful to get sleepy, be sure not to schedule *aerobic* exercise into your day too close to your bedtime. Exercising vigorously within two hours of going to bed may make you too energized to go sleep. It is important, though, to get aerobic exercise during the day so that your body is truly tired and ready for sleep.

Do not let your bedtime ritual become a compulsion. It is a simple structure that can be varied as circumstances and your needs change, even day to day. If the rituals last more than ten to fifteen minutes, or if you feel compelled to do them just right, or at exactly the same time— fearing dreadful outcomes if you don't do it just right—consider being more flexible so you are not trapped by an obsessional routine.

Bedtime Rituals

Gloria was a thirty-five-year-old professional woman. She had struggled for many years with the symptoms of OCD. She had a complex bedtime ritual that could take several hours to complete. If the ritual was not done "properly," she would get very anxious and often would be unable to sleep. Her ritual involved checking many things several times—for example, the stove, the front and back doors, and the windows. Anything that interrupted her ritual would force her to start again. Unfortunately, the person who most frequently interrupted her ritual was her husband. She could not start her bedtime ritual until he came home, or she would worry that he had not properly checked all of the things that she already had checked, such as the lock on the door. After her bedtime process had started, he was not allowed to go out of the house, or even into the kitchen.

Her husband was her support person in her work to overcome her OCD. The two of them spent several hours reviewing her baseline ritual and discussing what a new ritual should involve. For example, they agreed that the process should not take longer than one hour and should not involve him. At first it was difficult for Gloria to make these changes, but with diligent practice, and the support and encouragement of her husband, she was able to reduce drastically the time it took her to get to sleep, resulting in marked improvements in the quality of her sleep and in her relationship with her husband.

It will take a while to retrain your insomnia-dominated brain to this new approach. If you are firm with yourself, as you would be if you were training a child or an animal, you will succeed. If you are unwilling to adopt a restricted sleep window, that is okay, too, but remember that you have chosen to sleep this way. Stop complaining and fighting about your chaotic sleep pattern and just figure that this is how you choose to spend those hours. If you have something better to do with that time than lying in bed awake, use some of those hours for better purposes. If not, be happy that at least you have the extra time to use in this way.

Be Consistent

Remember, as you learned with other aspects of the Anxiety Cure, you need to let go of worry to regain control of your anxiety-driven life. Trust your body to get the sleep it needs. Your job is to set up and maintain a healthy sleep window with enough hours in it. Give your body a chance to adapt to that sleep window.

Try to be consistent weekdays and weekends. When you shift your sleep window from day to day, especially when you shift your sleep time every weekend, you are doing the equivalent of flying over several time zones each weekend. It is like flying across the country or even to Europe for the weekend. Is it surprising that your body has trouble adapting to that time zone shift each week?

Sleep

Sleep is normal, natural, and unavoidable, like breathing and eating. Sleep is also subject to being disturbed by anxiety, again like breathing and eating. In the Anxiety Cure, we encourage you to let go of your anxiety-driven abnormal sleeping (as well as abnormal breathing and eating) so that you can slip into more healthy patterns that you can maintain over long periods of time. If you worry less about insomnia and daytime sleepiness, you will have fewer of these problems. Your worry machine drives your insomnia.

Medicines to Treat Insomnia

Some people with anxiety benefit from the occasional use of sleep medication. As with medication use for anxiety that is not related to sleep problems, we encourage you to think of medication as a tool to help you live a full life, not as a mark of failure. Whether or not you choose to talk to your doctor about the possibility of using sleeping medications, we suggest that you also use the nonmedication suggestions in this chapter. Medication on its own will not solve your sleep worry if you are expecting to have eight hours of unbroken, anxiety-free sleep every night. It is important to help the medication work by setting up realistic expectations. Ask your doctor how often you may use any sleep medication you are prescribed, as different doctors take different approaches to short- and long-term use of sleep aids. Similarly, if you want to take an over-the-counter sleep medication, be sure your doctor is aware of that, too. Some people do well with occasional use of over-the-counter sleep medications, but it is important not to use them without a doctor's knowledge and approval while you are on other medications.

The medicines used to treat insomnia are the same medicines used to treat daytime anxiety. This is a surprise to many people, who assume that sleeping pills are "knockout" pills. The pharmaceutical companies recognize this public perception, so they market different medicines for daytime anxiety and insomnia. For example, Valium (diazepam) is used in the daytime and Dalmane (flurazepam) at night, even though both are long-acting benzodiazepines that could be used in reversed roles with no problem. Similarly, Xanax (alprazolam) and Halcion (triazolam) are two short-acting benzodiazepines, the first marketed for daytime use and the second for nighttime use. Those medications could also be reversed, except Halcion is so short-acting that it is not practical for daytime use.

These same antianxiety medicines used for daytime anxiety also work to reduce insomnia, not because they knock you out but because they reduce your worry. They are "antiworry" pills. When your worry is reduced, your previously worried brain lets your tired body go to sleep. This is how sleeping pills work. That is why Valium, Xanax, and Klonopin are good sleeping pills.

Medication for insomnia can be particularly useful if you have nocturnal panic attacks. Panic attacks can occur during sleep, with or without dreaming. Sleep panic is often especially troubling and may occur with little or no mental content, meaning you feel panic but have no specific worried thoughts. Nighttime panic can cause or complicate insomnia because the anxious person fears panic and comes to fear sleep because it may lead to panic during sleep. Knowing you have medication available to help you in this situation is particularly comforting as you work to reduce your fear of sleep.

Using medicines to reduce insomnia is fine, if that helps you sleep better. There is nothing wrong with using antianxiety medicines every single night for insomnia any more than there is anything wrong with using these medicines every single day. Anxious people do not escalate their doses of antianxiety medicines over months or even years of everyday use, and similarly neither do anxious people who use antianxiety medicines to sleep better. If you find that your use of antianxiety medicines at bedtime escalates beyond the usual therapeutic dose (which you will find in the medicine package's insert, the *Physicians' Desk Reference* [*PDR*], or from talking with your pharmacist or doctor) and/or if you use the techniques that we have taught you and nevertheless you continue to have troubled sleep, it is wise to consult with your doctor.

We want you to rethink your suffering from anxiety. That includes rethinking daytime and nighttime worry. We want you to be less afraid of your anxious symptoms and to be more confident that they will pass if you do not fight them and if you do not add your fearful thoughts. Stop feeding the dragon, and he will drift away from you.

CHAPTER 16

Anxiety and Addiction

Addiction, like depression, is commonly coexistent with anxiety. About one-third of people with addiction also have an anxiety disorder, while about one-sixth of people with an anxiety disorder also have an addiction to alcohol or another drug. Far more common than actual addiction among anxious people who take medication, however, is the mistaken belief that they are addicted to their medicines when they are not addicted at all. This distinction between actual addiction and fear of addiction is crucial, since treatment for the two problems is completely different.

Fear of Addiction to Antianxiety Medication

Anxious people are often afraid that they will use a medicine, it will work, and then they will be "hooked" on the medicine. Depressed people who find Prozac or Zoloft helpful sometimes fear that they are hooked or addicted and when they cut down or stop they find that their symptoms of depression return. Even more commonly, anxious people who find benefit in medicines, especially the benzodiazepines such as Xanax or Valium, fear they are addicted, because when they stop the medicine, they feel more anxious or have more insomnia. Feeling addicted when you are not addicted is one more blow to your already damaged self-esteem.

It is important to understand clearly that needing medication to function well is not the same as addiction. Imagine a person with myopia (nearsightedness) who relies on eyeglasses to see. The analogy was used in Chapter 4, but we review it again here for readers who have not seen it before. The nearsighted person could be described as "glasses dependent," since if the glasses are removed, the person would do almost anything to get the glasses back. But this person has not lost control over his use of eyeglasses. Neither of the following hallmarks of addiction are present: he does not continue to wear glasses despite problems caused to himself or others by his use of glasses, and there is no dishonesty.

Now think about the agoraphobic person taking Prozac or Xanax. Does the medicine help the person live a better life the way the glasses help the myopic person? Is the agoraphobic person honest with his or her doctor and others who have a reason to know about his or her medicine use? Clearly, the typical anxious person taking medicines, including the benzodiazepines, is similar to the person using eyeglasses in that there are terrific benefits and no problems for each in using the respective medicines or eyeglasses.

Withdrawal Symptoms

The fact that the anxious person using a medicine may have withdrawal symptoms on rapid discontinuation is not a factor in making the distinction between addiction and nonaddictive medicine use. Many medicines produce withdrawal symptoms on abrupt discontinuation (such as high blood pressure medicines, antiepilepsy medicines, and antidepressants), even though they are neither addictive nor abused by alcoholics or people addicted to drugs.

We recommend that you use medicines for your anxiety disorder if the medicines improve the quality of your life. If you can function fully without medicines and not have too much distress, so much the better. If you find that without medicines your functioning is limited and/or you have significant distress because of your anxiety disorder, then you should at least try using medicines. Do not let inappropriate fear of addiction scare you away from medicines that can make a big difference in your life the way glasses can help the nearsighted person.

Addiction to Antianxiety Medications

Some people who are alcoholics or drug addicts do abuse antianxiety medicines. They use these medicines at high doses and right along with their usual quantity of alcohol and other drugs. They often get medicines from many doctors and lie about their medicine, alcohol, and other drug use. For such people, these medicines do not help much because their anxiety problems are substantially worsened by their continuing use of alcohol and other drugs. Alcoholics and drug addicts use high and usually unstable doses of antianxiety medicines along with alcohol and other drugs, and they do not get good responses. Anxious patients who are not addicted to alcohol and other drugs usually use these medicines in low and stable doses (that is, they do not use above the level normally prescribed by doctors), and their doctors are fully informed about their use of medicines (as well as about their use of alcohol and other drugs). See Table 1 on page 65 for maximum dose zones. Nonaddicted anxious people typically have good responses to these medicines at low doses. We have never seen anyone who was not previously an addict to alcohol and other drugs who became addicted to these drugs as a result of using them as directed by their physicians. The only people we have seen who have had addiction to these medicines had prior personal and family histories of addiction to alcohol and other drugs.

Dealing with Addiction

Having dealt with the inappropriate fear of addiction to antianxiety medicines, let us focus on what to do if you have an addiction problem. If your use of alcohol is excessive or if you use illegal drugs, you have a problem that needs attention. If you use more medicines than your doctor prescribes, if you are dishonest with your doctor about your use of medicines, if you steal or forge prescriptions or get medicines from multiple doctors without telling each and every one of them what medicines you are using, then you are an addict. If you use more alcohol than makes sense for you, if you have good reason to stop drinking but find it hard to do, if you have negative consequences in your life from alcohol or other drug use, then you need help in overcoming your addiction.

If you have a problem with alcohol or other drugs, there are many experts in the field of addiction who can help you. One way to find expert assistance is to ask for help from a friend or relative who has a problem of alcoholism or drug addiction. You can also go to free Alcoholics Anonymous (AA) or Narcotics Anonymous (NA, the twelve-step program for drug addiction) meetings and ask for referrals to good therapists in your area. The people at these meetings are experts in using the local providers of health care services. Ask their advice. Another good way to get help is to call the American Society of Addiction Medicine (ASAM) at 301-656-3920 or on the web at www.asam.org to find the names of physicians in your area with expertise in addiction.

Addiction is a real disease, and like anxiety disorders, it can be overcome. We want you to be able to recognize addiction in yourself and others (including family members) and to know what to do when you see it. If you are concerned about another person's addiction to alcohol and other drugs, we suggest you go to some local Al-Anon meetings. Al-Anon is the twelve-step program for family members and friends of addicted people. As with AA and NA, phone numbers for Al-Anon are listed in your local telephone directory; you can call for information about the times and locations of nearby meetings. Like the anxiety disorders, substance-use disorders—addiction to alcohol and other drugs—does not cure itself like the common cold. On its own, addiction just gets worse. If addiction is your problem, you need to clearly identify the problem of addiction to alcohol and other drugs and take positive action to regain control of your life.

Although we have seen some recovering alcoholics and drug addicts who have used these medicines in nonaddictive ways over long periods of time with no relapses, because the benzodiazepines are subject to abuse by alcoholics and drug addicts, we do not recommend using them in the treatment of either recovering alcoholics or drug addicts. Today there are many good medicines to treat anxiety with no abuse potential for active and recovering alcoholics and drug addicts. The antidepressants are the best place to start, as they offer a wide range of choices with broad antipanic, antianxiety, and anti-OCD benefits. For insomnia, Desyrel (trazodone) is a sedating antidepressant that can usually be used in relatively modest doses (25 or 50 mg before bed). BuSpar is a good alternative to the benzodiazepines for daytime anxiety. When thinking about the treatment of anxiety in people comorbid for addiction, recall that these people can participate fully in the nonpharmacological treatments for anxiety, which have shown great success in recent years.

Twelve-Step Programs

One clear benefit alcoholics and drug addicts have, compared to nonaddicted people with anxiety, is that they can use the full power of the twelve-step programs, working the program by using a sponsor and the twelve steps. This reduces the anxiety and panic because of the support these resources offer. In itself, stopping drinking and drug use reduces anxiety, panic, and depression. Sobriety, when prolonged, helps the addicted, anxious brain heal.

The twelve-step programs are a modern miracle. One of our goals is to encourage people with addictions to use these programs. We also want nonaddicted people to learn how to help addicted people (whether they have anxiety or not) find their ways to, and then fully use, these programs. We ask nonaddicted readers, whether they have an anxiety disorder or not, to call their local AA or NA telephone number to learn the times and locations of a few convenient open meetings. Go to one so you can understand how these wonderful programs work. Open meetings are open to all those interested in learning about alcoholism, whether or not they have a drinking problem. Plan to arrive at the meeting fifteen minutes early, introduce yourself by your first name, and let your hosts know you have come to learn about addiction and recovery. Sit next to someone who can explain what is going on. You can learn about these programs from reading not only *The Selfish Brain— Learning from Addiction*, but also *A Bridge to Recovery—An Introduction to 12-Step Programs*, both written by Robert DuPont, the latter coauthored with his colleague John P. McGovern, M.D. *A Bridge to Recovery* is written for nonaddicts who work in all major American disciplines, such as education, health care, religion, and the criminal justice system, so they can learn how they can use the twelve-step programs in their everyday dealings with alcoholics and drug addicts, and their families.

At the age of fifty a psychiatrist who is also our patient lost her beloved husband to cancer. This woman did not have a problem with alcohol or other drugs. She joined a grief program and also began therapy to help her cope with her feelings of loss. She also turned to a friend who was a longtime member of Alcoholics Anonymous. She said that she sought out this friend "because I have learned that people in AA live on a higher, more spiritual level than other people, and I felt that then, after my husband's death, I especially needed this level of support to carry on my life." If you understand that woman's thinking, then you understand how we think about twelve-step programs and the potential for spiritual rebirth that is part of the recovery from alcoholism and drug addiction.

Imagine a doctor going into two wards in a busy hospital. One is the cancer ward, the other the ward for people addicted to alcohol and other drugs. The doctor first goes to the cancer ward, telling all the patients "I have good news. Although your disease will kill you if we leave it untreated, you can be cured. If you will go to a meeting once a day for about an hour, and if you will follow the few steps the program recommends, including quitting drinking and the use of drugs, your disease can be arrested so that you will live a full, normal life." Then the doctor takes the same message to the addiction ward.

Think how those two groups of patients would react. The cancer patients would react as if the doctor were a saint offering deliverance. Gladly and eagerly they would do what the doctor said. Now think what the reaction would be in the addiction ward. Most addicted people pooh-pooh such advice, returning to their addictive substance use as soon as they are released from the hospital. Like people returning to abusive lovers, they convince themselves "this time it will be different."

Why is there such a difference when both diseases are painful and frequently fatal? The addicted people suffer from a little voice in their heads, which we call their addictive disease. This voice whispers to them, "It's okay to use alcohol and drugs. Other people don't understand you. This time you can use just a little. This time you can control your use. This time there won't be any bad consequences when you use. This time no one will find out. This time your body won't be hurt. This time listen to me, not to them!"

Whether addicts are weak-willed or strong-willed, whether they have good or bad characters, they are subject to this subversive inner voice. It is terribly hard for them to say no to that voice, to admit that they suffer from the disease of addiction, and that the only way they can regain sanity is to give up their abusive lover, go to meetings, and work the twelve-step program. We have tremendous respect for the difficult time addicted people have getting well. We know just how hard it is and how often addicted people succumb to the tempting voice of their disease. We know just how easy it is to go back to that abusive lover. For many addicts, the disease of addiction ends only when their addiction claims their lives.

On the other hand, we have seen many addicted people get well. That usually means not only no more alcohol and drug use, but also regular participation in NA and AA. We have sympathy for addicted people because we respect the power of their disease. We are hopeful for every addicted person, since we have seen lasting recoveries of addicts at all stages of this dreadful disease. It is never too early and never too late to get well from addiction, whether the addiction occurs with or without a comorbid anxiety disorder. We also want to be sure that worried anxious people do not mislabel themselves as addicted and because of this mislabeling deprive themselves of the benefits medicine can bring to them.

PART FOUR

Anxiety over the Life Span

CHAPTER 17

Anxiety and Friends, Family, and Support People

The person who has the symptoms of anxiety is not the only one who suffers in a family struggling with an anxiety disorder. Many of the high costs of phobic avoidance are paid by family members. A vacation is a lot less fun if your friend, child, spouse, or parent has a phobia that prevents him or her from going along or that turns the joyous experience of a vacation into a torture for the anxious person and, because of this suffering, for everyone else.

Sometimes frustrated friends and family think the clinically anxious person is malingering or trying to manipulate them to get his or her own way in difficult situations. This may have some truth as the anxiety takes over much of the person's life, but in the end it is never the whole, or even the most important, part of the story. This is because anxiety is so terribly painful. No one would choose to have an anxiety disorder, no matter how desperately he or she sought to manipulate someone else to do something. The pain of the anxiety is simply too great to permit that sort of manipulation.

It is hard for children to understand why their phobic mothers or fathers do not drive them to school or to after-school activities the way other children's parents do. Even when a friend or family member tries to understand and to help solve anxiety problems by talking with the anxious person, the words of the anxious person can be confusing and disturbing because this is not a rational disorder. If the kitchen is a mess, why does a mother with OCD not allow her teenage son to clean it? How can a teacher understand that a child would restrict the intake of liquids all day at school because he or she is so scared of going into a bathroom without windows? It is often hard not to be angered by the explanations given for phobic behaviors.

Our family's confrontation with an anxiety disorder was relatively brief and had a happy outcome, as Caroline no longer has symptoms of the claustrophobia that plagued her as a child. Brief though this interlude was, however, it clearly had a profound impact on our lives, and as a result the anxiety disorders have become the focus of our professional work. Each of us has incorporated the techniques that are used in the Anxiety Cure into our own lives not only to deal with our own anxieties but also to deal with many of life's problems. Each of us has devoted much of our professional lives to helping people with anxiety disorders. Not only have our experiences helped us in our professional work, but we also have learned from our experiences to respect the suffering that is part of anxiety disorders while maintaining a tough-love stance—filled with hope, no matter how many prior efforts have failed—to overcoming these disturbing problems.

Frustrating Attempts to Help

One of the first signs of trouble for friends and families confronting anxiety disorders is often the control over the behaviors of others that anxious people exert in order to decrease their intense anxieties. These attempts at control may include incomprehensible tasks that make others feel unimportant or enslaved by the anxiety dragon, an unreasonable taskmaster. Friends and family members are being victimized as they are pulled into the anxious person's world. The passion surrounding this type of irrational behavioral control can be intense, often leading to the capitulation of nonanxious people, who would rather yield than suffer through the worry of having done something "wrong." Powerful feelings of fear and anger can erode relationships, alienate friends and family members, and, ultimately, cause all concerned to feel alone, rejected, and hopeless. This is a common but terrible consequence of allowing the anxiety, fear, and panic to become more real and more important than the caring bonds among friends and family.

Most anxious people try to hide their manipulations of their friends and family members because they know their needs are unreasonable. All too often, friends and family members are either oblivious to the deep-seated irrationality behind certain requests or preferences or they are willing to give in to get along. Only in extreme situations is the anxious person willing to come out and label the request for what it is: a do-or-die requirement for any sort of peaceful family life. The power of the anxiety disease is so great that no matter how loving and easygoing the anxious person is in other aspects of family relationships, when it comes to phobic avoidance or obsessive-compulsive rituals, no compromise or reason can be tolerated. This is a surefire recipe for family crisis.

Imaginary Victims

Mary was a twenty-four-year-old woman with OCD. She had a terrible fear that while she was driving, or even riding as a passenger in a car, she would hit or witness the hitting of a pedestrian. This had been a problem for her since she was sixteen years old when she took a driver's education course that showed a movie about drinking and driving. The movie ended with a scene of a pedestrian having been struck and killed by a hit-and-run driver. At the time she came to us for help, Mary did not drink at all for fear that she suddenly might have to drive. She lived in the city, so she could usually take the subway. Her mother drove her to her part-time job on the weekends. Whenever Mary had the obsession that her mother had hit a pedestrian during their drive to work, her mother gave in to Mary's request to turn around and retrace their route to search for the imagined victim. This took them so much extra time that they routinely took twice the ordinary driving time to get to their destination. Mary's mother had to choose between going on a fruitless search or enduring the pain and anger of the anxious passenger. Years before she had chosen the easy route of going along with Mary's fear, although the mother knew the search was pointless. This had become so much a part of their lives that they rarely discussed the fact that Mary's request was outrageous and wasteful.

In situations where this type of behavioral control has gone on for many years, it may seem normal to the nonanxious friends and family members to do things in odd ways. They may have adapted to cover up the anxiety problem by ignoring the strange ways that they are all forced to act. Often families in which this has happened are quite isolated socially, because often they are defending the anxious person from the scrutiny of the rest of the world.

Families and friends who have protected a person with an anxiety disorder have a difficult task during treatment, as they have to unlearn all of the unreasonable, protective, and limiting behaviors that they performed previously. Instead, they have to see that their protection is keeping the anxiety disorder alive and that it is a disservice to an anxious person to give in to the tyrannically anxious feelings because it reinforces the anxious person's perception that this behavior is acceptable. *Once friends and family members stop giving in to the unreasonable demands of the anxious person and begin to do things in a more healthy manner, anxiety and stress will lessen for both the anxious person and for those who care about that person.*

This reduction in anxiety is especially true for nonanxious family members and friends who have been supporting the anxiety, since these people often do things the "wrong" way. They do not have the powerful, irrational internal feelings that would dictate the oddly specific way in which things must be done, and they are repeatedly being taken to task for this by the distressed anxious person.

Stop Supporting the Anxiety Disorder

No longer supporting the anxiety disorder can be easy for some friends and families, but for most it is a difficult process filled with moments of uncertainty. If the person suffering from an anxiety disorder is motivated to overcome the disability of the anxiety-driven behavior, then this process is much easier.

Mary sought help in a crisis because her job transferred her to the suburbs, which necessitated her driving to work daily at the same time that her mother developed an illness that forced her to restrict her driving. What had been a stable pattern for Mary and her mother for years suddenly collapsed, and both of them had to confront the fact that Mary was unable to continue as before, when she had been relying on her mother. Mary's mother felt bad when she realized that her loving support of her daughter had allowed Mary to stay relatively free of anxiety but only at a high price. Mary suffered because of her limited life, especially socially. Once she sought help, Mary worked hard on learning new techniques and practicing new behaviors because she was motivated to keep her job. Mary's mother was extremely supportive of her and praised her hard work. This story ended successfully, with the daughter able to drive herself directly to her destination without having to retrace her route and without severe anxiety.

In situations where a friend or family member has decided not to tolerate the dragon's dictates any longer, but where the anxious person is not a willing participant, there will be many difficult decisions to make. It is easy to imagine how this story would have gone if Mary had not wanted to change her behavior. Her mother would have been caught between her desire to help her daughter live a normal life and her desire not to upset her anxious daughter. This sad dilemma happens frequently and leads not only to breaks in friendships and family bonds but also to increased limitations and increased suffering for the anxious person. It is truly important to keep the message of tough love for the anxious person and anger at the anxiety disorder dragon's tyranny clear at all times.

Once Mary's mother learned about OCD and how to treat it, she could say that it was out of love for her daughter that she no longer drove her to work. She learned that trying to minimize the symptoms of anxiety at the time they first occurred by giving in to Mary's illness in reality had prolonged and intensified her daughter's suffering. If, despite the best efforts of friends and family, the anxious person insists on continuing to give in to anxious thoughts, it may be time to move on without that person.

What if Mary's mother had learned about the treatment for OCD and shared her knowledge with Mary, but Mary had not wanted to confront her fears? If her mother then decided to move to another city to convalesce from her illness, that would be an example of moving on and forcing the anxious person to change the present anxiety-driven behavior.

The most common example of this type of situation is in families where one member has agoraphobia or a flying or driving phobia, and a family vacation, an out-of-town wedding, or another obligation is scheduled months in advance. It may be necessary for the family to choose to go on the trip and to lovingly encourage the phobic family member to join them but not to alter their plans if the anxious person chooses not to attempt to confront his or her fears. It is important to stress that this is done out of a desire to help the anxious person get well and to show that there is no reason to give in to the fear. If the dragon is allowed to control the family's activities, then the dragon not only puts the anxious person in prison, but also the entire family is held hostage.

There may be complicating reasons why a person fails to get well from an anxiety disorder. For example, posttraumatic stress disorder (PTSD) can be complicated by depression, addiction, or legal and financial consequences of the event, such as liability lawsuits and disability payments. Work on PTSD with the Anxiety Cure may be severely hampered if there are financial reasons for a person to benefit from having the anxiety problem. People who have secondary gains from PTSD and other anxiety disorders associated with liability have a conflicted motivation for recovery: if they get better, they lose the "perk" of having the problem. This is important to evaluate early on in your recovery because we have found that people with secondary gains do not fare well in terms of long-term recovery from their anxiety disorder. One way to handle this is to settle the lawsuits before trying to begin to get well. That solves the problem of secondary gain. People who are receiving disability payments for an anxiety disorder have a more difficult problem and may need to get off the disability before they can get well.

Friends and family members can be a major source of hope during the recovery process because they are not bound by irrational anxious thoughts and feelings. Instead, healthy friends and family members can offer their own realistic assessments of a situation in an effort to reeducate the anxious person about the risks involved in a particular situation. For example, Mary's mother told her daughter that when Mary was not in the car, she herself *never* feared hitting a pedestrian while driving and *never* turned around to retrace her route. This was a great surprise to Mary and a big step forward in her process of recovery.

Support Efforts to Get Well

Friend and family confrontations about anxious irrationality can succeed only when nonanxious family members accept the intensity and reality of the suffering of the anxious person. Mary's mother did not feel anxious about hitting a pedestrian when she drove. She did not have obsessions, and she did not have panic and dread when she drove. Mary did have terrible thoughts and painful feelings. Only when Mary's mother respected those serious, painful thoughts and feelings, and just how hard it was for Mary to confront them, could Mary begin, in small steps, to confront her fears.

Friends and family members cannot help anxious people by minimizing their suffering or by humiliating them. The thoughts and feelings of the anxious person are real, not imaginary. They are false alarms of the anxious brain, false signs that are experienced as more real and more important than any other part of the anxious person's life. It is only with time and great effort that anxious people can reclaim their lives from being hijacked by the anxiety disorder dragon. Friends and family members need to be patient and respectful, as well as firm and supportive, as they gradually confront the anxious person's pathological thoughts and feelings.

What Do You Tell People?

Many people with family members who suffer from anxiety disorders are confused about what to tell others about the problem, especially what to tell children about their parents' anxiety problems or what to tell other children about their anxious child's problems. While there is no point in wearing a figurative signboard advertising any illness, including anxiety disorders, it is generally wise to let people know the facts if they will be interacting with someone who has an anxiety disorder. That means telling teachers about children's anxiety problems and family members about anxiety disorders. It sometimes means telling employers if the anxiety disorders show up in workplace behaviors. See Chapters 8 and 18 for more thoughts on whom to tell about anxiety disorders and what to tell them.

It is important not to let outrage at the anxious person drive you apart. Instead, both of you should be angry at the anxiety disorder. Think of the dragon as your common adversary. Use your outrage to fuel the family's recognition of having a shared problem and finding a good family-based solution. Together you can act out new, healthy responses to the dragon's distorted message. Do not let him take back the new freedom you are finding. As a united family, you can be strong for one another, and you can be your own best teachers.

There are rewards for a family that has gone through this process together. Just as everyone suffers with the person who is limited by anxiety, so also does everyone benefit once the anxiety is conquered. As one wife whose husband recovered from severe agoraphobia put it, "I never knew we could be so happy or that we could have such a wonderful life together."

Provide Hope

We ask you to be patient and to build hope for a better life for your anxious person. Getting well starts with acknowledgment of the disease, with acceptance of the pain and the losses that are caused by the disease. Without that pain, and the honest acceptance of it, it is not possible to make the effort needed to get well. In that important sense, the pain of an anxiety disorder is constructive. It is motivating, or it can be. The next step is hope. Your anxious person has to have hope that life can get better, that he or she can get well. Without hope, even with pain, your anxious person will not do the work needed to get well. The third necessary ingredient is to see a path to getting well. That is what the Anxiety Cure offers.

How to Be a Support Person

When a person is ill with a physical disease, be it a broken bone or a long-term chronic illness, there is usually a support person to offer care. Because anxiety disorders, and mental health problems in general, are often not acknowledged to be as serious as physical ailments, there is seldom a recognition of the need for a support person. Far from being given encouragement for the hard work that you do to support your anxious person, you may instead have been unsure of your role in his or her recovery, and you even may have been accused by others of prolonging the illness.

The support person is vital to the Anxiety Cure program. Without you, the program works much less well. A support person can be a parent, a child, a spouse, a friend, or a neighbor. We want you to learn how to be helpful in the process of recovery. You do not have to be an expert in anxiety disorders or a genius in the treatment of mental disorders to have a success with the Anxiety Cure. As a support person, you need patience and persistence. You need to respect your anxious person and his or her efforts to succeed in the program.

Choose to Accept or Decline Being a Support Person

You may find that you have unintentionally become a support person—for example, if your child has developed an anxiety problem—or you may have been specifically recruited for this job by your anxious person. Either way, we ask you to think carefully about taking on the tasks that we outline here. It is not in the interest of either your anxious person or you to take this responsibility if you feel upset or overburdened by the obligation. Sometimes being too close to the problem could keep you from being empathetic and prevent you from understanding the necessity of some important recommendations, such as breaking up the work needed into manageably small steps. Carefully read through this chapter to see what is expected of you and then have an honest conversation with your anxious person about your willingness to fulfill this important role. If you would rather not be a support person, remember that there are other ways for you to help your anxious person, and there are other people who can be his or her support person. Even if no other candidates seem possible to you right now, be sure to review Chapter 8 about selecting a support person to get new ideas.

Responsibilities of the Support Person

To be useful as a support person, you must be genuinely interested in the welfare of the anxious person and be willing to take the time to learn how to help. There are two main commitments that support people must make to be effective:

1. Take the time to understand the anxious person's problems.
2. Make time for a regular practice to overcome these problems.

To learn more about anxiety, you should start by reading this book. You will learn that anxiety diseases are complex, painful, humiliating, and ever-changing. Nevertheless, anxiety disorders are ultimately understandable and manageable. Words like panic and obsession will take on new meanings for you as you see just how powerful these experiences are. They are not similar to the ordinary anxiety experienced by people who do not suffer from anxiety disorders. The painful feelings of clinically significant anxiety are so devastating that they bring even the strongest people to their knees.

Respect, but do not fear, these distressing thoughts and feelings. Above all, respect your anxious person for what he or she is up against and for whatever efforts he or she makes to get well. Acknowledge that you do not understand his or her feelings and (unless you have an anxiety disorder yourself) that you never will fully understand them. Even though you do not understand the experiences of your anxious person, with help from the Anxiety Cure program you can understand the disorder and what it takes to get well. You will not understand your anxious person or be able to help him or her unless you honestly respect the great suffering and disability these disorders cause.

Practice, Practice, Practice

As we discussed earlier in this book in Part Two, your anxious person must practice in his or her discomfort zone at least once a week in order to get well. We ask that you participate in at least one practice session a week. Initially, this may mean simply meeting to talk about the problem, which in itself may cause your anxious person to be in his or her discomfort zone. Ultimately, practice will require you to accompany your anxious person to the anxiety-provoking situation to practice. During these practice sessions, ask your anxious person to describe his or her feelings every step of the way. Ask him or her what you can do to be helpful. The best way to be helpful changes rapidly, so you will need to understand how to be the most helpful at each specific time during practice sessions. You will be surprised by just how beneficial it is for you to be there, being both supportive and encouraging. These practice sessions should last at least thirty minutes to give you time to use the Wizard Wisdom antianxiety strategies you learned in Step 2.

You do not need to have answers. If you join your anxious person in becoming a student of anxiety, you will have been tremendously helpful. Ask what his or her feelings and thoughts are as the practice goes on. Ask what you can do to help. Remind your anxious person how you see the situation at the time. Tell your anxious person how he or she looks to you during practice. You will be surprised that your anxious person thinks he or she looks bizarre or distraught, although you and any other outside observer are unlikely to see any manifestation of the inner panic. It is likely to be surprising (and reassuring) to your anxious person that he or she looks pretty normal, even though feeling a high level of panic. If your anxious person asks you a question you cannot answer, say that. No one expects you to be an expert. Your job is to be patient and supportive while you learn from your anxious person more about the problems that anxiety causes.

During this practice time or at a different time, we ask that you review the journal entries or practice sheets that your anxious person will use to record his or her practice and future goals. Your job is to be supportive, encouraging, and patient. Progress may be slow at times, but that is fine. As long as there is regular and repeated practice, there will be progress. Always give praise and always give outs. That means that when your anxious person asks you to let him or her get out of a situation, you always say yes.

An out is different from an excuse or fleeing a situation. While it is wrong to avoid an unpleasant activity due to anxiety, it may be necessary to ask for a six-month delay in jury duty, for example, to permit an agoraphobic person to practice for the experience. That practice usually involves visiting the court and jury setting and watching the process. The principle is always to break the task down into small steps and to repeat them over and over until they become manageable, if not easy.

During practice and as you review the practice journal, be sure to show sincere interest and optimism. Keep the warming fire of hope alight at all times. Do not be harsh or judgmental. Do not say, "Go do it. Don't be a wimp!" Say instead, "I know it is hard for you, and I am sorry about that. Can I help break it down into smaller steps for you to practice?" Your job is a hard one in the sense that you need to be both firm and gentle at the same time. You need to be persistent and patient, too. We have tremendous respect for the challenges you face in dealing with your anxious person. We hope that you and your anxious person can find the serenity of recovery and the gift of self-esteem that comes from doing a hard job well.

Seek Professional Help for Troubling Situations

Sometimes a person with an anxiety problem is unwilling to do the work needed to get well. Although he or she suffers and lives a crippled life, there can be too much fear or worry to enable effective action to solve the problem. Such a person has our sympathy because we are aware of just how terribly painful these illnesses are. Anxious people who suffer without working on a cure are among the most difficult people to help.

Most anxious people will use this program effectively and practice on a fairly regular schedule. If, however, your anxious person does not practice regularly, which this program encourages, then as a support person, you have no good moves. If you criticize or pressure your anxious person to practice, this will lower his or her already low self-esteem. If you accept the passivity and avoidance and find ways to make life easier for the anxious person despite the disability caused by the disease, then you are enabling the disease to continue to control the anxious person's life. Either way, with criticism or avoidance, both you and your anxious person lose.

It is important to remember that you are a *support person*—ultimately, this is your anxious person's problem, not yours. Point out the bind that you are in and, to help with your work, suggest finding a psychiatrist or therapist who specializes in treating anxiety disorders. Perhaps some medicine or help from an experienced professional therapist can get both of you back on track. Recall that support people can be helpful in most situations, but you are not likely to be able to handle the most difficult problems by yourself. Do not hesitate to get help if you feel over-whelmed.

Four Trouble Signs for Support People

When to seek professional help:

1. Your anxious person is not practicing in his or her discomfort zone regularly.
2. No progress is being made toward achieving your anxious person's goals.
3. Your anxious person's anxiety level has not dropped in practice set-tings, even with repeated exposure.
4. You feel overwhelmed and unprepared to deal with your anxious person's level of distress.

CHAPTER 18

Anxiety and Your Work Life

Anxiety has a profound impact on work life. In the past you may have limited your choice of jobs or chances for promotion to appease your anxiety dragon. Perhaps you chose a job based on its proximity to your home, a subway, or a familiar street. Once you have begun to recover from an anxiety disorder, you may find that the job that you tolerated because it allowed you to avoid anxious situations no longer fits your needs. Prior to the Anxiety Cure, you may have tried to reduce stress by having a job that was easy for you. This strategy almost always ends up actually increasing anxiety symptoms, as you find that you have too much time to worry while at work.

Or in contrast, perhaps to reduce your anxiety, you may work more than you would like to. Some anxious people find that the time they are on the job is mostly anxiety free, as concentration clearly must be on work, not on anxious thoughts. This helps block anxious thoughts and keeps the hours at work relatively clear of anxiety. Worry about work when away from your job coupled with reduced anxiety while at work can make work the major focus of your life to the exclusion of friends and family as well as leisure activities. If your work has been affected by your anxiety disorder, chances are you have had a problem balancing work and play in your life. You may want to review Step 7, Structure Your Life without Anxiety, to think about what parts of your life could use development as you fit your job into your life.

Avoid Avoidance

Whether you work too little or too much or you are in a job that does not challenge you to grow, if you are in a job that does not allow you to be exposed regularly to your anxious situations, then you are missing a daily chance to practice your anxiety cure at work.

Fear of Driving

Amanda was a twenty-nine-year-old teacher with a driving phobia. She chose to teach at a school that was on her husband's way to work so he could drop her off and pick her up every day on his way to and from his office. This meant that Amanda had to stay at work from 7:30 A.M. until 7:00 P.M., even though her job ended at 3:00 P.M. The school was locked at 5:00 P.M., so Amanda had to walk to a local public library and wait there for her husband. Occasionally, however, her husband had to travel out of town or the library was closed for various reasons. This created a crisis for Amanda, who worried about how she would get to and from work.

As she used the eight steps of the Anxiety Cure, Amanda gradually began to drive herself to work. She found, however, that when she had setbacks, she would again rely on the old pattern of having her husband drive her and pick her up.

Amanda had hoped to return to graduate school one day, so in order to see how she would like a particular course of study, she decided to take classes while she was still teaching. This positive choice forced Amanda to drive herself to work, since she needed to get from her teaching job to the university campus. Amanda found that her anxiety went down once she knew that falling back on relying on her husband to drive her back and forth to work was no longer an option. She knew she would drive herself, and even if she had some anxiety, she used the techniques she had learned to move forward with her day. She was surprised to see that she had previously put a lot of energy into choosing whether or not to have her husband drive her. Once it was not a choice, she simply drove herself and felt a lot less anxious.

Additionally, Amanda found that she had spent time during the day, especially after the school day ended as she waited for her husband to pick her up, thinking of excuses not to drive places with friends or figuring out how to get places when her usual avoidance strategies broke down. Once she was back in graduate school driving herself, she had no time for this type of worrying. She felt less anxious during the day, even though she was much busier.

Evaluate Options

Once you stop making anxiety-driven decisions and instead seek to make choices based on what is best for you, you will find that there are more options for employment than you had imagined. This does not mean you have to be busy with paid employment or be in a terribly hard job. Everyone has different priorities. You may want to volunteer at a museum or spend time fishing or playing volleyball in a league. To overcome the dragon, you need to choose how much you work, what work you do, and where you work. You are then in charge of your life.

Low self-esteem is a common problem with people suffering from anxiety problems. This in itself can cause you to avoid work for which you are well suited. Be sure not to sell yourself short. Talk with your friends and family about your skills and interests, and consider doing the work in a book like *What Color Is Your Parachute?* (see Suggested Additional Reading) or taking a career-development class at your community college. *You may be so accustomed to limiting your choices about work because of anxious avoidance that you are unfamiliar with thinking of all the choices that you have.*

Urge for Perfection

Maria was a forty-five-year-old homemaker with GAD. Her two sons were in high school, a time when she had always planned to return to paid employment to begin saving for their college tuitions. Maria had put all of her attention into her husband's career, moving when he needed the family to move for a better job and caring for their children while he worked long hours. Without realizing what was happening, she spent more and more time worrying. Her efforts to eliminate her worries led to her attempts to become the perfect homemaker. For example, she packed her sons' bags for camp a week ahead of time to be sure they had all the clean clothes they needed. She cooked elaborate meals for religious holidays, and she spent hours studying the family's ethnic heritage to bring more traditions into her sons' lives.

This drive for perfection, however, did not make the dragon happy. Instead, Maria felt she had no self-esteem because she did not have a college education and a paying job. She found, however, that eighteen years of being out of the workforce had left her feeling that she had nothing to offer an employer. On one hand, she wanted to return to school or to find a job. On the other, her inner worry machine undermined her self-confidence so thoroughly that she was afraid to make a start.

For Maria, as for many people with anxiety disorders stuck in work that does not suit them economically, socially, or intellectually, it is important to upgrade work skills with the Anxiety Cure by looking nonanxiously at the alternatives open to you. Maria used the Anxiety Cure program to make tentative progress toward preventing worries from dominating her life.

She prioritized finding a job and spent two hours a day learning about job options and practicing her office skills. She began to assign household chores to her family and tolerated their less-than-perfect results. Maria managed the anxiety that these changes caused her, noticing that overall her anxiety was actually lessened by reducing her perfectionistic tendencies. She went on a job interview. In preparation, she role-played the interview with a friend. Her friend had encouraged her to act as though she were confident of her abilities.

To her amazement, Maria landed a job at a large corporation. Within a matter of months, her efficiency and hard work had won the approval of her bosses, earning her a promotion. Maria's self-confidence soared as she found that the busier she was with the new opportunities that she had chosen, the less her anxiety bothered her.

How to Relate to Bosses and Coworkers

Throughout the Anxiety Cure we recommend that you be honest about your anxiety with friends and family. These people who care about you can be enormously helpful as you work to get free of your anxiety. We have stressed, however, that honesty about anxiety does not always extend to bosses and coworkers. Think of the difference between the relationships you have with your friends and family and those with your bosses and coworkers as being like having a private face versus having a public mask. In many ways, everyone differentiates between private and public relationships. For example, we dress differently around our friends and family from the way we do at work. We may talk differently and say different things about our personal experiences. A man whose wife has left him, for example, may remove her picture from his desk and simply ask the human resources department to take her name off of his insurance policy. While his boss and coworkers know there is trouble at home because the wife no longer calls him and her photograph is gone, most people at work respect his privacy and do not ask him the details about this personal problem.

Often people with anxiety do not think through what they want to say (or not say) to employers or coworkers. The long-term employment implications of a panic attack can seem insignificant while you are having one. At a less anxious time, think through how you want to handle anxiety at work. If your anxiety symptoms are noticeable, like sweating or shaking, people may ask questions out of concern for you. How do you want to answer? Right or wrong, remember that there is still a stigma about mental health problems. What you say to one well-meaning colleague can easily become gossip. While we never recommend lying, a careful choice of words may be necessary to maintain the professional, public mask that you have chosen. If physical symptoms like sweating or shaking are a noticeable problem, for example, it may be necessary to say something like "I have a little trouble with that now and then. My doctor is trying to help me with it. Thanks for caring, but I am really all right." This reassures your concerned coworker, and while it is not a lie, it does not specifically explain the anxiety that is the cause of your physical symptoms.

Think about what to tell people on a need-to-know basis. Keep in mind that no one is as focused on you as you are. No one is going to notice your lack of concentration and physical symptoms as much as you are.

In general, anxious people are far more critical of themselves than other people are. No matter how much you sweat or shake, for example, it is unlikely that anyone at work will notice because they are too busy thinking about themselves to think about you (as you are too busy thinking about yourself to think much about them!). Assume that they do not notice your anxiety unless someone says something. If they do, the most important thing you can say is that you know about the problem but that it is not as serious as heart disease or other major medical problems.

Some people are always open about having an anxiety problem and tell us that they have not had difficulty at work even with this self-disclosure. We also have found that some people who disclose too much information about having an anxiety problem end up with limited job responsibilities. This may happen out of the employer's fear of overwhelming the anxious person or not wanting the job to be mishandled because of anxiety. Either way, the anxious person can end up being deprived of opportunities to advance. Prior to the Anxiety Cure this may have been an acceptable trade-off for you: if you tell people at work about having anxiety then you will have more escapes if anxiety strikes, even if it means limiting your future.

Remember that outs are always available even if people around you do not know you have anxiety. They just take a little more planning and creativity than escaping does. Using outs also means that you will have to come back to the situation that has been a problem in the past. This is helpful for your anxiety recovery. In general, then, your public face will help you decrease your anxiety and increase your self-confidence as you see that you can function even though the people around you do not know about, or cater to, your anxiety problem. In this way, your anxiety problem is similar to most other health problems: it is mostly a private matter.

If your anxiety gets in the way of your work, consider talking with your Employee Assistance Program (EAP) counselor about the problem if your employer has an EAP. Do not use your anxiety problem as an excuse to get special benefits that everyone else wants. We were asked to consult on a case of a woman who said she had claustrophobia and therefore needed an office with a window. Her position and seniority did not qualify her for a window office. When we offered her help with her claustrophobia so she could get along without a window, she refused. She did not want to get well; she wanted a window office.

In another situation, a man claimed he failed an oral test because of social phobia. His employer let him take the test three times, twice with his therapist present. He used medicines as needed. He functioned well in many social settings at work, including making presentations. Passing this oral exam was a requirement for his job. When his employer rejected his claim that he be excused from the exam, he sued for discrimination because of his anxiety. He lost the case, as we believe he should have. His problem was not social phobia but not knowing the material.

Assess Whether to Work Alone

Different jobs can be especially good or bad fits for people with anxiety problems. Working alone presents a unique set of problems and opportunities, and with the growth in telecommuting, it is important to pay special attention to this possibility. Parents who choose to stay at home with their children face the dilemma of working alone or working with adults. The line between avoidance as phobic response and avoidance for personal preference can be blurry when it comes to working alone. Are you choosing this type of work so you do not have to confront your anxiety of public speaking or because the opportunity is a good one for you?

Open Your Mind

Work, like most other areas of your life, is not a one-time decision. Thankfully, most of us get many opportunities to do different types of work. Open your mind to different possibilities and even try different work options and environments and different levels of private faces versus public masks. Above all, keep a record in your journal of how each change affects your anxiety level. This will enable you to decide whether the changes you make have any overall benefit or not and will give you ideas about which direction to go next.

Peter

Peter, a thirty-one-year-old with social phobia and spontaneous panic attacks, had a difficult time with this choice in his chronic anxiety. In the ten years after he graduated from college, Peter had seven different jobs and was fired from three of them. He left two jobs because he had panic at work and could not face going back into that situation. Two other jobs he left because he had conflicts with coworkers and did not want to work with them anymore.

Peter recently faced the fact that he was an alcoholic. He sought help in a crisis, having been fired from a job because his drinking was out of control. He was afraid he was going to be evicted from his rented room because he had been unable to pay the rent.

Peter began intensive work on his addiction, attending Alcoholics Anonymous meetings daily, working toward ninety meetings in ninety days, a standard path to recovery. With so much energy focused on his recovery from alcoholism, he needed a way to make money to pay the rent before he could work on his anxiety problems. He found a job as a legal transcriber, which he could do from home. He began working long hours to earn the money to pay his overdue bills. For Peter, this ability to work alone solved a short-term problem of needing a steady job that would not be threatened by his anxiety problems. But this job did not help him recover from anxiety; it merely marked time until he could do the work he needed to get well. This type of interim bargain with the dragon can be fine if a short time is needed to prioritize other areas. In Peter's case, he decided to begin working on his anxiety after he had been clean and sober for ninety days.

At that time he reevaluated his anxiety and realized that without even being aware of it, he had been doing practice for his social phobia daily—at AA meetings. He built on that success by continuing to do legal transcriptions from home in the evenings to pay his bills and volunteering at his church office part-time during the day, where he wrote grant proposals for a program to assist needy children. This volunteer work helped him feel more confident about his ability to work with others. He felt appreciated for his writing skills. He felt good that he was helping others through his work. Instead of seeking a different job, he chose to continue this combination of working from home and volunteer work, which he found to be a good balance. It is not necessary to challenge yourself in every arena of your life to live your life fully. If working alone allows you to do other things you would not be able to do with regular office work, then it may actually help you regain control of your life.

Laura

Laura was a forty-five-year-old woman with OCD who worked from home assisting her husband with his business. She used this home-based business as an opportunity to avoid driving. She went out only when her husband drove. She did not socialize with other people other than eating an occasional meal at her parents' home. Her husband initially supported her choice to leave her office job to help him full-time as his business grew, but he found that more and more of their time was taken over by Laura's rituals and avoidance. He sought help because she did not recognize that this was a problem.

Working from home had allowed Laura to stop ignoring her obsessions and instead to devote more and more time to them. Maintaining her public mask in her office job had prevented her from completely submitting to anxiety. Working at home, she could let her husband see all the anxiety she had. He worked with her to give the anxiety what it wanted. The result, sadly but predictably, was that anxiety increasingly dominated the lives of both Laura and her husband when she worked at home.

CHAPTER 19

Anxiety and Aging

Although anxiety disorders affect people of all ages from early childhood until death, the older anxious person faces several specific problems. We use the term "older" because these problems may be encountered at any age from midlife on and are not just a concern for the elderly. An anxious person who has a disability from a car accident at age thirty faces some of the same dilemmas as a much older retiree. The dilemmas of aging and anxiety revolve around the realities of human mortality. For the anxious person, any sign of physical decline is an opportunity for the worry machine to spin out of control, predicting terrible problems in the immediate future. This process of fear of bodily decline makes aging a time fraught with the potential for upsurges in anxiety. Additionally, friends and family can be hard-pressed to cope, as there is often some basis to the worry at this stage of life. Most families marshal resources of time and money to solve the presenting medical and/or social problems of aging without realizing that in many cases it is worry, not declining health, that cripples the aging anxious person.

Unfortunately, focusing on the anxious person's physical health is like reassuring him or her that nothing is wrong. It leads the anxious person to try harder to convince those around him or her that something *is* wrong, since he or she feels so bad emotionally. This leads friends and family to feel exhausted by the endless expressions of worry that know no end and that fail to respond to reasonable reassurances.

For example, Charles was a fifty-two-year-old executive at a major corporation. He earned a good salary, his social life was based on business acquaintances, and he looked forward to retiring at sixty with a nice pension. Charles had been a worried person all his life. His worry was helpful at work as it made him detail oriented, punctual, and determined to produce a good result. Without warning, his corporation was purchased in a hostile takeover, and he lost his job with no severance package and no prospect of a pension for many years. His wife had worked part-time, but when Charles lost his job, she quickly picked up more hours and was gone from home all day during the workweek. Charles found himself alone at home and overwhelmed with his unleashed worry. He could not find a job in his field. He realized that being hired as a middle-aged executive was unlikely. A year after he was fired, Charles began to deliver pizzas in the evening to earn some extra money and to leave his days free for developing his own consulting business. The consulting business was slow to develop, so he spent most of his time sitting alone at his desk at home, worrying and obsessively sorting bills and papers.

Charles's wife sought help for him, as she found his anxiety and depression to be unbearable. Finally seeking help for problems he no longer thought he could handle on his own, Charles used the Anxiety Cure techniques along with medicine to reduce his anxiety and depression. After several months of treatment, he developed a new way of looking at his life. It was not the happy life he had dreamed of—a life leading to retirement, playing golf, and a second home in a retirement community. That dream was gone. Charles saw that he now had years of freedom that he had never expected. He began to plan how to use the time to his best advantage and to see this crisis as an opportunity for a new, good life. He accepted what had happened to him and looked for the real opportunities this unchosen life had for him and his wife. When he did that, he was able to help more at home (a role reversal that pleased both him and his wife), and he enjoyed the new experiences his fledgling consulting business brought to him. He spent more time with his children and grandchildren.

Retirement

Retirement is imagined by most people to be a golden time—the light at the end of the tunnel of work. Freedom from financial worries, child-rearing tasks, the drudgery of work, and all the time in the world to pursue leisure activities. The tanned, fit senior playing golf on a beautiful green with a group of healthy friends is a common fantasy. Yet for most anxious people, the reality of retirement is a world away from this idyllic picture. The jobs and responsibilities of work life, as well as responsibilities for children, that were imagined to be the causes of anxiety suddenly are gone.

Many anxious retirees are devastated when, with the increased open time, their anxiety levels soar. External responsibilities helped contain their anxiety.

With those responsibilities gone, anxiety has free rein to dominate your whole life. You have more time to feed the dragon with your worries.

As you can see from other parts of this chapter, suddenly new sources of anxiety are present in your life as you age. They join the familiar stable of worries that have been with you throughout your life. The added worries of retirement are a shock to most people, causing embarrassment as friends and family who are still working enviously assume you are having the time of your life. And what explanations for this unhappiness can you offer? No one seems to listen or to take your worries seriously, even though they feel so real to you.

Some people who have never had significant trouble with anxiety find retirement triggers the onset of their anxiety disorder. Some people immediately return to the workforce to once again blame anxious feelings on job stress and to contain anxiety with ever-present responsibilities. Others give in to the anxiety and lose precious years to worry and the demands of the voracious dragon. We suggest that retirement be viewed as an opportunity for practicing your antianxiety techniques on many fronts. Especially use the ideas in Step 7, Structure Your Life without Anxiety, and work to build your own dragon armor specifically tailored for this part of your life.

This is your life, not the dragon's. Do not let him convince you that there is a reason he must have your life now. Whatever is going on in your life—whatever sadness, physical problems, or financial concerns—the worry machine will make it worse if you let it. Do not be ashamed of the troubles retirement causes for you, and do not hide them from people who care about you. This does you and them no good. Simply talking about your fear of fear can help you sort out the real worries from the exaggerated worries and can reduce your anxiety tremendously.

What is the difference between "real" worries and "exaggerated" worries? Real worries are ones that a nonanxious person in the same situation would have. Real worries are solvable problems that respond to practical solutions. Exaggerated worries are worries that nonanxious people would not have in similar settings. Exaggerated worries are not solvable in practical ways. They flourish regardless of practical steps to reduce them. You can work on your anxiety and bring your retirement closer to the idyllic experience you had hoped for if you build working on your anxiety into your retirement plans. Use your anxiety as a springboard.

The Elderly and Medicines

As with other types of medicines, there are special considerations for people age sixty-five and over using medicines for anxiety. *Usually, the same medicines that are useful for younger people with anxiety will be useful for older people as well, but elderly people may need lower doses.* See the table below for typical dosages of antianxiety medicines for older people. You will need to be monitored more closely by your prescribing doctor than a younger person because side effects can be more serious. For example, the drowsiness that can accompany using a benzodiazepine can lead to a fall, which could have devastating consequences (such as a fractured hip) for an older person.

Be sure to talk to your doctor about any special concerns that you have before you begin taking medicine, and report side effects promptly so adjustments in dosages can be made. Also be sure to tell all your doctors what medicines you are taking to avoid problems of drug interactions. If you are taking any medicine, whether a prescription or an over-the-counter medicine, check with your doctor before taking any other medicine, even if you have used the medicine previously.

Typical Doses of Medications Used to Treat Anxiety in Adults (Ages 65 and Older)

Antidepressants	*Dosage*
Celexa (citalopram)	10–40 mg/day
Effexor (venlafaxine)	75–150 mg/day
Lexapro (escitalopram)	5–10 mg/day
Luvox (fluvoxamine)	50–150 mg/day
Paxil (paroxetine)	5–20 mg/day
Prozac (fluoxetine)	5–10 mg/day
Serzone (nefazodone)	100–300 mg/day
Tofranil (imipramine)	25–100 mg/day
Zoloft (sertraline)	25–100 mg/day
Benzodiazepines	*Dosage*
Ativan (lorazepam)	0.5 mg 1 to 3 times/day
Klonopin (clonazepam)	0.25 mg 1 to 3 times/day
Serax (oxazepam)	10–15 mg 1 to 3 times/day
Tranxene (clorazepate)	3.75–7.5 mg 1 to 3 times/day
Valium (diazepam)	2 mg 1 to 3 times/day
Xanax (alprazolam)	0.25 mg 1 to 3 times/day

On the other hand, it is important not to shy away from using medicines if that is what you and your doctor decide would be best for you. There is no reason to try to tough out the anxiety problem. You will not get extra credit for not using a medicine. The goal of the Anxiety Cure is for you to live a full life without restriction because of anxiety. If you can do that without a medicine, great. If you cannot do that, then you are probably unwise to forgo using the medicine simply because you are older or because you do not want to use a medicine. Even worse, if you are morbidly afraid of taking a medicine, you are giving in to the dragon. Review the risks and benefits of medicine in Step 6, Evaluate Your Need for Medicines and Therapy, with your friends and family prior to assuming that medicine is not for you. If you are having troubles that are related to anxiety, such as difficulty concentrating, medicines may significantly improve your problems.

Fear of Death

Worry about death is a problem for many anxious people of all ages. This problem is especially likely to strike later in life as more people close to you die and as your own inevitable death approaches. Death, which felt almost impossibly remote when you were a young adult, can feel frighteningly close as you age. Death is the ultimate loss of control. Death feels lonely—you are alone in death. The prospect of being in a coffin, even in death, may seem terribly claustrophobic. These typically anxious fears are all the more troubling to many anxious people because they are so obviously unreasonable.

You may worry that your physical symptoms of anxiety mean that there is something wrong with you that your doctors cannot find. One patient who had this type of worry said that she had a "cardiac neurosis." Yet having a severe case of this fear of anxious symptoms can make you feel as if you are almost dead already because you are so constrained by what you can and cannot do because of anxiety. People with OCD commonly have terrible images of death and feel that if they do not do their rituals, then horrible things will happen to them or their loved ones. These fixations on death are all the more horrible because you fear death so terribly. It is clearly one more example of how the dragon can scare you better than any horror movie, because the terror is made by your own brain to control you with your own worst fears.

You will die. All living things will die. Accept death—your death—to free yourself from the fear of death, so you can live whatever life you are fortunate enough to have.

If you spend all of your time worrying about your anxiety, there is no room to enjoy being alive. What, then, is there really to fear in death if you are hardly living your life now because of anxiety? You will be dead a long time, and worrying about death will simply diminish the possibility of enjoying the life that is left to you.

We have seen over and over the delight a person who has suffered from anxiety problems can feel when the anxiety is under control. Mark, a sixty-year-old lifelong agoraphobic, said he felt reborn as a nonanxious person when he worked with the Anxiety Cure. He felt sad about the years of his life he had spent trapped by his fears, but mostly he felt awed by the chance to spend the remainder of his life without those terrible fears. Mark was like a kid in a candy store—life offered so many wonderful possibilities he could hardly decide where to start.

Tips for Friends and Family

If an older friend or relative has anxiety symptoms, you may have struggled to know how to approach the problem or how to seek help. Perhaps you knew that anxiety was a problem for years, but now it seems worse than ever. This may be simply an unmasking of an old problem. If, as sometimes happens, this is a brand-new problem in an elderly person, there may be a physical cause of anxiety. In this case, it is important to point out your concern to the anxious person's doctor so medical evaluations can be made.

Many people who are past midlife will resist acknowledging the problem that they have with anxiety. Often it is such a long-standing problem that it seems not only unchangeable but also to be an intrinsic part of the person. The anxiety problem may have some medical basis (like a heart condition) that makes the anxious person believe the problem warrants the amount of worry and attention that is devoted to it.

As a supportive friend, you can be of great assistance in gently helping your anxious person see that he or she does not need to feel so bad. Try to help your anxious person see that the potential gains justify the effort needed to make a change. If using the Anxiety Cure, or seeing a therapist, or trying a medicine does not help, what has possibly been lost by trying? And there is much to gain when it succeeds. A new perspective can reveal just how wonderful life is again or, in some cases, for the first time. Sympathize with your anxious person about the terrible feelings anxiety produces. Physical ailments are difficult, and aging can be painful and distressing. But there is nothing so bad that worrying will not make it worse.

GLOSSARY

acceptance   The one-word antidote to anxiety disorders. Accept the painful feelings and worried thoughts but do not accept avoidance as part of your life. Acceptance is active and difficult, it is not a passive or weak response to anxiety.

addiction   Loss of control (initiated by continued use despite problems) and dishonesty (denial).

agoraphobia/panic disorder (PD)   Spontaneous panic attacks coupled with situational panic as well as pathological anxiety, with or without significant avoidance. The fear of being alone when perceiving great inner danger.

anticipatory anxiety   A type of pathological anxiety. The fear of panic feelings. Anticipatory anxiety often leads to avoidance (or phobia) of situations that are associated with panic.

anxiety   The body's signal of possible future danger, an emotional early warning message.

avoidance   The phobic response to stay away from panic-producing situations, even though you would do these things if you did not have anxiety.

cure   Knowing what is wrong and knowing what to do about it. When anxiety no longer impedes your life.

depression   A mental disorder characterized by feeling hopeless, helpless, and blue or despondent. May be a single episode, a chronic condition, or recurrent over many years.

desensitization   Practice in a fear-generating situation so that the second fear is progressively reduced.

discomfort zone   Anxiety is measured on a scale of 0 (no anxiety) to 10 (the worst anxiety possible). The discomfort zone represents midlevel anxiety of 4 to 7.

dragon   The anxiety dragon personifies the fear of the fear, the second fear. This is a mythical creature. Dragons do not exist outside of thinking, and neither do anxiety disorders.

false alarm   The brain-based first fear that causes the flood of anxious symptoms. These are normal bodily responses at an incorrect time.

first fear   Biological surge in adrenaline that causes the physical symptoms of anxiety.

generalized anxiety disorder (GAD)   General pathological anxiety without panic attacks, phobic avoidance, or pathological shyness, as well as without obsessions and compulsions.

obsessive-compulsive disorder (OCD)　Obsessions that are repugnant, unwanted, and intrusive thoughts leading to efforts to reduce this discomfort with compulsions, or ritual senseless behaviors, like checking or repeating a word or number over and over.

pathological anxiety　Normal anxiety that occurs when there is no generally understandable danger.

posttraumatic stress disorder (PTSD)　Intense fear after a traumatic event. Characterized by flashbacks to the event.

practice　Voluntary, repeated exposure to the fear-generating situation.

quality people　People who care about others and their feelings. Usually characteristic of people with anxiety disorders.

recovery　The process of getting well from an anxiety disorder.

second fear　Fear of the first fear, the biological flash of anxiety symptoms. Fear of the fear.

separation anxiety　Fear of being apart from a safe person. A diagnosis of childhood anxiety disorders. Agoraphobia in adults is sometimes called adult separation anxiety, as the anxious person fears being away from a safe person if anxiety strikes.

setback　A recurrence of panic and severe anxiety after a period of relatively mild, or even nonexistent, anxiety problems. A setback can be demoralizing if it is not expected. Accept and allow the panic to return. A setback can be a springboard to new growth and new learning.

situational panic　A linked response of a specific situation to panic feelings. A biologically based brain response. A first fear that triggers further anxious thoughts and, usually, avoidance.

social phobia　Fear, panic, and anxiety of embarrassment. May be limited to public speaking or may be part of a global shyness.

specific phobia　Fear and anxiety of panic in a specific situation, such as fear of heights, medical procedures, claustrophobia, or insects or snakes.

spontaneous panic　A biologically based brain response. A first fear that triggers anxious thoughts that are not linked to any specific situation. "Out-of-the-blue" panic.

stress　Any change is stressful because it means a new mental and physical adaptation. Stress can be painful, but it also can lead to growth.

support person　Any person who is chosen by a person with an anxiety disorder to help with practice sessions. A support person supports the process of recovery.

worry machine　The characteristic of anxious people to focus on "what-if" problems in thinking about the future. The worry machine imagines only bad outcomes.

SUGGESTED ADDITIONAL READING

Anxiety Disorders

Davidson, J. R., and H. Dreher. *The Anxiety Book: Developing Strength in the Face of Fear.* New York: Riverhead Books, 2003.

Markway, B. G., C. N. Carmin, C. A. Pollard, and T. Flynn. *Dying of Embarrassment—Help for Social Anxiety & Phobia.* Oakland, Calif.: New Harbinger Publications, Inc., 1995.

Ross, J. *Triumph over Fear—A Book of Help and Hope for People with Anxiety, Panic Attacks, and Phobias.* New York: Bantam Books, 1994.

Weekes, C. *Hope and Help for Your Nerves.* New York: Hawthorne Books, 1969.

———. *Peace from Nervous Suffering.* New York: Hawthorne Books, 1972.

Wilson, R. R. *Don't Panic—Taking Control of Anxiety Attacks*, rev. ed. New York: Harper Perennial, 1996.

Obsessive-Compulsive Disorder

Chansky, T. E. *Freeing Your Child from Obsessive-Compulsive Disorder.* New York: Three Rivers Press, 2000.

Foa, E. B., and R. R. Wilson. *Stop Obsessing! How to Overcome Your Obsessions and Compulsions.* New York: Bantam Books, 1991.

Rapoport, J. L. *The Boy Who Couldn't Stop Washing—The Experience and Treatment of Obsessive-Compulsive Disorder.* New York: New American Library, 1989.

Schwartz, J. M., with B. Beyette. *Brain Lock—Free Yourself from Obsessive-Compulsive Behavior.* New York: HarperCollins Publishers, Inc., 1996.

Addiction/Problems with Alcohol and Other Drugs of Abuse

DuPont, R. L. *Getting Tough on Gateway Drugs: A Guide for the Family.* Washington, D.C.: American Psychiatric Press, 1984.

———. *The Selfish Brain: Learning from Addiction.* Washington, D.C.: American Psychiatric Press, 1997.

DuPont, R. L., and J. P. McGovern. *A Bridge to Recovery—An Introduction to 12-Step Programs.* Washington, D.C.: American Psychiatric Press, 1994.

Ford, B., with C. Chase. *Betty—A Glad Awakening.* Garden City, N.Y.: Doubleday & Company, Inc., 1987.

Depression

Burns, D. D. *The Feeling Good Handbook.* New York: Penguin Books, 1989.

Family Relationships

Wolin, S. J., and S. Wolin. *The Resilient Self—How Survivors of Troubled Families Rise above Adversity.* New York: Villard Books, 1993.

Career Planning/Financial Planning/Money Problems

Bolles, R. N. *What Color Is Your Parachute 2003: A Practical Manual for Job-Hunters and Career Changes.* Berkeley, Calif.: Ten Speed Press, 2002.

Miedaner, T. *Coach Yourself to Success.* Lincolnwood, Ill.: Contemporary Books, 2000.

Quinn, J. B. *Making the Most of Your Money: A Comprehensive Guide to Financial Planning.* New York: Simon & Schuster, 1997.

Medicines/Diagnoses

American Psychiatric Association. *Diagnostic and Statistical Manual of Mental Disorders (DSM-IVTR)*, 4th ed. Washington, D.C.: American Psychiatric Association, 2000.

Appleton, W. S. *Prozac and the New Antidepressants.* New York: Plume (Penguin Books USA Inc.), 2000.

Medical Economics Data Production Company. *Physicians' Desk Reference (PDR).* Montvale, N.J.: Author, 2002.

Norden, M. J. *Beyond Prozac—Brain-Toxic Lifestyles, Natural Antidotes & New Generation Antidepressants.* New York: HarperCollins Publishers, Inc., 1996.

Religion/Spirituality and Getting Well

Adams, J. R. *So You Think You're Not Religious? A Thinking Person's Guide to the Church.* Cambridge, Mass.: Cowley Publications, 1989.

Kurtz, E., and K. Ketcham. *The Spirituality of Imperfection.* New York: Bantam, 1994.

Young, J. E., and J. S. Klosko. *Reinventing Your Life—How to Break Free from Negative Life Patterns and Feel Good Again.* New York: Plume (Penguin Books USA Inc.), 1994.

RESOURCES

Many of the following organizations offer a wide variety of material on anxiety disorders, including general information, books, articles, and pamphlets. Write or call for further information and, where appropriate, local meeting times and locations of support groups. Support groups may also be available online at some Internet sites.

Anxiety and Phobia Treatment Center
The P.M. Newsletter
White Plains Hospital Center
Davis Avenue at East Post Road
White Plains, NY 10601
914-681-1038

Anxiety Disorders Association of America (ADAA)
8730 Georgia Avenue, Suite 600
Silver Spring, MD 20910
240-485-1001
www.adaa.org

National Institute of Mental Health
Anxiety Disorders Education Program
www.nimh.nih.gov/anxiety

Emotions Anonymous (EA) International Services
P.O. Box 4245
St. Paul, MN 55104
612-647-9712

National Alliance for the Mentally Ill (NAMI)
200 North Glebe Road #1015
Arlington, VA 22203
703-524-7600

National Anxiety Foundation
3135 Custer Drive
Lexington, KY 40517-4001
606-272-7166
www.lexington-on-line.com/naf.html

National Self-Help Clearinghouse
Graduate School and University Center of the City University of New York
365 Fifth Avenue, Suite 3300
New York, NY 10016
212-817-1822
www.selfhelpweb.org

Obsessive-Compulsive Anonymous
P.O. Box 215
New Hyde Park, NY 11040
516-739-0662
www.hometown.aol.com/west24th/lindac.html

Obsessive-Compulsive Disorder Foundation, Inc.
337 Notch Hill Road
North Branford, CT 08471
203-315-2190
www.ocfoundation.org

Recovery, Inc.
802 N. Dearborn Street
Chicago, IL 60610
312-337-5661
www.recovery-inc.com

Clinical Trials

www.adaa.org
www.clinicaltrials.org
www.clinicaltrials.gov
www.dupontclinicaltrials.com

INDEX